QUILTING

Averil Colby

QUILTING

B. T. BATSFORD LTD London

First published 1972
First paperback edition 1978
© Averil Colby 1972

ISBN 0 7134 2665 9

Printed in Great Britain by
The Anchor Press Ltd, Tiptree, Essex
for the publishers
B.T. Batsford Ltd, 4 Fitzhardinge Street, London W1H 0AH

CONTENTS

Acknowledgments		vi
List of Illustrations		vii
Foreword		ix

1 Origins — 1

2 Materials — 20

3 Tools and Equipment — 30

4 Patterns: Wadded Quilting — 40

5 Patterns: Flat, Cord and Stuffed Quilting — 67

6 The Sixteenth Century — 82

7 The Seventeenth Century — 91

8 The Eighteenth Century — 104

9 The Nineteenth Century — 128

10 The Twentieth Century — 150

11 Gathered Patchwork — 167

Appendix A	*Notes on Wadded Quilting*	170
Appendix B	*Notes on Flat Quilting*	181
Appendix C	*Notes on Cord Quilting*	186
Appendix D	*Notes on Stuffed Quilting*	193
Appendix E	*Notes on Gathered Patchwork*	195
Appendix F	*List of Template Drawings*	198
Notes		199
Bibliography		206
Index		211

Acknowledgments

The Author and Publishers would like to thank the following for giving permission for quilting in their possession to be photographed for reproduction:
The Director of the American Museum in Britain, Bath, for figs 142, 143. Mrs Ursula Brock, Tolleshunt d'Arcy, for figs 154, 155. Mrs R. A. Burtt, Minchinhampton, for figs 156, 157, 175, 176, 178, 179, 180, 181, 182. The City of Bath Corporation (Museum of Costume) for the Frontispiece, and figs 102, 103, 122, 123. Miss Katharine Daniel, Horsington, for fig 121. Mrs Douglas Edwards, Newton Ferrers, for fig 153. Mr and Mrs Morris Mendus, St David's, for fig 145. Mrs Nigel Morgan, Solva, for fig 135. Roger Warner, Esq., Burford, for figs 106, 111.

For giving permission for photographs of quilting in their possession to be reproduced:
The Director of the British Museum for fig 1. The Director of the City of Manchester Art Gallery (Gallery of English Costume) for figs 115, 120, 135. Civici Musei Veneziani d'Arte e di Storia, Venice for fig 110. The Council for Small Industries in Rural Areas for figs 141, 149, 152. C. O. von Kienbusch, Esq., New York, for fig 109. Mrs Mary Lough, Witton-le-Wear, for fig 159. Le Ministère de L'Information, France, for fig 140. The Director of the National Museum of Wales (St Fagan's Folk Museum), for fig 144. The Photo Archives of the Leningrad Department of the Institute of Archaeology of the Academy of Sciences of the u.s.s.r., for figs 3, 4. The Director of the Bowes Museum, Barnard Castle, for figs 147, 150, 151, 158. The Director of the Royal Ontario Museum, Toronto, for fig 139. The Smithsonian Institution, Washington, D.C. for fig 148. The Trustees of the Victoria and Albert Museum, for figs 6, 11, 20, 100, 101, 104, 105, 108, 109, 112, 116, 117, 118, 119, 129, 134.

For permitting drawings to be made of quilting in their possession:
The Director of the American Museum in Britain, Bath, for figs 15, 54, 55, 79. The Director of the Bowes Museum, Barnard Castle, for figs 22, 23, 25, 32, 33, 34, 35, 45, 58, 59, 125. Mrs R. A. Burtt, Minchinhampton, for figs 183, 184, 185. The City of Bath Corporation (Museum of Costume), for fig 87. Miss Katharine Daniel, Horsington, for fig 89. Mrs Mary Lough, Witton-le-Wear, for figs 26, 36, 52, 53. Mr and Mrs Morris Mendus, St David's, for fig 24. The Director of the National Museum of Wales (St Fagan's Folk Museum), for figs 28, 30, 31, 41, 44, 64, 65. The Photo Archives of the Leningrad Department of the Institute of Archaeology of the Academy of Sciences of the u.s.s.r., for fig 2. Miss Jessica Stone, Eltham, for figs 113, 114. The Trustees of the Victoria and Albert Museum, for figs 8, 9, 10, 60, 75, 76, 77, 78, 83, 84, 88, 90, 91, 95, 96, 97, 98, 107, 124, 126. Mrs Norah Vivian, Wadhurst, for figs 161, 162.

For permission to reproduce illustrations from their books.
Mrs Ruth Finley, for figs 80, 81, 82. Mrs Elizabeth Hake, for figs 27, 38, 39, 40, 85, 136, 137, 146. Charles ffoulkes, Esq., for fig 5. Modern Language Association and R. S. Loomis's *Arthurian Legends in Medieval Art,* 1938.

For permission to reproduce patterns from their transfers:
The Embroiderer's Guild, London, for figs 48, 92, 93.

Illustration nos 160, 163, 164 are in the author's collection.

The words of *The Quilting Party* are reproduced by permission of Francis Day and Hunter Ltd, London W.C.2.

Negative numbers of prints which can be obtained are given in the chapter notes on pp. 199 *et seq.*

LIST OF ILLUSTRATIONS

		page
	Eighteenth-century silk quilt	*Frontispiece*
1	Carved ivory figure, *c.* 3400 B.C.	5
3	One end of a funerary carpet, *c.* first century B.C.	7
4	Detail of previous figure	7
6	Sicilian quilt with scenes from the Tristram Legend, *c.* 1395	14
7	Titles of scenes on previous figure	15
11	Ivory diptych of the Flight into Egypt	18
20	Scene of a German needlework school, *c.* 1700	39
99	German arming doublet, sixteenth century	85
100	German linen quilt, sixteenth century	89
101	Flat quilted embroidered coverlet, seventeenth century	92
102	Woman's embroidered waistcoat, *c.* 1680	95
103	Woman's jacket, *c.* 1690	95
104	Part of a linen robe, seventeenth century	95
105	Linen pillow sham, late seventeenth century	96
106	Man's quilted linen cap, late seventeenth century	98
108	Portuguese cotton quilt, seventeenth century	101
109	Panel with representation of the Last Supper, *c.* 1700	105
110	Man's cotton lappet cap, Italian, eighteenth century	107
111	Man's cap, early eighteenth century	107
112	Section of man's cap before making up, mid-eighteenth century	107
115	Three linen caps for children, eighteenth century	109
116	Side and back of a child's cotton cap, eighteenth century	109
117	Cuff of linen coat sleeve, mid-eighteenth century	110
118	Man's sleeved linen waistcoat, eighteenth century	110
119	Detail of previous figure	111
120	Baby's linen jacket, late eighteenth century	113

121	Satin christening long coat, late eighteenth century	113
122	Woman's lappet cap, early eighteenth century	117
123	Part of a satin petticoat, early eighteenth century	117
129	Detail of quilt from Great Tangley Manor, early eighteenth century	122
134	Embroidered linen quilt, 1703	125
135	Cotton quilt, Welsh, said to be 1770	129
138	White cotton satin stays, nineteenth century	133
139	Japanese firefighting clothing, 1868–1912	135
140	Cradle lined with satin, made for the King of Rome, c. 1811	136
141	Cotton quilt typical of South Wales, c. 1940	138
142	American white stuffed quilt, 1821	141
143	American white stuffed quilt, early nineteenth century	142
144	Cotton quilt, probably made for a marriage, nineteenth century	144
145	Cream cotton marriage quilt, c. 1885	145
146	White linen quilt, 1807	146
147	Red and buff cotton strip quilt, late nineteenth century	147
148	American cotton block quilt, 1866	148
149	Cotton quilt marked by Miss Sanderson, c. 1900	150
150	Pink and white cotton basket quilt, early twentieth century	151
151	Cream sateen quilt for Allenheads, 1903	152
152	Welsh cotton quilt, c. 1940	155
153	Silk christening jacket, 1955	155
154	Apricot silk child's coat, Damascus, late nineteenth century/ early twentieth century	156
155	Pink cotton child's coat, Damascus, late nineteenth century/ early twentieth century	156
156	Cream silk cushion cover, 1959	157
157	Part-worked panel with patterns in back stitch	158
158	Blue and pink cotton poplin quilt, 1958	161
159	Pink shantung marriage quilt, 1966	162
160	Cream and pale yellow poplin quilt, January 1968	163
163	Cotton gathered patchwork quilt, 1967	168
164	Detail of previous figure	169
175	Sampler of flat quilting	184
176	Reverse side of previous figure	185
178	Sampler of quilting cord with Method I	188
179	Reverse side of previous figure	189
180	Sampler of quilting cord with Method II	190
181	Reverse side of previous figure	191

FOREWORD

Needlework of all kinds has alternating periods of popularity and eclipse during its history, and quilting is no exception, but the extent of its acceptance as the answer to so many needs, has given it a more continuous existence than most. It has come commonly to be associated with bed quilts but the nature of its structure has given it enough toughness and resilience at one end of the scale, to be used for carpets and armour, and at the other end, a capacity for delicate work and patterns, which has made it suitable for babies' clothing.

Examples of all types of quilting recognised today, can be traced back far beyond present-day work, and the earliest evidence we have shows it then as an established, and not an emergent or experimental, work. Like other needlework with a traditional background its true origins are lost, but everything points to it having had its beginning in the East and, travelling by the Oriental trade routes, to have spread gradually to Asia, Europe and the West.

Until the beginning of the present century, all records mention the work as 'quilting' but within the last 50 or 60 years, various labels have been attached to the different types – such as 'English', 'American', 'Italian' – none of which is justified, as the methods and many of the patterns are considerably older than the civilisations of any of these countries. In the hope of identifying them clearly in this book, the kind of padding used to make each type has been given as the description. The so-called 'English' or 'American' quilting is referred to as 'wadded' quilting, 'Italian' as 'cord' or 'corded' quilting, and 'stuffed' quilting is used to describe the work which sometimes has been called 'Trapunto'. This last title may have some justification if we can go by the earliest known example of stuffed quilting, which is attributed to fourteenth-century Sicilian work.

Quilting in England and Wales can be said just to be holding its own in 1970. Sixteen years ago, when doing research on the history of patchwork, I saw between 200 and 300 quilts in the homes of people who had inherited or made them, in all parts of the country. During the recent three years I went over much the same ground again to find what I could of quilting, but with different results. The owners of many quilts had been persuaded to sell them, as there has been a demand for 'old' quilts, especially with patchwork tops; many people had moved from their old homes into new and smaller houses or bungalows, and had had to part with their quilts and frames for lack of room, and a number of the older quilters had died or given up quilting.

A few quilters, however, still are making traditional quilts and some are teaching also in classes organised by Women's Institutes, the Embroiderers' Guild and so on. Some individual teachers of embroidery in London and the provinces, have included quilting among their subjects, encouraging students to experiment with the work which includes freehand patterns, adaptations of designs intended for other embroidery, and machine quilting, the results of which will be interesting to see in work of the future; at present most of it is in the sampler stage. I have been most grateful to those teachers and students who have shown me their work and methods, and to none more than Mrs R. A. Burtt of Minchinhampton in Gloucestershire. She has lent me all her teaching samplers and some of her finished work to use as illustrations and given me unlimited help and advice whenever I asked for it.

The material for this book has been collected from many sources, as I am only the latest of many who have been interested in the history and uses of quilting. I learned quilting early in the 1930s and since then, in any work I have undertaken, I have had very generous help from Miss Muriel Rose, to which she has added much more for my latest research, and I am most grateful to her. Among writers in this country, Mrs Mavis FitzRandolph and Mrs Elizabeth Hake also have been more than generous with their help. Mrs FitzRandolph has answered many questions for me over a number of years and much of the information in my book is based on that in her *Traditional Quilting*. Mrs Hake has kindly given me permission to reproduce some of the illustrations from her book, *English Quilting*, for which generosity I am greatly in her debt. In my search for patterns, I have been overwhelmed with the loans or gifts of templates from many quilters, or from the descendants of others, from which to make line-drawings and I thank them all again, collectively, for giving me the opportunity to see and make use of them.

All the museum authorities have been most generous in answer to requests for help. Mr Ffransis Payne of St Fagan's Folk Museum, Cardiff and Mr Frank Atkinson of the Bowes Museum, Barnard Castle, gave me their untiring help over Welsh and North Country quilts in their respective collections, and I should like to thank also Mr Richard Foster, Folk Life Assistant at the Bowes Museum. Miss Anne Buck, Keeper of the Gallery of English Costume in Manchester, allowed me to see all the quilting collections in her care, as well as having special items photographed, and has given much of her time, help and advice over several years. I am grateful also for all the help I have received from the Department of Textiles of the Victoria and Albert Museum, and especially the Keeper, Mr Donald King and Miss Santina Levey, Research Assistant, who has given so much practical help as well as her time and interest, to my work. I should like to thank Mrs Mines, the Chief Costume Assistant to the Museum of Costume at Bath, who has gone out of her way to help, and made it possible for me to have a colour photograph of the quilt on the frontispiece. The Director of the American Museum, also at Bath, has been kind enough to allow me to study the quilting there and I am grateful to him and also Miss Constance Holland and Mrs Margaret Irwin, who bore the brunt of my many enquiries. My thanks are due also, to Mr Christopher Wall of the National Trust, for making it possible for me to see the quilts at Hardwick Hall, and also Mr L. J. Keen, House Steward at Hardwick, who could not have done more to help.

I owe much gratitude to the Area Librarian, Mr Farmer and to the staff of the Winscombe branch of the South Western Region Library System. Mr Farmer never failed to get any book I needed and where it was not possible, he had photostat copies made of relevant passages, or borrowed microfilm books for me to study and provided facilities for me to do so at the library. The microfilm books were kindly lent by the Bodleian Library.

I am immensely grateful to Miss Grace Cansdale who has done the typescript of this book, and to Mrs Arthur Lee and Mrs Howe of Churchill who have so kindly done the drawings for me. As always, I have to thank my kind and patient publisher. Mr Samuel Carr has given me help and advice at all times, doing much of my work for me and never reminding me, that once again another promised script is long overdue.

Langford   Averil Colby
Somerset

1 ORIGINS

Tradition is described as 'a custom which has been handed down from ancestors to posterity',[1] but to reverse tradition and trace back a custom to its beginning is much more easily said than done and when the subject being traced is needlework, there is little hope of the recorded tradition being an unbroken one. In the first place the hazards are too great for textiles to survive for any length of time. They have many natural enemies – those of wear, tear and moth – and they are the most easily destroyed of our possessions in the event of natural and national calamities – fire, tempest, flood, and war in all its degrees – which can affect the life of a country. Cherished objects can survive for a generation or two but tradition goes back further than that in most needlework and, from the early examples which we have now, it seems that the safest place to hide and store relics and evidence of the occupations of past peoples, has been in their tombs and burial places. Certainly when making a search in the twentieth century into the history of needlework, it is remarkable how often an early example owes its survival to an ancient burial custom many centuries before.

Surviving examples of the work of any age are the most satisfactory evidence, however few and far between they are in time, but failing these, the missing years must be filled with written records and representations of it, in such things as paintings, carving, sculpture and so on. Household inventories and wills have provided invaluable records of different kinds of needlework for hundreds of years; diaries have contained good descriptive detail, although at times it seems that sentiment may have added a little colour to a stated fact, especially when a description is that of needlework which was commonplace in the daily life at the time of writing. Sometimes a social historian will refer to some type or aspect of needlework, but this is rare; and sometimes a past poet, writer or essayist – all more observant than many other people – may describe an embroidery or occupation which gives an indication of the existence in his time, of whatever needlework is being sought; but the final history must be written from all the collected pieces of evidence and put together as truthfully as the lapse of time will allow.

From the earliest days of quilting the lapse of time is very long indeed – certainly for 6,000 years and probably more – but it is inevitable that the so-called 'mists of antiquity' will have clouded the years, and as far as quilting is concerned the clouding is caused to some extent by the indiscriminate use of the word 'quilt'. In the last hundred years or more, it seems that almost any kind of bed cover is likely to have been referred to as a quilt, whether or not any quilting has been included in the making of it. Descriptive references, such as 'patchwork quilt' or 'embroidered quilt' have tended to be misleading but this has arisen, undoubtedly, from the practice of adding quilting to other kinds of needlework in order to secure a lining, or an interlining, or to enrich a pattern, or for all these reasons, but it is a misnomer which has led to many a false trail in carrying out research into quilting itself – a subject which has so many variations within its own tradition.

In common with all kinds of needlework, quilting has acquired a number of differentia in its traditional career through history, according to the demands of need and fashion, and, where each development has been acceptable, gradually it became recognised as part of the tradition. So far as we know, the earliest work consisted of two outer layers of fabric with a layer of soft padding stitched between them; but somewhere along the road, an alternative padding of cord or thick thread was used as a means of producing a different kind of pattern which had a raised outline on the surface, instead of one caused by the depression of stitching through padded material. At some time also, it was discovered that the kind of pattern made with cord between two layers of fabric, could be made by stitching the cord to the back of a single thickness so firmly, that it raised the front surface. The effect on the front of the work in either method was identical and they could not be distinguished unless the wrong side (the back of the work) could be seen, so both became looked upon as quilting.

Other methods worked their way in. Two layers of fabric stitched together in an all-over repetitive pattern, was counted as quilting; so too, was work in which the pattern was stitched first through two outer thicknesses, and after it was completed, small pieces of soft padding were inserted (generally from the back) in order to raise and give extra emphasis to parts of the pattern.

The stitching in all types of quilting is more consistent than the methods of pattern-making, however, and running stitch and back stitch are the recognised traditional processes from the earliest days of the work. Embroidery has been – and is still – used as an additional surface decoration to the corded and flat types of pattern. Usually it is of a floral nature and in colour, and is worked in chain stitch, but corded quilting on linen, combined with patterns in drawn and pulled stitches, and carried out in white or self-coloured linen thread is found, especially in eighteenth-century work.

In common with other traditional needlework, it is impossible to trace back quilting to its inception and original use, but the necessity for some kind of protection, rather than a means of decoration, probably led to its invention. The basic principle in the construction of the work is that of sewing together layers of material laid and stretched on top of one another, thoroughly, evenly and methodically, ensuring that at no place can they become detached, thus in effect creating a new fabric. That the sewing stitches happened to produce a kind of decoration did not affect their practical purpose, but probably this kind of involuntary bonus, which may have had the irresistible attraction of 'two for the price of one', helped to encourage the development of the work.

From the little evidence we have up to now, it appears that the earliest work contained a thick, soft padding. Was it then, invented in the first place as an economy to strengthen and preserve worn fabrics, perhaps of animal skin or some woven material? Its nature suggests that of a protective covering and in the first place, was the object to be protected the human body? But if so, there is nothing to show whether it was to be shielded from cold, heat or physical harm. There is no conclusive evidence even, to indicate from which part of the world the work came originally or we might have some idea as to whether its obvious insulating property was intended, in a garment, to keep the wearer warm or cool. If quilting was applied first to a garment of a wrap-round character, such as a cloak might be, it could have been used at night also, either as a warm covering or a protection from a hard floor or bed. Or was it used first perhaps, as a kind of mattress? Or a carpet? Or was the original piece of quilting a padded cover to protect the head or body in combat? So far we know the answers to none of these questions, but we do know without doubt, from examples and records, that this versatile kind of needlework has been adapted to all these purposes. In Northern countries floor and bed covers and clothing have been quilted with thick interlinings between outer layers of fabric; in temperate climates thinner padding or cord took the place of thick padding and in Eastern countries, where fine bed quilts and quilted carpets were common, outer garments also of thin cotton or silk, with a fine cord as padding, have kept out the heat of the sun. Quilted garments in many countries were worn as armour until they became inadequate as a defence against heavier armaments than the mace, sword, arrow and spear.

Some light on the use of quilting about 2,000 years ago, may be shown by the derivation of the noun 'quilt', from the Latin *culcita* or *culcitra*, meaning 'a sack, a mattress or cushion, filled with feathers, wool or hair and so on, and an object which could be used for lying upon or as a covering for warmth'.[2] Varro, a writer on husbandry in the first century B.C., relates the word to *calx*, the 'heel', meaning to tread down or trample, hence to press down or press in; he writes of 'tomentum in culcita culcare' – to press down or press in the stuffing (*tomentum*) into the mattress and it seems that some kind of quilted bedding was in use in his time, or at least developed from then.

But it seems more than probable that garments of quilting were worn more than 3,000 years before that, from the evidence of a small carved ivory figure in the possession of the British Museum. The figure was found by Sir Flinders Petrie in the Temple of Osiris at Abydos in 1903, and is that of a king of the Egyptian First Dynasty, wearing the Crown of Upper Egypt and wrapped in a cloak or mantle, on which the carved patterns are characteristic of a quilted textile. The garment hangs stiffly and not in the soft folds of a single thickness of material and although there must be a degree of doubt without definite proof, it does seem that the faithfulness in the carving to the likenesses of the cloak and of the wearer may be believed (1).[3] In *Needlework Through the Ages*, Mrs Antrobus (Mary Symons) gives reasons for this belief; in the first place the carving is taken for a good likeness of the King – 'The workmanship is remarkably fine and the figure is no doubt an accurate portrait of the king represented'[4] and so it seems reasonable that if the likeness to the king is good, so too, will his apparel be shown faithfully. The pattern is carved in deep relief and does not suggest a surface decoration of applied work or embroidered thread and in the opinion of Mrs Antrobus – 'it is more likely that the patterns represent quilting for which a linen thread would be used. The deep carving, moreover, suggests the quilting of one layer of material over another, or even of more than one; the raised character of the carved pattern produces an effect identical with that of quilting over a soft yielding substance like wool or down . . . this robe might have been designed for a ceremony at which white only was permitted, and this would add strength to the quilting theory'.[5] The lozenge or diamond pattern is common to all kinds of decorative needlework but it is especially characteristic of traditional quilting patterns, with a consistent history up to the present century, so it does seem that, with good reason and argument for quilting, we can take it that this figure represents a very early example of it.

As the garment is shown as the apparel of a royal person, it is clear that this quilting was no rough peasant work but a skilled and established form of needlework, and of sufficient standing to be thought worthy of high

1 *Carved ivory figure of a Pharaoh of the Egyptian First Dynasty, wearing a supposedly quilted mantle. c. 3400 B.C.*

estate, its worthiness emphasized by the possibility of the mantle being of a ceremonial nature. Similar carving on other figures of this and later dates, suggests an accepted use of quilting for outer garments.[6]

An early example of quilting as a floor covering – probably the earliest surviving example of quilting at all – is a carpet in the possession of the Leningrad Department of the Institute of Archaeology of the Academy of Sciences of the Union of the Soviet Republics (3, 4). It was discovered by the Koslóv expedition of 1924 and 1925, and is thought to have been made during the period of the first century B.C. and the second century A.D. Writing of this also, Mrs Antrobus remarks, 'this carpet was actually found on the floor of a tomb, just as it might have been used in a tent or mountain stronghold of a great chieftain during his life',[7] showing again that the standing of quilting was one of importance.

Of particular interest in regard to present-day quilting, is the pattern on the central part of the carpet. It consists of a repetitive series of large clockwise and anticlockwise spirals, with smaller scroll patterns joined to them and filling the intervening spaces, to make a continuous pattern. The narrow border surrounding the quilted centre contains a row of geometrically shaped interlocking patterns, outlined with a closely stitched twisted thread and quilted to the foundation. The chief border is coarsely quilted in diagonal and cross diamond lines, upon which are applied, in brown-, purple- and white-coloured cloth, a number of symbolic tree and animal shapes. The high order of artistry and skill in the animal forms show that a long cultural tradition lay behind the work at the time when it was done. Not only are the patterns full of life and vigour but the attention to detail and the way in which the work is carried out, give proof of a practised and long-standing tradition; the fine concentric lines of back-stitched quilting, different in pattern in each animal, represent the differences in the natural coat of each beast and in outlining the bone and muscle structures, emphasis is given to the implied movement in the vital struggle in each group (2).

2   *Detail of figure 3. A border group of gryphon tearing a reindeer*

But however unique the applied patterns are, the scroll and spiral designs of the centre panel are noteworthy also, in that – with the cross diamond or lozenge pattern on the Egyptian mantle (1) – they are still in use in twentieth-century quilting, and so probably have the longest and most consistent record of any in the tradition.

The next thousand years of quilting history represent a period of drought as far as records are concerned. Having reached the heights of perfection and social importance which were attached to the royal mantle and the funerary carpet, and the practical domestic inference of Varro's observation, it is unlikely that it died out as a form of decorative and household needle-work in the parts of the world where it had flourished. It is even probable that other examples, which would bridge the interval, still exist and may be found, but always the frailty of textiles has to be taken into account and set

3   One end of a small funerary carpet, showing a scroll and spiral patterned ground, with groups of wild beasts and arboreal patterns on the outer border. Scytho-Siberian, first century B.C.–second century A.D.

4   Detail of figure 3. A border group of a wild beast falling on a yak

against the possibility of finding surviving specimens of the work itself, so we have to be content with written records. This evidence, too, is scarce, but accounts of European and English work do exist, not only of domestic work (as might be expected), but there exist records which deal in detail with the use of quilting in the construction of defensive body armour. It is improbable that domestic quilting played as small a part in the textiles of the Early Middle Ages as written evidence suggests, but the fact remains that it is with accounts of quilted fabrics for military wear that this period is most represented, and a fairly consistent picture can be built up from records, inventories and the works of contemporary writers and poets, of the uses and construction of quilted armour, from the time of William the Conqueror and the Crusades at the end of the eleventh century.

In its construction it has only a distant relationship to the fine needlework recognised as quilting in later centuries, but the basic principle of stitching together two outer layers of fabric with layers of soft padding between them, is the same. There is, however, something about the quality of honest purpose in the making of armour, with no fine stitching, no decoration – just strong linen or canvas, strongly sewn in straight lines, with tough thread, which had to be well done or it failed in its vital purpose – that gives to the tradition of quilting, a backbone not possessed by any other kind of domestic needlework.

Early armour for light troops often was made of leather, or of quilted linen or similar fabric, which was stuffed with various kinds of padding. This proved a reasonable, although not complete, defence against the weapons of cut and thrust – the sword, the spear and the arrow – and even when body armour was strengthened by chain or plate outer defence, fabric armour was worn as well, until the time when the wearing of any armour became almost useless in the face of pistol, musket and cannon shot.

Quilted armour had several advantages over that made from metal; the garments were lighter and less cumbrous on long marches, they were more easily put on and off, and the cost was less than that for chain mail or plate armour to the soldier, and to the knight by whom he was employed. An early kind of armour was the Jack, a sleeved coat, described as a humble form of the Brigandine (5). Both were composed of two outer fabric layers and contained stuffing and small plates of metal, but in the brigandine the plates had to be riveted to the foundation, overlapping upwards for ease of movement, by a professional armourer; in the jack the plates were of metal or horn and enclosed within the padding, and the whole was laced together in a kind of rough quilting through rows of spaced holes punched through from side to side of the coat, the lacing appearing on the outside as lines and

5   *A figure wearing a jack, seen in Memling's Chasse of Saint Ursula. Late fifteenth century*

triangles. This work was more on the domestic level and could be done by the wearer himself or by his wife.[8] Nevertheless, it must have been a tough and not ineffective defence when it was well made, as according to an account of a riot during Wat Tyler's Rebellion (1381) the rioters tried to destroy a jack belonging to the Duke of Lancaster, and to do so, had to hack it to pieces with swords and axes.[9] Although *The Faerie Queene* was not written until 1579, the virtue of quilted armour was recognised by the 'Gyant Monstruous' who –

> wore no armour, ne for none did care,
> As no whit dreading any living wight;
> But in a Jacket quilted richly rare
> upon checklaton he was straungely dight;[10]

The jack had a long record in armoury, probably because of its reliable toughness and what would be called nowadays, its 'do-it-yourself' quality, and the numerous references to it show that it must have been a well-tried and familiar defence. The story of Sir Walter Scott's *Marmion* was set round the Battle of Flodden Field in 1513 and in relating the account of the battle, he describes the weapons used and the contemporary defensive armour worn against them. After a description of the men-at-arms 'heavily sheathed in mail and plate' and mounted on 'Flemish steeds' –

> On foot the yeoman too, but dress'd
> In his steel-jack, a swarthy vest,

> With iron quilted well;
> Each at his back (a slender store)
> His forty days' provisions bore,
>   As feudal statutes tell.
> His arms were halbert, axe, or spear
> A cross-bow there, a hagbut here,
>   A dagger knife, and brand.[11]

The knights and men-at-arms in chain mail and plate armour, outwardly were better equipped for combat when metal had largely superseded the all-fabric defences, but the quilted garments were retained and worn also, under or over the outer armour. This was partly to absorb at least some of the shock of hard blows on the metal, but also as a bodily protection from the armour itself, the weight of which was considerable and could cause bruising and chafing whether worn in or out of battle. Very little seems to have been written of the discomfort of armour by the men who wore it, but in a letter to his daughter Margaret, when she was Regent of the Netherlands (1510–19), the Emperor Maximilian I thanked her for some fine shirts and linen which she had helped to make for him – 'and we are overjoyed because you have taken thought for our person; and when this year we are wearing our armour which is hard and heavy, then our heart will be comforted with the good feel and gentleness of the fine cloth'.[12]

Other garments worn under or over metal armour were the Gambeson, the Haketon, the Pourpoint and the Habergon. The last was a sleeveless jacket, usually of plate or mail, but sometimes it was padded and quilted, and it appears that the habergon also could be made at home. The young Damzell, Britomart, inspired by stories of the warlike Angela, and so determined to follow her example to help her hero Artegall –

> That she resolv'd, unweeting to her sire,
>   Advent'rous Knighthood on herself to don,
>   And counseld with her Nourse, her Maides attire
>   To turn into a massy habergon,
> And bad her all things put in readinesse anon.[13]

In a later book of *The Faerie Queene*, the Amazon Redagund wore a habergon of mail over a quilted garment, described in some detail as she prepared herself for battle with Artegall –

> And the Amazon, as best it likt her selfe to dight
>   All in a Càmis light of purple silke
>   Woven uppon with silver, subtly wrought

And quilted uppon satin white as milke,
Trayled with ribbands diversly distrought
Like as the workeman had their courses taught;
Which was short tucked for light motion
Up to her ham, but when she list, it rought
Down to her lowest heele, and thereuppon
She wore for her defence a mayled habergon.[14]

But all her preparations were wasted, her armour failed her and she had to rely on trickery to get the better of the knight.

The gambeson was worn sometimes as a substitute for metal armour, but more usually it served as a padded undergarment, especially beneath the mailed habergon. It was a kind of doublet made from leather or thickly quilted silk or linen, and when worn under armour, it rose above the metal at the neck, to prevent chafing. In this and all quilted armour, the quality and toughness of the stuffing was of equal importance as the outer fabric as it was virtually the last defence from blows to the body. It is likely that the gambeson needed the skill of a professional to make, as in some accounts of 1286 – *Comptus Ballivorum Franciae* – there is an item relating to the use of cendal and tow for stuffing a gambeson,[15] and in 1322, another item in the *Chamber of Accounts, Paris* reads 'Item. Adae armentario 40sol.4d. profactoris gambesonorum', suggesting that a woman professional by the name of Ada, was employed in the making of fabric armour.[16]

Other fabric body armours were the haketon, a sleeveless, stuffed and quilted jerkin and the pourpoint, a stuffed and quilted doublet, both worn under mail or plate. Quilted linen caps were worn under heavy metal helmets and shinpieces, gauntlets and the gorget were lined and padded, often with quilting. With all the various layers of hard and soft armour, each apparently protecting the other, and the knight or soldier as a kind of kernel in the centre, the twentieth-century layman is helped a little to know in what order they were put on in the fourteenth century, by the accounts of the knights in Chaucer's *Canterbury Tales*. From *The Prologue* it seems that the habergon of the knight was of mail, as it had stained his fustian jupon or surcoat, presumably with rust.

But for to tellen yow of his array,
His hors was gode, but he was not gay
Of fustian he wered a gipoun
Al bismotered with his habergoun:
For he was late y-come from his viage
And went for to doon his pilgrimage.[17]

And later in Chaucer's own *Tale of Sir Thopas*, the knight was prepared for battle –

> He dide next his whyte lere
> Of clooth of lake fyn and clere
> A breke and eek a sherte;
> And next his sherte an aketon
> And over that an habergon
> For percinge of his herte.[18]

Over all this, he wore also, a fine steel hawberk, a helmet, a white surcoat, leather shinpieces and carried a sword and spear.

It is not surprising that surviving examples of quilted armour are rare. The weight alone, of chain mail or plate worn over it, would have shortened its life considerably, and with plate the likelihood of damage was even greater. The risks of wearing armour over anything but a suitable under-garment are stressed in some military orders of the late sixteenth century – 'No armed man should weare any cut doublets, as well in respect that the wearing of armour doth quicklie fret them out and also by reason that the corners and edges of the lames and jointes of the armours doo take such holde uppon such cuttes as they do hinder the quicke and sudden arming of men.'[19] This implies also, the need for quilted armour to be in good repair, not only from damage by the metal but from sweated moisture inside and rusty damp penetrating from the outside armour, so with all these hazards the evidence which remains is understandably scanty. Very little seems to have survived of the fabric armour of Chaucer's time (towards the end of the fourteenth century) but we have in England one well-known example in the quilted surcoat or jupon worn at that time by the Black Prince. Until a few years ago, it hung, with his helmet, gauntlets and shield, over his tomb in Canterbury Cathedral, but for its preservation it has now been replaced by a replica. The original coat was of red and blue velvet on which had been applied the Royal Arms of England embroidered on linen, and the whole was quilted, with a lining of fine buckram, in vertical lines.

The heat and lack of ventilation of fabric armour caused much discomfort, and the more so if the garments were ill-fitting. This was recognised by the professional linen armourers; they had already the sole right to cover armour and to make stuffed and quilted armour, padded and quilted helmet linings, and so on, but realising the need for some knowledge of tailoring in their work, the existing *Linen Armourers* – a guild distinct from the *Armourers* – were instituted as *The Fraternity of Tailors and Linen Armourers of Linen Armour of St John the Baptist in the City of London*, during the reign of Edward I.

in 1272.[20] The Charter was confirmed by each succeeding monarch up to and including James I, who is supposed to have had such a fear of death by treachery, that he wore always a protective quilted doublet. Henry VI granted a right of search to the guild, which allowed them to inspect shops and workshops and to confiscate any work which did not come up to their standards, and in the reign of Henry VII, the guild became *The Merchant Taylors Company*, with the granting of the Charter which is held by the Company to the present day. A connection of some interest between this Company and the detailed knowledge of early fabric armour shown in references to it in *The Faerie Queene* is, that Edmund Spenser was educated at the Merchant Taylors' School, of which his father was a free journeyman, and must have been familiar with the foundation and history of the Company.

If records are proof of importance, then domestic quilting of the eleventh, twelfth and thirteenth centuries does not seem to have had the same standing as quilted armour over the same period. This is hard to believe. Most references to quilted bed covers are in inventories and household accounts, and so presumably they belonged to upper-class families, but it is unlikely that this kind of bed furnishing was not used in poorer homes. Sewing women employed in the big houses came from families of dependents on the estates, doing much of the quilting as part of their work and, as with other kinds of needlework which have begun at this level in society, it must have found its way quite soon into cottage life where it was skilfully adapted to the same needs in less costly materials. As regards quilted clothing, if fabric armour worn by the foot soldier could be made in his home, something of the same kind, such as a warm and weatherproof jerkin, could have been made economically, from partly worn clothing perhaps, for other members of the household.

Towards the end of the thirteenth century, the few references there are to quilted bedding are thinly scattered and not very descriptive, but where they do exist they seem to imply that quilts as bed covers, far from being rare, were an accepted kind of furnishing. In 1290, 'Maketh a bed . . . of quoiltene [quilting] and of materasz'[21] infers that the quilting was a covering and not an underlay or mattress; a little later, in about 1300, 'cowltes and covertures'[22] (quilts and bed clothes) are mentioned in a poem, and another reference in 1320, to 'Foure hondred beddes of selk echon, Quiltes of gold there upon'[23] is on the scale of furnishing necessary for a palace.

Towards the end of the fourteenth century, examples of domestic quilting are more in evidence, and of these, three known examples of bed quilts – all of Sicilian origin – have survived. Two of the quilts were made as a pair;

6　One of a pair of quilts showing scenes from the Legend of Tristram, quilted on linen with brown thread. Sicilian, c. 1395

7 *Descriptive titles of the scenes from the quilt on figure 6, with translations from the Sicilian dialect*

COMU LU AMOROLDU E VINUTU IN CORNUVALGIA CUN XXXX GALEI How Amoroldu has come into Cornwall with forty galleys	COMU LU AMOROLDU FERIU TRISTAINU A TR[A] DIMENTU How Amoroldu smote Tristainu by treachery	SITATI DE IRLANDIA Cities of Ireland	COMU LU AMOROLDU FA BANDIRI LU OSTI IN CORNUVALGIA How Amoroldu has proclaimed the expedition into Cornwall
COMU TRISTAINU DAI LE GUANTA ALLU AMOROLDU DE LA BACTAGLIA How Tristainu gives the glove of battle to Amoroldu	COMU TRISTAINU FERIU LU AMOROLDU IN TESTA How Tristainu smote Amoroldu in the head	COMU LU INFA DELU AMOROLDU ASPECTTAVA LU PATRUNU How the servant of Amoroldu waited for his master	COMU LU RRE LANGUIS CUMANDA CHI VAIA LO OSTI [IN] CORNUVALGIA How King Languis commands that the host go into Cornwall
COMU LU AMOROLDU FA SULDARI LA GENTI How Amoroldu has the men hired	COMU TRISTAINU BUCTA LA VARCA ARRETU INTU ALLU MARE How Tristainu thrust the boat back into the sea	COMU TRISTAINU ASPECTA LU AMOROLDU ALLA ISOLA DILU MARU SANCA VINTURA How Tristainu waits for Amoroldu in the island of the sea Sanca Vintura	
COMU LU RRE LANGUIS MANDA PER LU TRABUTU IN CORNUVALGIA How King Languis sends for the tribute to Cornwall	COMU [LI M]ISSAGIERI SO VINUTI A[LLU] RRE MARCU P [ER] LU TRIBUTU DI SECTI ANNI How the messengers have come to King Marcu for the tribute of seven years		COMU LU AMOROLDU VAI IN CORNUVALGIA How Amoroldu goes into Cornwall

one is now in England, in the possession of the Victoria and Albert Museum and the other in the Bargello at Florence. The third quilt is somewhat different in the arrangement of the patterns, although the subject is the same as that on the pair; the quilt is in private ownership at Florence.

The chief patterns on the quilts were inspired by the legendary life of Tristram, shown in a number of pictorial episodes, and the similarity in the treatment and design of all the quilts points to them having a common source, probably that of a workshop. The scenes on each of the paired quilts are not in sequence but were chosen seemingly at random, the pictured narrative following on from one quilt to another and back again. Some episodes are enclosed in a series of rectangular compartments down the middle sections of the quilts, and others on the surrounding outer borders, on three sides only, are larger and contain more detail (6). A descriptive inscription in Sicilian dialect of the action and characters portrayed in it, accompanies each episode. All three quilts are discussed at length by Mr Roger Loomis in *Arthurian Legends in Medieval Art*[24] from which translations of the relevant inscriptions on the London quilt are given (7).

This quilt is the one with which we are the most familiar in England and we are fortunate in the fact that it is complete, measuring 122 inches in length and 106 inches wide; each rectangular compartment in the middle part, with its surrounding border, is approximately 36 inches long and 29 inches wide. The Bargello quilt, unhappily, has lost two of its middle compartments, the border on the right side and the upper end of the left border, but the pair are in remarkably fine condition, having survived for nearly 600 years; convincing evidence is given for them having been made for the marriage of Pietro di Luigi Guicciardini and Laodamia Acciaiuili, which took place in 1395.[25]

A study of the quilt in London shows the quilted patterns worked with back stitch through two layers of heavy linen, making in fact something weighty enough to be more appropriate as a hanging, than as a bed cover under which a comfortable night could be experienced. The outlines of the principal figures – the knights, kings and other characters, the horses, ships, castellated buildings and so on – were stitched in brown linen thread which emphasises their importance over the secondary patterns, for which a natural linen thread was used. The narrow borders surrounding the middle compartments are decorated with groups of small formal leaf patterns (8) and

8   *Detail of the small borders on figure 6*

the wide outer borders, contain a series of scenes without formal divisions, but stems of ivy leaves and berries, vine rods with bunches of grapes and leaves (9), branches of oak leaves and acorns, flowering sprays of roses (10) or lilies, as well as other similar but smaller patterns, separate the larger scenes of the knight's adventures. The quilted patterns were raised with a cotton padding, probably by the method known now as 'stuffed quilting' (Appendix I) and the smaller details quilted after the padding was done.

Evidence of quilted garments of an everyday kind being worn about the beginning of the fifteenth century is given by a small carving of ivory. It is Milanese in origin and about 1400 in date, and shows the figures of the Holy Family on the Flight into Egypt, of which Joseph is wearing a coat quilted all

9 *Detail of the grape and vine pattern separating two border scenes on figure 6*

10 *Detail of a scrolling rose and leaf pattern which separates several border scenes on figure 6*

over in a simple cross diamond pattern (11). The garment is loose fitting and has the look of easy comfort, fitting almost to the neck without a collar but with a short front opening from the top, which would allow the garment to be pulled over the head; the sleeves are long and the only fastening appears to be a cord or belt round the waist, over which the top part of the coat is pulled to give a bloused effect, so that the cord is not seen. The carving is in very small scale but clear in every detail and is of a section in a pierced ivory diptych, showing 12 scenes from the life of Christ mounted against a back-

ground of illuminated vellum, in a frame of intarsia of coloured woods and bone. It is in the possession of the Victoria and Albert Museum, and because of the size and delicate detail in every other respect, it can be taken that the coat is a faithful representation of a real garment. Its simplicity, and that it is worn by a man of humble circumstance, suggests that it was of the kind worn by the Italian peasant of the time; clearly it is of wadded quilting but not thickly interlined, as the coat hangs in soft folds.

Descriptive comments and documentary records of quilting in domestic use by the end of the fourteenth and throughout the fifteenth centuries, also become a little easier to find, but whether it is because bed quilts were more plentiful, or whether more records have survived, it is not possible to know. In the fourteenth-century *Romance of Arthur of Lytel Brytayne*, 'a rich quilt wrought with coten, with crimson sendel stitched with thredes of gold',[26] describes a bed cover of crimson silk, either woven or embroidered with gold and quilted with cotton thread, but whether or not it refers to work done in this country, there is no telling. From the time of the Crusades especially, Eastern silks and embroideries found their way to Europe and to England, and it is possible that a description such as the 'rich quilt' may have been of Eastern origin. Work of the Middle Ages was notable for its richness and lavish use of gold thread and, although generally this was ecclesiastical in purpose, it was not wholly confined to work for the churches. A mention in about 1450 suggests that some quilts were of a more humdrum quality and looked upon as essential bed furnishings – 'Thei lay down to slepe upon the grasse for other quyltes ne pilowes hadde their noon',[27] and here there is an indication that quilts were used as underlays. In an inventory of Durham Priory, taken in 1466, one entry concerns a quilt embroidered with the Four Evangelists but no other indications are given as to materials or whether or not the pattern was made by quilting. Most probably the 'Four Evangelists' were worked as a surface embroidery on a quilted ground. As a final note to fifteenth-century quilts a record of an imported one comes, unexpectedly, among items in the cargo of a trading vessel during the year 1498–9, taking tin, hides and fish from Cornwall to France, and bringing from Brittany return cargoes of, among other things, manufactured cloth. 'A typical return cargo was that of the *Julian* of St Brieuc, bringing 200 pieces of linen, 300 of canvas, 3 bolts of canvas, 3 pieces of checker ray and 1 quilt valued at 3s. 4d.'[28]

By the time references, inventory entries and other evidence of the existence of early domestic quilting have been analysed, very little descriptive material is left. As happens from time to time, an 'old' quilt is given in an inventory or a list of household furnishing, but this may mean either that it is of value because of its age, or that it is so worn and threadbare that it is useless and included only by a conscientious clerk or assessor. Neither is it clear in many records as to whether the quilt or quilts are of earlier work than the date of the reference itself; a quilt recorded in the eighteenth century, may well have been made one, or even two, centuries earlier. Quilted clothing is, perhaps, somewhat less difficult to date with any certainty, as its periods of popularity and use are at the mercy of fashion, and so can be tracked down and identified with more accuracy.

2 MATERIALS

However scanty early descriptions and references may be, our knowledge of the kind of materials used, which are described either by inference or direct statement, depends on the keenness of eye or the interest, of the observer. Because of the need for clear identification, inventories of household goods and wardrobes can be relied upon for reasonable accuracy about details, but in very early records, which consist of representations of quilting, such as the carvings on ivory or stone (1, 11), or just a plain statement mentioning 'a quilt', we are left with nothing more substantial than a guess that the textiles quilted were those which were common to the countries in which the work had been done.

Materials appropriate to the different ways of doing quilting, have varied according to the purposes for which it has been intended, but as a general rule the top layer has been of finer quality than the lower layer or back of the work. In quilting terms used today, it is customary to refer to the right side of the work as the *top* and the underlayer as the *backing*, with the interlining where appropriate, as the *padding*, and although there is no evidence that these terms were in use before the twentieth century, they are understood readily nowadays and, as far as this book is concerned, are used to describe all early as well as contemporary work.

Padding

The character of each type of quilting is given to it by the kind of padding with which the patterns are raised, and when the padding – generally referred to in old records as 'stuffing' – is of wool, cotton wool, rags and so on, the implication is that the work had been intended for warmth and not necessarily decoration. The padding of the early examples illustrated on figures 1 and 5 has been discussed already, but some early records of English quilting are more specific about the materials used. An item in a wardrobe account in the reign of King John, dated 1212, was for the payment of 12 pence for a pound of cotton for the stuffing of a haketon belonging to the King.[1] Cotton or linen were tougher than wool for padding fabric armour and not liable to moth damage; nevertheless, wool is mentioned a number of times in connection with protective body armour. Wool soaked with vinegar also has been recommended as the padding for a gambeson, for the purpose, so it was said, of providing increased resistance to iron, and although a comment on this idea – 'that it was probably done to keep out vermin'[2] – no doubt has some truth in it, it has another possible and significant application. In *Historia Naturalis* (A.D. 77), Pliny the Elder states that 'The old Romans assigned to wool even supernatural powers . . . and besides dress and protection from cold, unwashed wool supplies very many remedies if dipped in oil and wine or vinegar, according as the particular need is for an emollient or a pungent remedy, for an astringent or relaxing one, being applied and frequently moistened, for dislocations and aching sinews.'[3] There must have been many aching sinews enclosed in armour, for which relief would have been welcome and, with the possible addition of supernatural protection thrown in, this custom may well have continued.

Regulations for the padding and stuffing of medieval quilted armour were strict, as the materials were out of sight and could not be inspected and it was necessary to prevent the use of old rags and bad materials. In *Comptus Ballivorum Franciae* in 1286, cendal and tow are mentioned in an item for stuffing gambesons but the cendal probably was used as lining behind the quilted tow. In 1311 other regulations stipulated that new cotton materials must be used for padding, although 'old linen' was allowed between the folds.[4] In the Low Countries in the middle of the fifteenth century, the pourpoint was stuffed with cotton waste 'to the thickness of four fingers', as being more easily compressed than folds of linen material;[5] some French army regulations of 1450, gave 29 or 30 thicknesses of linen encased in deer-skin for the making of jacks.[6] Cotton padding was used for some silk-covered arming doublets in the sixteenth century (p. 84), and flax was used for a German military skirt (p. 84).

Padding for domestic quilting is mentioned in the fifteenth century for which 'flockes' was used, and Fabyan couples the use of this with linen outer covers – 'Like as, for quilts, ticks and mattresses, the flax of the Cadurci in Fraunce hath no fellow; for surely the invention thereof, as also of flockes to stuff them with, came out of Fraunce.'[7] Also in the inventory taken on the death of Sir John Fastolfe in 1459, an item was listed of 'j Pettecote of lynen clothe stoffyd with flokys.'[8] At this time 'flokys' probably would have been all wool, but of inferior quality from that used for spinning. A 'good thick quylt of cotton or els of pure flockes or of cleane woole' was recommended for the making of a nightcap in 1541 (p. 83) and all of these types of padding were recognised as suitable for quilting at that time.

Cotton had been imported in quantity into England since early in the fifteenth century, but there seems to be no record of it as padding for bed quilts, until the 'India quilts' and other cotton merchandise from the Far East, became fashionable in the seventeenth century (see Chapter 7). Wool, however, was in good supply in England during the early days of recorded quilting, and for domestic quilting it is likely that the rough wool left over from shearing, as well as pieces left on the briars in the fields, were washed and used for padding, much as it has been in rural areas up to the present century. No serious mention in literature is made of the material which lay between the outer layers of a quilt, and although poets and playwrights have had quite a lot to say about the outward appearances of quilts from time to time, only one seems to have let loose his imagination on padding material. In Philip Massinger's play *Maid of Honour*, produced in 1632, the following lines occur –

> Quilts fill'd high
> With gossamer and roses, cannot yield
> The body soft repose, the mind kept waking
> With anguish and affliction.[9]

With the exception of imported quilts, most of the surviving eighteenth-century wadded quilting was padded with a thin layer of natural wool, while cotton cord or thread was used for the patterns in cord quilting. There is mention sometimes of cotton padding being used for skirts or robes; part of a sixteenth-century farthingale received extra padding of cotton to supplement the cord (p. 94). Petticoats, waistcoats and jackets for women made of wadded quilting, usually contained wool padding. A number of petticoats in the eighteenth century were padded with wool which had been dyed blue; whether this was a fashionable craze for a time is not certain, as no specific mention seems to have been made of it, but it appears to have been used often under white or cream materials, and possibly this was intended to give an undertone of colour to – or perhaps to take up the colour of – an overskirt. It has been suggested that the blue-dyed wool may have been the surplus from another piece of work, but too many petticoats contain it for it not to have been intentional. Another theory is that natural-coloured wool tends to give 'a slightly dirty look' through thin silk of a pale colour.[10]

During the nineteenth century, records and surviving examples of quilting show that various kinds of material were used for padding, and the choice lay sometimes with a need for economy. Economy to the point of meanness, was one of using paper for the padding of bed quilts supplied in the Poor Law Institutions and hospitals. They were no doubt warm enough and better than none at all and often enough the tops were made of red and white patchwork squares, on which texts were embroidered; they were known as 'hospital' and, sometimes, 'scripture' quilts.

Economy for domestic quilts consisted in making use of odd lengths or pieces of woven materials, such as woollen garments no longer serviceable, which were unpicked and the pieces laid in layers and smoothed as much as possible between the outer covers, before quilting. Disused blanket made good padding and was easy to sew, and quilts containing it still remain in some Northern districts, in South Wales and in Northern Ireland. Some Welsh quilts, with an interlining of Welsh flannel in the piece, are both light and warm and the patterns on them seem to be especially finely quilted, perhaps because of the even thickness of the padding; others of a rough nature contain mill puff.

The most usual kinds of padding have been either cotton wadding, or washed and carded wool, not only in Britain and America, but in all countries where quilting has been practised. In Britain, the kind of padding has been governed to some extent by whichever sort was most easily come by. Generally speaking wool has been found in quilts from South Wales, the south-western counties, Westmorland, Cumberland and the Isle of Man, where sheep-raising was common and wool could be had almost for the gathering, and the counties lying within reach of manufacturing towns – Durham, Northumberland and Yorkshire – have had plentiful supplies of cotton wadding which was reasonably cheap to buy. These are by no means hard-and-fast rules, and quilts made in all districts since about the middle of the nineteenth century can be found with either wool or cotton padding. A soft cotton padding, known as 'domett', sometimes has been used for cot and cradle quilts and some garments.

Padding for American quilts largely has been of cotton grown in that country, but before the time of the Revolution wadding as well as quilts were imported from England. Eighteenth-century shipping records mention both in cargoes of textiles; in 1727 'Quilts, Ruggs and Waddings' were listed in such a cargo, of a ship from England which landed on 22 June in that year.[11] Wool padding has been used also for American quilts but there has been a preference for cotton as it is cleaner to prepare, and there is no risk of staining from oil as in ill-prepared wool; for present-day work 'cotton quilt batt' can be bought for the purpose. Other kinds of padding which are recommended are pre-shrunk blanket for lightweight quilts, and Dacron polyester batt or double thickness of cotton for a thicker padding. A recent book on American needlework recommends for quilted cushions, 'a piece of flannel, worn-out blanket, bathrobe (almost anything soft will do)'.[12]

Synthetic materials for padding, gradually are taking the place of those made with natural fibres. Even the older generation of traditional quilters is coming to use Courtelle and similar materials, which are reasonably cheap to buy by the yard and are easy to quilt through (159). There is no trouble in spreading this padding evenly, as there is with wool or wadding and two or more layers can be used for extra warmth. It washes and dries quickly and well, but in spite of all these advantages, nothing is equal to clean carded wool as regards warmth and maintaining the good appearance of the patterns. Perhaps there is something in the belief of the supernatural powers of wool.

Whatever kind of padding is used, it is important to keep the original freshness of the work after several years of wear, and the secret lies in washing carefully and choosing a day with a certain amount of breeze – and not a strong wind – for drying. The quilt should be shaken from time to time to loosen the fibres in the padding, and afterwards hung in a warm atmosphere to dry out completely. No ironing should be necessary.

Wool and cotton only have been used for cord and stuffed quilting and there seems to be nothing to suggest that any inferior or economic kind of padding has been used at any stage. Neither is there any early written description of either type of quilting in which we can identify the kind of padding, but from examples which have survived, tufts or cord of either wool or cotton fibres have been found (6, 108). While wadded quilting has been looked upon as cottage work since the early part of the nineteenth century, cord or stuffed quilting have been regarded as an occupation or a fashion of the well-to-do since the early eighteenth century. Bed covers of wadded quilting were intended for warmth and those with corded patterns were of a less practical nature in this respect; but for fitted clothing, such as waistcoats, caps and the like, closely quilted cord gave a pleasant stiffening to linen, cotton and silk, and sufficient warmth where wadded quilting would have been cumbersome and well-nigh stuffy to wear (106, 110, 111, 118, 119). That cord and stuffed quilting require a degree of skill to carry out and are slow to do, has not recommended the work to everyone, but its relative rarity adds to its attraction for others.

Nowadays cotton is used for both types of quilting. Firm cotton cord gives good results for linen and cotton, and it can be bought for little cost and in different thicknesses – a thickness appropriate for most materials costs only a few pence a yard.[13] Candlewick and upholstery cord are recommended for cord quilting in America, where the work is more popular than in Britain. Little or no stuffed quilting is done in Britain, but instructions for doing it, illustrated with recently made examples, are given in some American needlework books.[14] Teased wool or cotton are recommended for the padding.

A kind of needlework known as *shadow quilting*, is made of soft, semi-transparent materials, such as muslin or fine silk, in the manner of cord quilting, but instead of cord a thick coloured wool, or wool and nylon as used for knitting, is threaded between the outer layers (see Appendix C). The wool should not be of pale colours, but bright enough to show faintly through the top material. Like cord and stuffed quilting, this work is not reversible.

Top and Backing Materials

From the earliest records, linen seems to have been used more than any other material for the outer covers of bed quilts, clothing and any other purpose for which quilting has been practicable, and although there is little indication as to any difference of quality, it is likely that this varied according to the appropriate need. The 'pettecote of lynen cloth' of Sir John Fastolfe – which would have been literally a 'petit' or short coat and not an underskirt – undoubtedly differed from the quality or strength of the linen used for his jacks (one of which was made of black linen), or for those of the dependants on his estate. Materials other than linen used for body armour of all kinds, varied from canvas, buckram, leather, deerskin, or chamois (99) and fustian, to silk for linings and quilted doublets (p. 84), and velvet for the surcoat of the Black Prince (p. 12).

Materials which were used as linings for clothing, often were suitable for outer covers of bed quilts and are mentioned in descriptions of both from an early date. Fustian had a multitude of uses; a twilled cotton material with a short nap, it too, was made in various qualities suitable for making 'sokkes for the Queen', as given in the *Privy Purse Expenses of Elizabeth of York* (1503), and other articles of clothing in inventories and accounts until the seventeenth century, as well as lining fabric armour and making either the top or lining of quilts; 'fustian down' was used for padding quilted upholstery (see Chapters 6 and 7).

Sarcenet, known also as sarsnet, sercennett, sarcinet and other various spellings, is a soft, silk material which is little different from the time it was first known in England in the thirteenth century. It is used still for linings, and records show that it was made into quilted and embroidered bed covers as late as the eighteenth century. Cendal (sendel or sendall), has been described as 'something of a mystery' as to its nature, but there seems little doubt that it was a kind of fine silk, made in several qualities suitable for different purposes. Apart from references to fabric armour and quilts, such as the 'rich quilt of crimson sendel stitched with thredes of gold' (p. 18), it is mentioned as a lining material in the fourteenth century, for the crimson and blue outer garments worn by the Doctor of Physic in *The Canterbury Tales*.[15] About a hundred years later, it was described as 'a thynne stuff lyke cypres; but yet was a thin stuff lyke sarcenett and of a raw kynde of silk or sarcenett, but coarser and narrower than sarcenett now ys',[16] which pleasant ramble leaves us not much wiser than before.

Another medieval material, mentioned in connection with quilting, was checklaton, sometimes ciclatoun. Sir Thopas of *The Canterbury Tales* wore a robe of ciclatoun, and Spenser was much taken with its rich appearance having given the Gyant in *The Faerie Queene* a jacket of quilted checklaton (p. 9), he described it elsewhere as a 'kind of quilded leather' (p. 87), but whether or not it was so, comments on its brightness suggest a rich material, possibly with gold thread woven into it. Lute-string – a corruption of 'lustring' – was a lustrous silk material of which quilts were made, and quilts of taffeta, sometimes described as 'chaungeable' (corresponding to 'shot silk' nowadays) appeared in inventories, suggesting that it was of a quality suitable for upper-class households.

Pertian or persian was another of the silk materials used for quilting and mentioned in eighteenth-century records, which was looked upon as appropriate for linings also. It was thin and soft much like the China silk of the quilts imported from the East, from which quilts and clothing were made. Towards the end of the eighteenth century when quilted clothing was still worn in England, the Reverend James Woodforde was so greatly impressed by the Oriental dress of a visitor to Oxford, that he described it in detail in his diary for 13 June 1775 – 'A Chinese man about 25 years of age came to see our College. . . . He had on his head a Cap like a Bell covered with a red Feather and tyed under his Chin, a kind of Close Coat on his back, of pink silk quilted, over that a loose Gown of pink silk quilted also, which came down to his heels, and over that a black Gauze or Crape in imitation of a long cloak, a pr of Breeches or drawers of pink silk and quilted also and a kind of silk Boots of the same colour and quilted also, and a pr of red Morocco slippers.'[17]

Until the beginning of the nineteenth century, quilting on silk and satin was recorded many times, and in some cases quilting was described as having some embroidered pattern worked upon it. This suggests that the work was not padded with wadding but, probably, was flat quilted without any padding. Unfortunately, it is possible only to assume that this was so, as early bed quilts of silk or satin have perished. Embroidery with cord quilting is possible because the padding is added after the embroidery and quilting stitches have been done (181). The most practical way of quilting over a surface decoration, is when this addition is done during the process of weaving, as in the case of the late seventeenth-century red and green silk flowered jacket shown on figure 103. Tops of silk or satin in wadded quilting, whether used for quilts or petticoats, relied on the quilting patterns for their decoration (Frontispiece).

By the end of the eighteenth century, when the quilted petticoat was no longer fashionable, cotton print had replaced silk and satin in popularity. Bed quilts still were made, but cotton patchwork, as well as the colour-printed patterns on the cottons, were a discouragement to the expert quilter, whose work could be seen to advantage only on the back of the quilt if this was of plain material. The use of patchwork had begun as a fashion early in the century as a means of using up the left-over pieces of the imported chints from India (p. 121). Before the end of the century a patchwork quilt was not only a fashionable possession, but making one was accepted as a genteel occupation for the well-to-do, in spite of the background of economy. Even the famous Miss Catherine Hutton, who made such a name for herself in all aspects of needlework in her time, was not averse to a quilt made from used garments. An entry in her journal for 31 July 1779, stated that she had 'Called upon my Aunt Perkins, who showed us several family antiquities, and promised me a bed-quilt that was a gown and petticoat of my grandmother.'[18] This must have been of patchwork. As she was given to enlarging at length on her own achievements, it is sad that she could not do the same for the work of others, or more might have been known about this quilt. Miss Hutton would have been about 22 years of age at the time, and so, at a rough estimate, the gown and petticoat could have been worn about 50 years before and made from some of the imported 'painted callicoes' or pintadoes.

The craze for patchwork had a lasting effect on quilting and from the beginning of the nineteenth century, cotton had taken the place of silk and satin for quilt tops. For a time quilting suffered a setback, as unpadded bed-spreads were more popular, but some good examples of quilted patchwork have survived from the early years of the century, probably made by diehard quilters in spite of the difficulties which they found in sewing through the patches. By the 1830s, however, they had turned the patchwork shapes to good account and adapted traditional quilting patterns to fit them (150). Some silk, velvet and satin patchwork bedspreads made towards the end of the century, have no place in quilting history; the materials were not worth the skill and labour of the work.

It is known that woollen materials were used for quilt tops in the eighteenth century, and a woollen material called 'calamanca', which had a glazed surface, was used as a backing for silk and satin petticoats. Often the wool for quilt tops was homespun. Examples of North Country farmhouse quilts of homespun are illustrated in *Quilting in the North of England* and *Traditional Quilting*,[19] and wool, grown on the Manx sheep, and spun and woven on the Isle of Man was made into quilts there during the nineteenth and early twentieth centuries.[20] A survey carried out in the island over a number of years, beginning about 1938, found that these quilt tops sometimes were made in chequered patterns of red and blue squares, and others like the North Country strip quilts, consisted of alternating strips of red and blue or green. Cloth or calico were used as backing materials and, as they were padded with natural wool, the resulting warmth must have been considerable.

Some quilts in South Wales were made of locally woven cloth, and a number of them had tops of Welsh flannel and a backing of calico or patchwork, with a leaning towards strong or dark colours. A Pembrokeshire quilt made about the end of the nineteenth century is typical of many others, with a backing of slate-blue Welsh flannel; the top is made of a patchwork of large and small square and rectangular pieces in dark purple, reddish purple, brown, and dark red, and the centre patches are joined by strips of blue.

An account of quilting done in Northern Ireland, written in 1959, describes quilts made there at the beginning of this century.[21] The information was collected in Glenlark, in County Tyrone, and referred to work done in the districts in the glen. The commonest type of quilt had a red–flannel top, also known as 'swanskin', which was two yards wide and bought locally. Sometimes red flannel would be used for both top and backing 'to produce a reversible article', while for other quilts, dyed blanket would be used for either top or backing, or for both. Backing material for flannel quilts 'generally was coarse cotton "flour pokes", prepared and dyed with factory-made dyes'. These quilts, padded with blanket, were heavy and warm but others of light weight were made with an unpadded flannel top and backing. Strangely enough, linen-covered quilts are unknown in the area.

In some parts of South Wales and the northern districts of England, heavy woollen fabrics such as suitings, factory samples, tailor's cuttings and samples, were used to make cloth or 'stuff' quilts in the nineteenth century and, in this century, as late as the 1950s. The pieces were joined in a rough kind of patchwork for both outer layers, with used and unpicked woollen clothing for padding. They were backed with a coarse unbleached calico or, even, ticking, and it was impossible to quilt them in the usual way. They were stitched through with a strong thread, either in long stitches in widely spaced lines from end to end and side to side, which had the appearance of sheep netting, or by knotting, a process in which isolated stitches through the quilt were made at intervals, and the thread ends tied in firm knots (12).

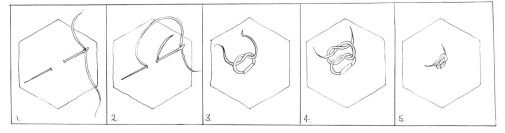

12   *Five stages of Knotting*

Outdoor working petticoats in the nineteenth and early twentieth centuries also were made of woollens, including homespun, but petticoats for ordinary wear were made from satin, silk, sateen and cotton, either white or coloured, which, sometimes, had printed patterns. Cotton for hard-wearing and economical bed quilts, and silk or satin for 'best', have been most popular for wadded quilting. Silk and satin are light and soft, and yield easily to the sewing, making the work go smoothly and showing the patterns at their best. The quilted cotton bed covers have little to fault in them, except to the critical eye of the 'old hand', who prefers a soft sheen (but not a gloss) to show off the patterns.

The kinds of material for top and backing, differ according to the method used for the work in hand. Sometimes a loosely woven fabric is needed for the lower layer, as in cord or stuffed quilting, when only one side of the work is seen (pp. 191, 193) but the same kind of material can be used for both sides of wadded quilting, when the patterns are seen on the reverse as they are in bed quilts. For quilted garments, such as dressing-gowns and bed-jackets, cushion and teapot covers and so on, which are lined inside, and the back of the quilting is not seen, a thinner backing material is sufficient.

Silk materials should be of good quality; crêpe-de-chine and silk shantung and satin which is not glossy, are well suited to quilting. Fine cotton and calico as well as fine linen (134) have made hard-wearing quilts and would continue to do so, as many of today's fabrics of cotton or linen are of the right texture and quality. Cotton poplin, in particular, makes good quilts which wash well, as the colours are fast.

Rayon, mercerised or synthetic materials are unsympathetic and stiff to quilt by hand and, even when machine-stitched, the results are not successful, except when commercially mass-produced for waterproof garments, hard-wearing coat linings and other inexpensive clothing.

Fine linen and cotton are still the most serviceable for cord-quilting; silk does not wear as well with the cord padding, but it is well suited to the softer materials used for padding in stuffed quilting.

3 TOOLS AND EQUIPMENT

The traditional item of equipment regarded as indispensable for working all types of quilting is the frame, and although the kind of frame differs according to the method used, its function is the same. This is to keep the several layers of material in place, evenly stretched and reasonably taut, while the patterns are being stitched through them, and when the finished work is taken out of the frame and the tension is released, they will appear in deeper relief. The methods of preparing or 'setting up' frames of all kinds, are governed in small ways by individual preferences but basically they are the same, and standard methods for use with each kind of frame are given in the appropriate Appendix.

In parts of the country where traditional wadded quilting once flourished the sight of a frame in use is no longer familiar and although it has not died out altogether, nowadays the place of the quilt frame, all too often, is in the attic or cupboard, taken apart, with the pieces tied together – sometimes wrapped in a dust-sheet, sometimes not – since the days when 'my grandmother' or 'my mother' used it. The reasons given for not throwing out a

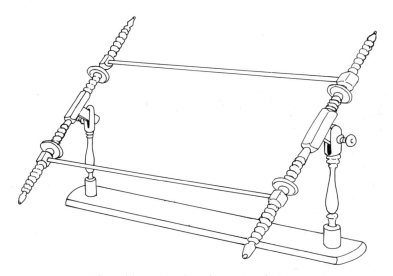

13   *Adjustable embroidery frame to stand on a table*

disused frame are generally sentimental ones, but sometimes there is a hope of putting it to use again with a chance of more leisure 'later on', or when the room now occupied by a growing family is no longer needed.

The matter of the space taken up by a full-sized conventional frame, especially during the time of preparation necessary for working on a large quilt is, no doubt, one of the reasons for the decline in quilting, although the same cannot be said for the making of smaller things, such as cot covers, for which smaller and lighter frames are adequate. These can be moved and put away out of working hours without disturbing the work, where a special workroom is not available. For even smaller things, especially those made with corded or stuffed patterns, an adjustable embroidery frame which can stand on the table or floor is practical and takes up very little room (13). The double-ring embroidery frame (14) or the back of a well-made picture-frame (157) often can be adapted and used, and are light enough to hold in the hand for working. A double-ring frame, which is supported on its own stand and

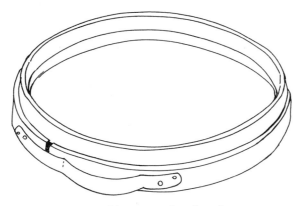

14   *Double-ring embroidery frame*

known as a 'quilting hoop', is used by some American quilters even for full-sized quilts; the work is done in small areas and the hoop moved as the work proceeds, but this method calls for especially careful preparation beforehand (Appendix A).

Frames intended for full-sized quilts need support strong enough to hold them steadily and at the right height for the worker, and the recognised traditional way to achieve this has been to rest the four corners of the frames on the backs of chairs of equal and convenient height, so leaving room for the work to be done at the sides. The chair backs should be flat at the top or, as with ladderback chairs, have well-placed lower bars, also flat topped, which can be used. In her book, *Old Patchwork Quilts*, Mrs Ruth Finley

describes the chairs which were used for supporting frames in America –
'The corners of the quilting frames were supported on the tops of low-
backed chairs, all the same height. Every household had a set of at least four
"quilting chairs", whose ordinary usefulness was confined to the kitchen.
. . . Many old chairs show a slight indentation across their tops where the
quilting frames rested, leaving their mark through the years.'[1]

In view of the amount of quilting done here and in America, it is surprising
that this improvised way of supporting frames was not only tolerated, but
continued to be so for as long as recorded work and methods have been
known; and frames which have attached, or especially intended supports,
seem to have been treated as phenomenal and worthy of mention. During
her research into the practice of traditional wadded quilting in England and
Wales (from 1928 to 1954), Mrs FitzRandolph found little evidence of any
but the conventional type in use, supported on chairs, either at that time or
in earlier years. She was told of a Welsh frame 'with its own legs',[2] which did
away with the need for other support, and Mrs Hake found another similar
one in north Devon which she describes, in *English Quilting*,[3] as being kept in
a room set apart from the work, which 'was always empty except for a
chair and a gigantic quilting frame (alleged to have been large enough to
have stretched a full-sized quilt) which stood on its own four legs, instead of
resting on chairs or tables such as was the custom with smaller frames'. But
there is more evidence of self-supporting frames in America and some are
illustrated in Mrs Webster's *Quilts. Their Story*,[4] and in *The Romance of the
Patchwork Quilt* by Mrs Hall and Mrs Kretsinger.[5] Another American frame
of this type is in the possession of the American Museum at Bath; it was
found in New Jersey and is dated as late nineteenth century (15).

A feature of these and apparently all self-supporting frames is that they have
a ratchet adjustment for altering the tension of the material and for rolling
the quilt as the work proceeds. But with the seemingly sole exception of one
found by Mrs FitzRandolph, the ratchet seems to be American in origin.
The English exception, which was found in Weardale, County Durham, was
said to have been made there at the beginning of the 1900s;[6] but as there is
evidence of American influence on some of the patchwork patterns in quilts
made in the same part of the county at the end of the nineteenth century, it
is quite possible that ideas for quilting frames came across the Atlantic also.

Frames and Wadded Quilting

With the exception of the double-ring, and adjustable frames generally
associated with all kinds of embroidery, the standard type of quilting frame is

relatively simple to make, and for anyone with a little aptitude for carpentry, it is straightforward enough to be made at home; otherwise a local carpenter or handyman could do the work. There is no evidence to show that, at any time, these frames have been made or sold commercially, and searching enquiries have not found any shop able, or even willing, to make and sell them today. Working drawings, however, are supplied by the Council for Small Industries in Rural Areas, for the conventional and ratchet types of frame; but those for the latter do not include any structure for self-support.[7] That the conventional frame has been in use for embroidery for at least 300 years is in no doubt, as the illustration on figure 20 comes from a German picture-book, *Curioser Spiegel*,[8] of about the year 1700, and shows two frames almost identical with present-day frames for quilting. Although the scholars are seen learning embroidery, it is known that quilting was done in Germany in the seventeenth century, so it is likely that the same kind of frame was used for that too, and the fact that it has survived without 'improvements' proves its worth and suitability for its job.

The frame consists of four straight lengths of wood (cut with the grain and never across it), two of comparatively sturdy construction, known as 'rails' or 'runners', and two, more slender pieces, called the 'stretchers' (16). The measurements of each may be varied according to the size needed – a small or medium-sized quilt or a cot quilt can be worked in a smaller frame than that required for one of full size, although some experienced quilters will use a large frame for a quilt of medium size. The essential thing is that the runners are long enough to take the full width of the proposed work, whether it is a bed quilt or a tea-cosy. Each runner must have at least two – and sometimes four – slots, cut through the thickness, which are wide and deep enough to enable the stretchers to be put through them. For a large frame, flat-sided timbers of 2×2 inches seem to be the average thickness, although a few may be a half inch more or less, and the length may be from six to eight feet, depending on the size of the work. Runners for some American ratchet frames are either round or octagonal, as in the one at the American Museum at Bath (15). A length of webbing of the kind used for light upholstery such as chair seats, and long enough to take the width of the quilt material, should be nailed firmly with short carpet-tacks to one side of each runner through which the slots are *not* made – that is to say, the webbing is attached to the top of the runner and the slots are cut through from side to side (17). The important point is that the measurements of the slots correspond to those of the stretchers. Lighter timber can be used for small frames – 1×1 inch will be sufficient – and a lighter webbing or a good braid is quite adequate, but it is still necessary for it to be fixed firmly to the runners,

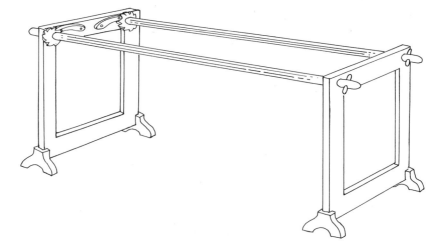

15   *Standing American frame with ratchets for adjustments*

as it is to this that the materials will be attached during the quilting. When fixing the webbing, it is advisable to put in the tacks in two rows, angled as for cabbage-planting in the garden (· . · · .).

The stretchers are lighter in weight, usually measuring from one to two inches in width and seldom more than one-quarter inch in thickness (for small frames even less), and it is necessary that they should fit easily but not loosely into the runner slots. The length is less than that for runners, 36 inches being a comfortable measurement for working. A series of spaced holes are bored through each end of the stretchers, sometimes in one row with holes about one inch apart (16), sometimes in two rows with the holes angled – the rows being one inch apart and the holes in each spaced at two-inch intervals (17). In some frames the holes are bored through the runners at right angles to, and also through, the slots, as in the early German frames (16, 20).

To complete the frames, four pegs of wood or metal are needed, which are used to hold the runners and stretchers in position when they are slotted together, by inserting them in the stretcher holes; as the sections of quilted pattern are completed, the pegs are removed for readjustments to be made and then replaced (Appendix A). Most pegs are of wood, slightly tapered at one end and made to fit snugly into the holes; they have, also, a shallow groove or neck at the top to allow for a length of string to be attached, so that they can be tethered to the frame (18c). Metal pegs are used sometimes, and as a rule, are about as thick as a six-inch nail (a not unusual substitute at times) with a loop at the top (18a). Once in a while pegs can be found in which pride

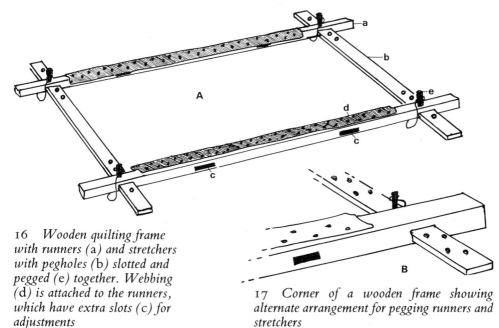

16 *Wooden quilting frame with runners (a) and stretchers with pegholes (b) slotted and pegged (e) together. Webbing (d) is attached to the runners, which have extra slots (c) for adjustments*

17 *Corner of a wooden frame showing alternate arrangement for pegging runners and stretchers*

of workmanship has been added to the ordinary straight shape and result in the kind of set made by a Hampshire carpenter in 1932 (18b). A screw adjustment for use in place of pegs, was found on a Weardale frame,[9] and iron clamps for the same purpose succeeded the wooden pegs in early American frames, but they do not seem to have been used at all in Britain.[10]

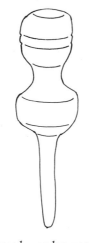

18 *(a) Metal peg*   *(b) Carved wooden peg*   *(c) Straight wooden peg with string*

The measurements given by Mrs Finley[11] and Mrs Peto[12] for frames used by American quilters, show them to have been more massive than the average British ones, where a nine-foot length is exceptional. In American frames the four strips of wood ordinarily were about an inch thick, two to four inches wide and some ten to twelve feet in length and, no doubt, clamps were more practical for these than wooden pegs; but for convenience and ease in working, and where space allows, the self-supporting frame with a ratchet adjustment has the advantage over all others.

Various kinds of wood have been used to make frames, but most are of pinewood, which lends itself to simple carpentry for those who are not professionals, although oaken frames are not uncommon and sometimes pinewood runners are used with stretchers of oak. Occasionally a cherished frame of mahogany has escaped the jumble sale, but these are rare, probably because the wood is hard and the frame unnecessarily heavy when finished; but whatever the wood, the runners and stretchers must be cut with the grain and be well prepared by planing and sandpapering, and finished with emery cloth. A smooth surface is an absolute necessity – and this includes the pegs if they are of wood; any trace of roughness might catch the materials and ruin the quilt.

Probably because of the difficulties connected with making, using and storing a frame, many a worker has tried, in one way or another, to quilt without it, but the skilled quilter would never be satisfied with any contriving or making-do without a frame. Accounts have been given of materials laid on a table, weighted at the corners with flat-irons or large stones, and quilted after a fashion,[13] and although it is possible only to guess, it is probable that fabric armour was held in the hand while the layers were stitched together. But this was rough though effective stuff, and perhaps the

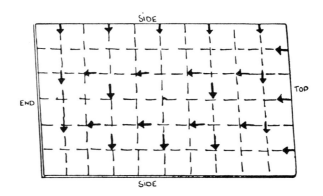

19   *Close lines of tackings necessary before quilting or knotting without a frame*

same may be said of any bed covers quilted without a frame. It is possible, however, to quilt small areas of material held in the hand, and quilts of patchwork which are composed of a number of sections or blocks – each usually about 12 to 15 inches square – can be made by quilting each block separately and joining them afterwards, but any method which dispenses with the conventional type of frame for quilting entails much more preparation beforehand, with close tacking or basting all over and through the layers of material, so that there is no possibility of them moving while the quilting is being done (19).

Frames for Flat, Corded and Stuffed Quilting

Frames which are suitable for wadded quilting are equally so for the methods used in flat, corded and stuffed quilting, especially for large pieces of work such as bedspreads; but in this country, work on such a scale is seldom, if ever, attempted nowadays. The principle of holding in place layers of material while the permanent stitching is done, is the same for all types, and even for the small piece of work it is an advantage to use a frame of some kind.

A simple piece of equipment for flat quilting is illustrated (157). It shows a light wooden frame which was once part of a well-made picture-frame, with neatly mortised corners to keep it rigid, and the materials attached to it with brass drawing-pins; any similar construction could be made at home satisfactorily, as long as its size allowed the quilting area to be kept free of the surround of the frame. In the example shown, the outer borders of the design measure $7\frac{1}{2} \times 8\frac{1}{2}$ inches and the frame measurements are $10\frac{1}{2} \times 12\frac{1}{2}$ inches; it is light to hold and work on, and small enough to be put away in a work drawer when necessary. Details for setting up and working are given in Appendix B.

A double-ring frame can be used for flat and cord quilting (14), but unless the pattern is small enough to lie completely within the boundary of the frame circle, it is not practicable for corded quilting, and a more satisfactory frame for this work is the type suitable for stuffed quilting (13), or that used for wadded patterns. Some highly skilled workers, no doubt, could do this without a frame, but none would recommend it as a general practice.

Other Equipment

After the frame, templates are the most important part of quilt-making equipment and quilters of experience acquire a large stock of them over the years, especially for wadded quilting. As these generally are made of cardboard, it is not unusual to find that basic shapes for favoured patterns are kept unused, from which new templates can be drawn as the working ones become soft and the finer points of the outlines have lost their shape. A cleanly cut outline can be achieved by cutting round the pencilled outline of the pattern which has been drawn on to cardboard, and sheets of template patterns can be supplied by the Council for Small Industries in Rural Areas at a small charge[14] (Appendix F).

A knife is the ideal tool for cutting the cardboard templates, and one well suited to this is a lino-cutting knife; it has a short, sharp blade especially shaped for the purpose and is invaluable for template-cutting. An excellent one with interchangeable blades can be bought quite cheaply at most good craft shops.

A good boxwood ruler, or a yardstick, or a large T-square will be needed for measuring and marking straight lines. Either tailor's chalk or a blue pencil (both favoured by experienced quilters since the nineteenth century) may be preferred by some for marking patterns for wadded quilting but perhaps the most satisfactory tool for this is a large yarn or rug needle. An ordinary HB lead pencil is often used for drawing the patterns for stuffed quilting, which is done on the back of the work (Appendix D).

Sheets of greaseproof-paper, and blue and yellow carbon-paper will be needed for those who make their own patterns, and a collection of transfers is necessary for those who do not.

Two pairs of scissors are advisable: a good pair for cutting out materials, and another for odd jobs (cutting thread and so on).

It is recognised generally that needles are preferable to pins for holding the work, and Mrs Fletcher, the well-known quilter in the North Country, recommends no. 9 between needles for this as well as for sewing wadded quilting, to the extent of having a stock of 'several dozen' available.[15] Most experienced quilters use the short *between* needle for sewing, the size used being that of individual preference as a rule, but the thickness of material and wadding has to be taken into account and, according to this, nos. 7, 8 and 9 are good ones to have on hand. For patterns which are stitched first and the padding or cord added afterwards, some workers prefer *sharps*, generally nos. 8 or 9, and a large-eyed blunt crewel type of needle will be needed for threading in the cord after sewing (Appendix C). The rug or yarn needle used for marking patterns in wadded quilting can be useful also for inserting the wool into stuffed quilting patterns in small areas, and a smooth stuffing-stick will be needed where a needle is not long enough (Appendix D).

.White tape will be needed for taping the sides of the quilt materials to the stretchers or embroidery frame; it should be not less than one inch in width (Appendix A).

20   *Scene of a needlework school taken from a German picture book* Curioser Spiegel, *showing frames in use identical with present-day types.* c. *1700*

4 PATTERNS: WADDED QUILTING

It is likely that, in the first place, quilting patterns came about involuntarily in the process of the work. Little experience in sewing is needed to discover that diagonal lines of stitching through layers of woven material hold them more firmly together than those which follow the straight woven thread; furthermore, that circular or spiral lines, although more difficult to accomplish, are even more useful for securing two or more thicknesses in place. Certainly patterns in quilting made by the diagonal line, the spiral and the scroll have the longest records of any that are found in present-day work, the first having lasted for upwards of 6,000 years and the other two for over 2,000 (1, 3).

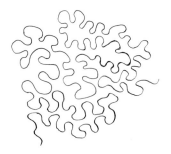

21 *Meander ground pattern*

In spite of the different methods of work used in quilting, there is a clear relationship between many patterns in all types – which shows that a good deal of borrowing and exchange of ideas has taken place in the past. In each type, however, there are characteristics which are not shared. The meander pattern (21) is found only in flat quilting, although it is associated with cord quilting patterns as a background (109), and some of the naturalistic types of shape found in wadded quilting have no counterpart in work padded with cord.

Quilting patterns have developed, or been taken from, many sources in the past. The geometrical types are related to mosaics of all kinds, from pavements to patchwork; and naturalistic shapes have been used where they appealed to the worker, and accorded with her competence in planning a pattern and ability to carry it out. Natural and formal outlines of flowers, fruit, birds, insects, animals and human figures are found in work of every century and, on occasions, those of ships, anchors, horseshoes, bicycles, houses, castles and many others. In common with design in much of today's needlework, that seen in quilting is sometimes freehand and experimental, and shows some loss of precision and rhythm, but, no doubt, it will be seen in better perspective in a few years' time. Patterns still made in the traditional shapes are unaffected.

Planning a design for needlework often has been beyond the scope of a worker whose skill in executing it was of the highest order, while others, with perhaps less ability for sewing, have been notable and professional designers, among whom men as well as women have been interested in quilting. Records of professional pattern-makers have survived, and quilting is among one of the sixteenth-century trades included in Thomas Newbury's *Dives Pragmaticus* (p. 84). Each line of the numerous couplets contains trades and occupations which are related:

Al occupacions to me must resort
To buy and then sell, to others comfort

Al Haberdashers, pedlers and makers of pinnes.
Al true Hoteliers and keepers of Innes.
Al Websters, Weavers, Shoremen and Fullers.
Al Carders, Spinners and sheepskin pullers:
Al Dyers, Drapers and Mercers lykewise.
Al Sylkemen and Semesters that I can devyse.
Al Broderers, Taylors, Quylters and Limners.
Al Upholsters, Brokers, Furriers and Skinners.

What lack you mistris; Come hither to me.

Professional pattern-makers advertised their skill and the names of many have been recorded until the end of the eighteenth century. The late seventeenth-century waistcoat illustrated (102), is inscribed along the shoulder – 'John Stilwell, Drawear, at ye Flaming Toorch in Russel Street Cou[rt]', and in 1706, an entry in Lady Grisel Baillie's household accounts was for five shillings paid to John Skugald the painter for 'drawing Grisie's peticoat' which is likely to refer to a quilting pattern; John Skugald was employed otherwise to paint the portraits of the family.[1] In London, pattern-drawing was included in the trade-cards issued by shopkeepers who sold haberdashery and drapery, a routine service which was encouraged by the fashionable use of quilting in both men's and women's clothing, as well as household furnishings. Francis Bishop, at the 'Sign of the Sun and Dove in King Street, Bloomsbury Square', described himself as a haberdasher, glover and pattern-drawer; Francis Flower at the 'Sign of the Rose and Woolsack' undertook to draw 'all Sorts of Patterns' and sold also 'shades of silk and worsted and canvas for working . . . all sorts of threads . . . with a great choice of linens; as Hollands, Callicoes, Cambricks, Lawns, Muslins, etc.[2]

In the middle of the century, Walter Gale of Mayfield in Sussex, recorded in his journal the drawing of a quilt pattern for a customer.

> '1750 Dec. 26th. I began to draw the quilt belonging to Mrs Godman. Dec. 30th. I finished the bed quilt after five days close application. It gave satisfaction and I received 10s 6d for the drawing.'[3]

This man made patterns for waistcoats (as well as for bed covers) for which cord quilting was fashionable, and it is very likely that Mrs Godman's quilt was drawn out for this work. Five days would be an excessively long time for drawing out a wadded quilt pattern but not too long for the finer detail needed in cord patterns.

Another eighteenth-century designer and maker of quilts was a Northumbrian, Joseph Hedley, whose working life began as a tailor's apprentice, when, no doubt, he learned quilting as part of his trade. Eventually he became known for his making and quilting of patchwork as well as 'plain' quilts, and is still something of a legend in the North Country, not only for his quilting but for the manner of his death in January 1825 which was by murder.[4] Although it is likely that he made cord-quilted, tailored waistcoats during the early years of his life, his reputation as Joe the Quilter was earned by his designs for wadded quilts, said to have been 'adorned with flowers and figured round'.[5] This description is borne out by a white cotton quilt attributed to him, in the possession of the Bowes Museum and although very worn and discoloured now, the elegance and quality of the patterns are still apparent. A deep, sweeping border pattern something like the *hammock* (42), capped at the top of each curve by a large shell (45), surrounds the edges on three sides; an inner border of a *running feather* (50) pattern surrounds a centre in which pots and sprays of flowers and leaves are reminiscent of the types in cord quilting. In spite of his reputation, Mr Hedley has been more admired than copied, as his influence does not seem to have spread to later work. Perhaps he was born before his time.

On the other hand, two pattern-makers born later in the century in which Joseph Hedley died, were to influence North Country quilt patterns for a long time, through their willingness and ability to hand on their knowledge. The first was a village shopkeeper in Allenheads, Northumberland, called

George Gardiner, and the other, one of his apprentices, was a Miss Elizabeth Sanderson, a well-known character who lived until 1934.[6]

Part of George Gardiner's reputation was due to his flair for trimming hats, and if they resembled, in a small degree, the results of his gift for quilt design, the ladies of Durham and Northumberland wore flowers and feathers on their heads.

Mr Gardiner's patterns have the richness and variety of a cornucopia, piled high with good things which never spill over. He had a fondness for feather patterns and scrolling, which he added to his work almost as a signature (22, 23) – traits of which can be seen also in the work of his successor, Miss Sanderson.

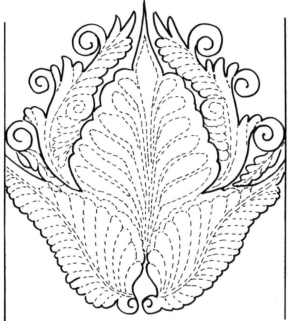

22   *An elaborate feather pattern typical of Mr George Gardiner's work*

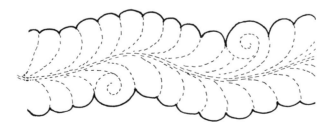

23   *Running feather with added scrolls*

No less famous in her time, Miss Sanderson became the best known of Mr Gardiner's many apprentices, and she continued, also, to take pupils and make quilt patterns, carrying the style of pattern into this century (149, 150). She was a skilled quilter in her own right, but her fame was for the quilt tops she drew out for other workers who, for one reason or another, were unable or unwilling to do their own, but prepared to pay for patterns from the hand of the master. As recently as the late 1950s, at least one quilt top she had drawn was treasured as an example of her work and had been kept unquilted. A number of her quilts have survived also (150).

Welsh quilters seem to have been more independent, preferring to quilt from their own stores of patterns, but one name stands out as being famous for her work during the last half of the nineteenth century – that of Mary Jones. She lived in the village of Panteg in Cardiganshire, making quilts and taking apprentices to help with the work. Some of her apprentices were still quilting 60 years after her death in 1900.[7] The itinerant quilters of South Wales, going from one house or farm to another taking their own patterns with them, contributed considerably to the continuity of Welsh traditional patterns during the nineteenth century (p. 139).

Pattern-drawing and instruction in quilting were services which were available to eighteenth-century American society also, and no doubt they had much the same influence on the style of work there as in England. An American counterpart of Walter Gale advertised in the *Boston Newsletter* in 1716, to say that 'at the House of Mr. George Brownell, late schoolmaster in Hanover Street, Boston, are all sorts of Milinery Works done . . . and Young Gentlewomen and Children taught all sorts of fine Works as Quilting . . .':[8] another instance it seems of an alliance between millinery and quilting. About 30 years later in 1747, another Boston advertisement stated that 'Sarah Hunt', dwelling in the house of James Nicol in School Street, also 'stamped Counterpins, curtains, linens and cottons for quilting with Fidelity and Despatch'.[9]

Of nineteenth-century quilters in America, it has been said that their finest patterns are 'largely original with the quilters themselves who plied their needles in solitary farmhouses and out-of-the-way hamlets, to which the influence of English ideas in needlework could not penetrate', bearing out what is true of quilting in this country, that many of the best patterns by now-forgotten workers, equalled or surpassed some of those made by the famous. Traditional patterns are not the work of one or two, but the steady accumulation of ideas collected and used with an appreciation of shape and proportion. The Hedleys, the Gardiners, the Sandersons and the Mari Pantegs light up the scene for a time with a magic out of the ordinary, but the 'ordinary' was there already for them to spur on and add to, but not to alter.

It has been a common custom among those who do any kind of traditional handwork, to describe patterns and processes they use with terms and names often obscure, without an interpreter, to any but themselves. Patchwork and quilting in England, Wales and in America are no exceptions to the custom. It is understandable, especially in work which has a mother-to-daughter kind of teaching and relies on example and memory, that some ready identification of a pattern is useful and that as the pattern is handed on and perhaps altered, so it is renamed. Some names are self-explanatory – 'rose' and 'shell' for instance, give an idea of the outline – but the interpretation of local patterns as 'Grandmother's Choice' or 'Betsy Jameson's Thing',[10] must be left to the friends and family of the Choice or the Thing.

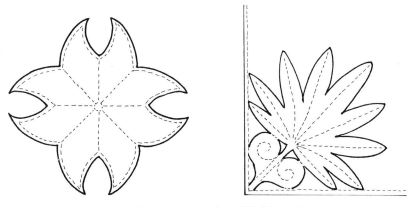

24   *Two patterns from Welsh quilts*

There appears to be no recorded naming of any quilt pattern before the present century, nor many written descriptions by which they can be recognised clearly. Quilt patterns mentioned by name in needlework books of the nineteenth century, refer to the patchwork tops of which they were made, but the term 'quilting' is explained in Caulfeild and Saward's *Dictionary of Needlework* as denoting 'Runnings made in any materials threefold in thickness . . . the Runnings being made diagonally, so as to form a pattern of diamonds, squares or octagons', and 'the Runnings may vary the design from the ordinary Plain Crossings.' It is stated also, that 'the diamond-shaped checkers produced in quilting were anciently called Gamboised', but it seems that quilt names were associated only with work done at home, and often their recognition did not spread beyond the parts of the country where quilting was practised as a part of necessary household work.

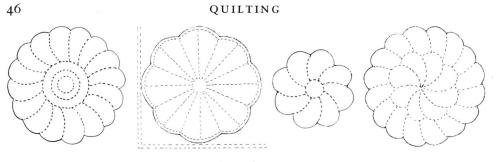

25   *Traditional rose patterns*

The circular rose shape is recognisable in all kinds of formal embroidery patterns, and no less so in quilting. In most cases in Great Britain it has a scalloped outline and any difference lies in the area within the outline; a number of these are shown in drawings (25, 31, 53, 57, 83, 91, 133, 151), and some small rose units used as fillings (26, 53, 62, 71). The same shape is illustrated on some quilts also (148, 159, 160). The heraldic Tudor rose was used in the eighteenth century (124) and is common in many nineteenth- and twentieth-century Welsh patterns, often as the chief unit in the centre and corners of a quilt; it is known sometimes as the 'Welsh rose'. In her work on quilting in the south-west of England, Mrs Hake found several realistic flower and leaf patterns, among them the dog rose and its bud (27).

Other formal patterns representing flowers, are known as the 'lily' and the 'tulip' (28, 29), and a number of small shapes which are a cross between the two and hard to classify, are no less decorative. Flower patterns come in

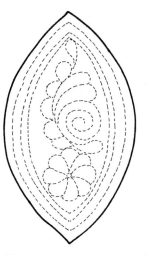

26   *Detail of figure 159, showing small rose filling*

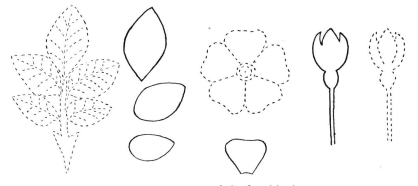

27   *Dog rose with leaf and bud*

28   *Tulip shape, sometimes called pineapple pattern*

29   *Tulip used as a corner pattern*

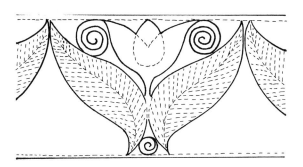

30   *Tulip incorporated in a border pattern*

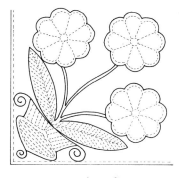

31   *Basket of roses*

sprays in all shapes and sizes, and nearly all are different; so too are the pot of flowers, basket of flowers (31, 90, 91), and the bouquet and the cornucopia (83), both of which have been more popular with American quilters (148).

Leaf patterns, whether realistic or formal, are common to all quilting and most are referred to simply as 'leaf patterns', although some are named. The cowslip leaf, honeysuckle, privet and elder, are named among North Country shapes, several being little different in outline to some feather patterns (32, 33, 34, 36, 37, 47, 125). Realistic leaf shapes are found in eighteenth- and nineteenth-century work of South Wales and the southern counties of England, where natural leaves were used for drawing the outlines; the horse chestnut is a favourite among Welsh quilters (24) and rose, ash, oak and ivy leaves (27, 38, 39, 40) have been used in sprays and garlands; a small shape resembling a laurel leaf is found in circular outlines (84). Nearly all leaf shapes contain filling patterns, some representing the ribs of a leaf, either curved or straight, and others have imaginative fillings with no relation to the outline, while others again are 'lined' as in some hammock and twist patterns (42, 43). Welsh quilters have used a pattern known to them as the 'Welsh pear' and to others as the 'Paisley pattern'. It is found in centre arrangements with a variety of fillings according to the worker's fancy (44, 141, 144).

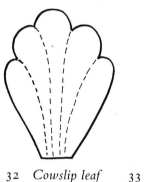
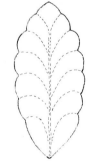
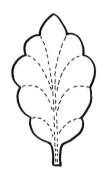
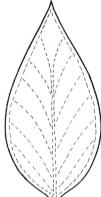

32   *Cowslip leaf*   33   *Honeysuckle leaf*   34   *Privet leaf*

35   *Elder leaf*

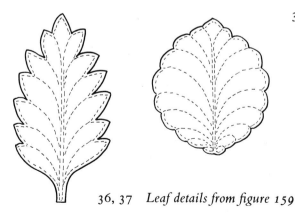

36, 37   *Leaf details from figure 159*

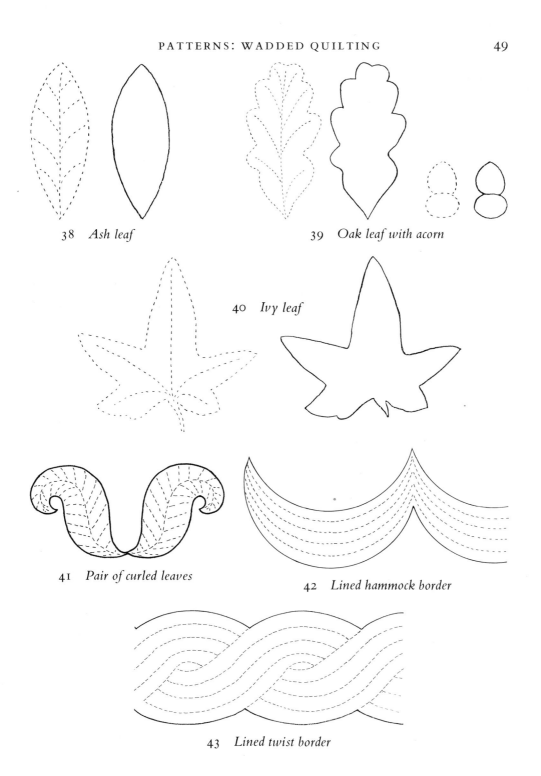

38 *Ash leaf*

39 *Oak leaf with acorn*

40 *Ivy leaf*

41 *Pair of curled leaves*

42 *Lined hammock border*

43 *Lined twist border*

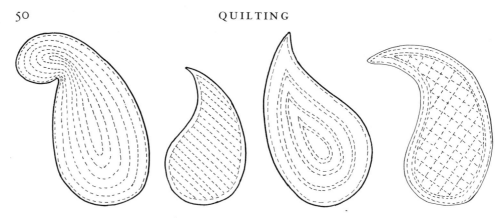

44 *Paisley or Welsh pear patterns with fillings*

The shell, with the outline of the heraldic scallop (45), is a familiar and historical shape in decoration which has not been as popular as others among quilters, and the few examples there are to be found show little variation. A small bed quilt, made in 1960, contained an elaboration of the shape used as the chief pattern (161); there was also a variation of the spiral pattern, in the form of a small whelk shell among the patterns, and a sea-wave on the border (46, 162).

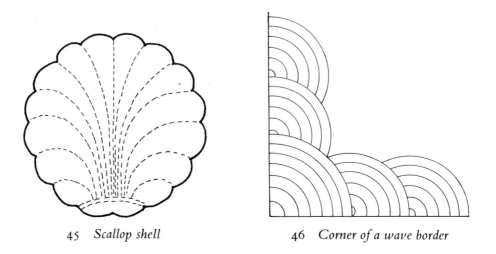

45 *Scallop shell*　　　　46 *Corner of a wave border*

Feather patterns are recognised as having the curled edges characteristic of an ostrich feather, rather than the smooth outline of a quill. The feather and the curled feather (47, 48) are used singly or in pairs in repetitive arrangements for centre and border patterns; and for border patterns only, the straight and running feather patterns are popular in North Country quilts (49, 50). The word 'feather' is added to a number of patterns with a simple outline to indicate the substitution of one that is scalloped, such as feather twist (160), feather circle or crown, feather wreath, feather hammock and so on (51, 52, 56). The border of a quilt made in 1968 shows alternating lined and feather twist patterns (160). Feathered patterns are popular in American quilting, especially the crown and wreath shapes; the feather pattern itself as compared with English versions, usually is made with a 'stalk' and has a more serrated outline (54, 55); it is referred to as 'Princess feather' in some quilt descriptions.

47 *Straight feather for wadded quilting*

48 *Curved feather suitable for all types of quilting*

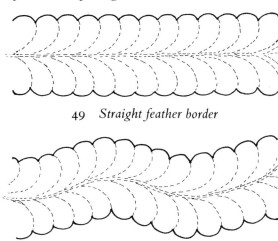

49 *Straight feather border*

51 *Feather circle or crown*

50 *Running feather border*

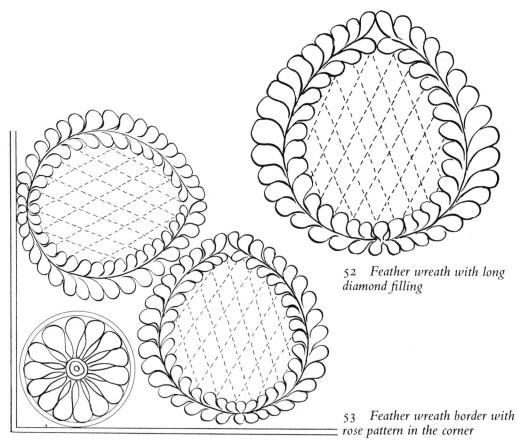

52   *Feather wreath with long diamond filling*

53   *Feather wreath border with rose pattern in the corner*

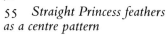

54   *Curled Princess feather as a centre pattern*

55   *Straight Princess feathers as a centre pattern*

The simple half-moon shape, known as the 'hammock' (57) is a repetitive pattern popular for borders as it can be adapted to fit a circular outline in the centre of a quilt, or a right-angled turn on the corner of a border (57). It has several variations – the lined hammock (42), and feather hammock (56); sometimes it has a twist included (58, 151) and often there is a decorative finial at the joining points of two hammocks (57, 58, 151). Patterns known as 'cord and tassel' are adaptations of the hammock shape of which there are many versions (59).

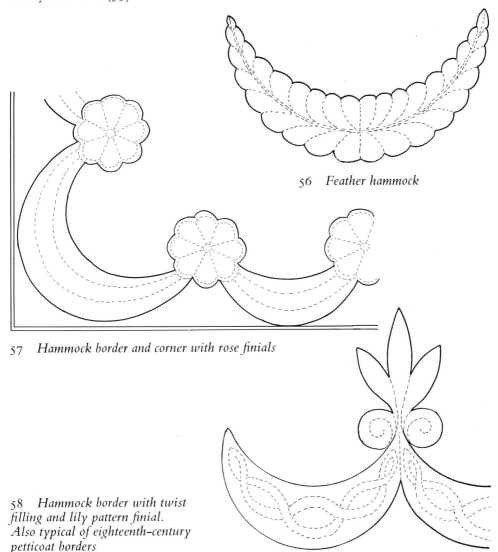

56   *Feather hammock*

57   *Hammock border and corner with rose finials*

58   *Hammock border with twist filling and lily pattern finial. Also typical of eighteenth-century petticoat borders*

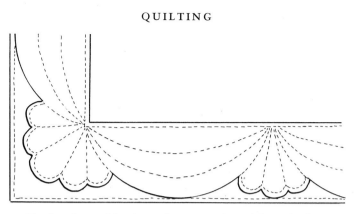

59   *Cord-and-tassel border and corner, adapted from the hammock*

Interlocking and 'endless' types of patterns are common to most kinds of needlework and they appear in quilting as the chain, plait and cable or twist, where a continuous pattern of the kind is appropriate, such as a border or surround for a centre pattern (Frontispiece, 60, 108, 135, 149, 151). This pattern is typical of others which are common to all types of quilting. An endless twist type of pattern was used on the crown of a small cream silk hat which was machine-quilted about the middle of the nineteenth century (61). Another of the interlocking shapes, which is popular among North Country quilters, is the true lovers' knot, decreed by tradition to be worked only on a quilt for a bride; an example can be seen in the centre and corners of the quilt on figure 159.

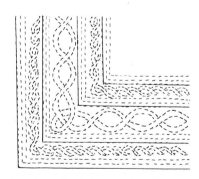

60   *Detail of chain and twist border and corner from figure 108*

61   *Machine-quilted crown of a silk hat with circular border variation of twist pattern*

The heart pattern carries with it the usual tradition of being symbolic of love and affection and there is no reason to doubt that when it is found among the patterns on a quilt, it was put there in accordance with this custom, and that the work was done for a baby, a child, a friend or a bride. It has been popular with all quilters, but nowhere more so than in Wales, where a variety of fillings have been added within the outline; a heart shape containing spirals is known as the 'Welsh heart' (156). Three Welsh quilts are illustrated, each showing different arrangements and fillings (141, 144, 145) and a number of fillings are shown in drawings (62). A quilt made during the late 1950s to commemorate a silver wedding anniversary (25 years), contained a border of hearts, each of which enclosed two interlocking rings (62). The string of small heart shapes was taken from the border of a cradle quilt and the pattern can be adapted to form a circular border (63).

62   *Heart shapes with various fillings*

63   *Small heart border taken from a cradle quilt*

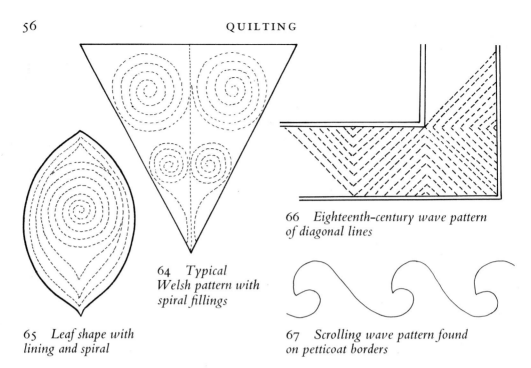

66 *Eighteenth-century wave pattern of diagonal lines*

64 *Typical Welsh pattern with spiral fillings*

65 *Leaf shape with lining and spiral*

67 *Scrolling wave pattern found on petticoat borders*

The spiral is a characteristic Welsh pattern and found in many quilts in South Wales, either as the chief pattern in straight or circular borders or in conjunction with other units in centre and border arrangements. A typical pattern of this kind is illustrated on figure 64, which shows in detail part of the border of a quilt (152); so also is figure 70 part of the border on another Welsh quilt (141). Four other Welsh quilts illustrated contain spiral patterns (135, 144, 145, 152). The close, fine lines of quilting and the exact repeated precision of the pattern is highly skilled work but is not uncommon in Welsh quilting where the name given to it is alas, the 'snail-creep'.

Another pattern known as 'sea-wave' has been especially popular among Welsh workers, although it is by no means exclusive to Wales and it is found as a corner or border pattern as a rule (46); it is referred to as the 'fan' also. Other so-called 'wave' patterns are lines worked in a zigzag pattern (66) which was used for a mid-eighteenth-century quilt and a simple kind of scroll which resembles a conventional wave shape (67).

There are many versions of the fan pattern which generally is used to fill a corner. Variety is given to the shape by different fillings and edges (68, 69, 135, 141, 144, 145). Another shape slightly related to the fan is the church window, in which the semicircle is part of the overlapping outlines which contain a number of other patterns; it is also another of the patterns which wadded, flat and cord quilting have in common (105).

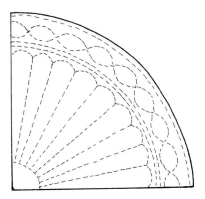

68 *Fan corner from eighteenth-century quilt*

69 *Fan corner. Detail from figure 135*

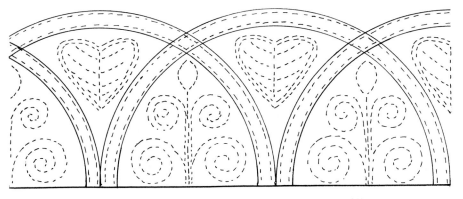

70 *Church window border with heart and spiral fillings*

71 *Church window border with rose, leaf and spiral fillings*

Fillings

Shapes recognised traditionally as filling patterns usually are geometrical, and in all quilting designs the use of filling is as important as the larger pattern units. There seems to be no convention governing their use in English and Welsh quilts, but for American quilts, in which all or part of the tops were made of patchwork – 'There was a general rule for which the majority of quilters had respect, elaborate and elegant quilting was most

72 *Geometrical filling patterns common to all types of quilting*

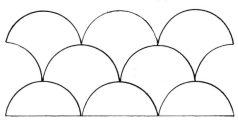

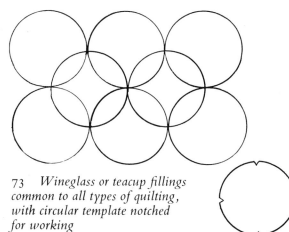

74   *Shell filling common to all types of quilting, with circular template notched for working*

73   *Wineglass or teacup fillings common to all types of quilting, with circular template notched for working*

effective when the patchwork pattern was unobtrusive in either form or color . . . geometric compositions demanded that the lines of the piecing be emphasised.'[11]

Filling patterns are made by small repetitive units in all-over arrangements which cover the background in and around larger units and like a shoal of minnows, penetrate all the holes and corners which cannot be occupied by anything larger. Templates are not needed for some fillings; those shapes made by straight lines can be marked along a ruler, yardstick or T-square, and consist of lines running either straight or diagonally in relation to the edges of the work, and crossing at regular intervals to make a trellis pattern. This is varied according to the angle at which the lines cross (72); the most familiar are the square or long diamond patterns which, to the uninitiated and the trade, have become synonymous with the word 'quilting'. Patterns with a circular outline need the guidance of a template or something which can be used as a tool for the purpose. The well-known wineglass pattern – in America teacup quilting – is a small network of over-lapping circles, and originally these two everyday things were used for marking the outlines (73). There is no reason why they should not be used still but for ease in marking, the handle of a cup can be something of an obstacle, whereas a wineglass has a stem in a good position for holding and the glass makes it possible to see what is going on underneath. Plates, cups, saucers, bowls and coins have been guides in the past for circular outlines and a saucepan has been heard of for the purpose but, presumably, after it had lost its handle. The small shell pattern can be made from a circular shape by marking half of it, and a circular piece of card, suitably notched (74) can be used for this as well as the wineglass.

Other small patterns, although not in the ordinary category of fillings, nevertheless are used as such within spaces other than background. Fillings in heart shapes, leaves and so on, have already been mentioned, but a ground filling which has not been as popular as it deserves, is one in which the ground is darned with small close running stitches; the lines of sewing are straight or slightly curved, and sometimes a combination of both (6, 97, 100). Some small patterns on garments and other areas, such as the ships and sails of the Sicilian quilt are well suited as fillings (75, 76, 77, 78).

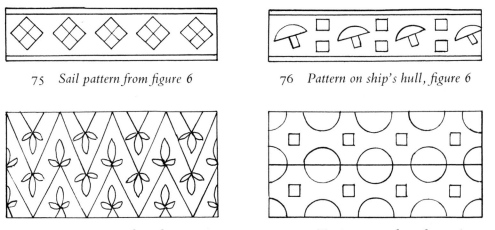

75   *Sail pattern from figure 6*   76   *Pattern on ship's hull, figure 6*

77   *Tunic pattern from figure 6*   78   *Tunic pattern from figure 6*

Some patchwork quilts are made in square sections or blocks, which alternately are plain material and patchwork, the plain squares having no other decoration than quilting patterns. It will be seen that the quilts on figures 148 and 150 were made in this way. The quilting patterns on the American quilt are stuffed (148), but the wadded basket quilt, made by Miss Sanderson, has quilting patterns on the patchwork squares as well (150). A similar pattern is illustrated in *Traditional Quilting*, in which the quilting patterns show a different basket pattern of fruit, flowers and leaves.[12] This type of block quilt is more popular in America, but many of the quilting patterns are identical with those in this country on similar quilts such as the feather circle, feather wreath and flower-spray patterns. A black and white American block quilt in the American Museum at Bath contains a quilted harp on the alternate plain squares (79); it is known as the 'Widow's Quilt'.[13]

Many American patterns are more realistic in character than English or Welsh patterns and often show subjects which are unconventional in comparison. The harp is not uncommon; pineapples have been popular (80) and a spider's web has been used as a pattern (81). Others are symbolic of American patriotism – the American Eagle (82) and clusters of stars representing the American Flag (142) have no parallel in English or Welsh traditions, although a quilt made in County Durham at the time of the Diamond Jubilee in 1897, had the head of Queen Victoria among the patterns.[14]

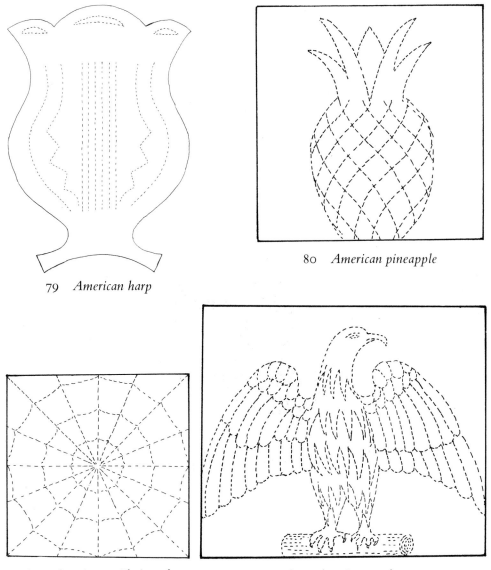

79 *American harp*

80 *American pineapple*

81 *American spider's web*

82 *American eagle*

83   *Cornucopia from eighteenth-century petticoat*

Ribbons, bows, cornucopias and flower and fern patterns were used on eighteenth-century quilted petticoats (83) but otherwise were more common to cord and flat quilted patterns.

A method of quilt-making related to patchwork, is one in which narrow lengths of material left over from other quilts are joined to make what are known as 'strip quilts' and, in these, the quilting patterns are adapted to fit the width of each strip. Alternate strips sometimes are made of patchwork,[15] but the example illustrated shows the reverse side of a quilt made from long pieces of red and buff coloured cotton in which the quilting has been done in patterns suitable for borders (147).

Pattern Arrangement

The design of a traditional quilt is made by the repetitive use of a number of pattern units. The units can be divided into those of major importance which are used to make the principal features, such as the centre of a bed cover and its borders, and secondary units which are smaller in size and are used for the spaces between the large patterns or narrow borders and so on. Thirdly, there are the filling or ground patterns which can be the test of a quilter's skill. When well done they must be faultless in shape and line but, badly done with uneven outlines or lines which are not parallel, a good quilt can be spoiled.

There is need for discipline in choosing the pattern units as there are almost unlimited ways in which they can be built up to make a good design. There are so many, in fact, that it is said that no two quilts have been made alike, unless deliberately as a pair.

Centre Arrangements

The outline of a centre arrangement can be circular, oval, rectangular or a square in which the sides may be parallel with the edges of a quilt or set crossways (84, 85, 135, 141, 144, 146, 149, 152, 158). Some quilts have no centre pattern, but the patterns are arranged in parallel rows from end to end as in strip quilts (147) or in a style popular in the eighteenth century and in a number of Welsh quilts, in which one or more units were arranged in a repetitive all-over pattern. A pattern such as this is shown on the christening cloak made about 1769 (121), which, with the exception of one small detail, is identical with that on an undocumented quilt in the possession of the Victoria and Albert Museum.[16] Occasionally a quilt can be found, on which

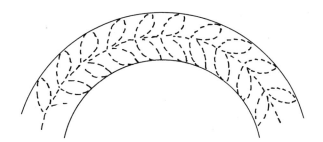

84   *Laurel-leaf pattern for circular or oval arrangements*

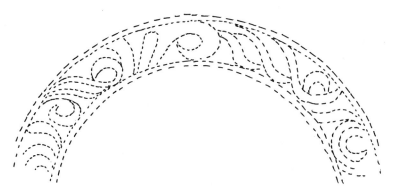

85   *Border pattern common in eighteenth century. Used here in circular shape, it is also on straight cross-banding on figure 121*

the border is of such depth that it reaches well into the middle, leaving room only for a small area of background filling instead of a more conventional design.

Borders

The chief border pattern often consists of repeats of the same units as those in the centre of the quilt (144, 159), although not necessarily on the same scale; sometimes a large centre pattern will have been reduced in size to fit a narrow border, and so on. There is no convention which governs the number of borders in one quilt, nor strictly speaking, the necessity of having one at all, although quilts without border patterns are rare. This does not apply to strip quilts which consist usually of border patterns only.

Although traditionally the outer border generally is related to the centre in design, many quilts contain two, three or more borders, each with a different pattern, none of which necessarily repeats any unit of the centre arrangement. Often they are not even similar in character, but where the border patterns are related, as illustrated on the Frontispiece, the gain to the whole design is clear.

Corners

The continuance of a border pattern on the corners without a break is a test of skill, as the tidy manœuvring of a pattern, such as a twist or running feather, is not easy. A saying that a broken cable pattern 'foretold a life cut short by disaster'[17] must have been disbelieved or accepted as an occupational hazard, if the number of occasions on which a pattern has been interrupted at a corner is any indication. The running or interlocking types of pattern often are broken just before a corner and the space filled with another small shape, before the border is continued on the other side. Some well-planned corners with continuous pattern, and others with a different pattern inserted, are shown on the Frontispiece and figures 86, 87, 88, 89).

Finish

Methods of finishing wadded quilting are given in Appendix A, but the decision on which method to use should be made at the time the design of the whole work is planned. If a covered piping cord or cross-cut binding are used, two or more lines of quilting, the same distance apart as the width of cord or binding, may be run along just inside the finished edges (172). If the

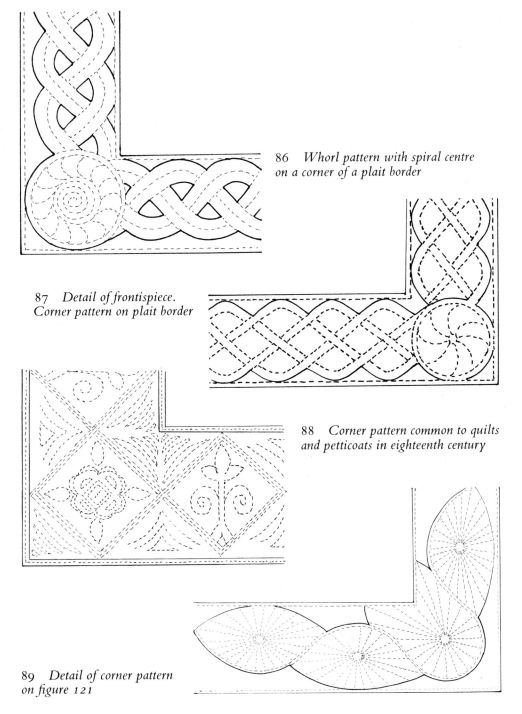

86   *Whorl pattern with spiral centre*
on a corner of a plait border

87   *Detail of frontispiece.*
Corner pattern on plait border

88   *Corner pattern common to quilts*
and petticoats in eighteenth century

89   *Detail of corner pattern*
on figure 121

edges are run together, the distance between the lines of stitches should correspond to the spacing of any parallel lines which may be included in patterns on the rest of the work.

Signatures and dates are found rarely among wadded quilting patterns but they can and should be incorporated in some part of them. Some quilters sign their work unconsciously by their style or by the repeated inclusion of a favourite pattern which becomes a characteristic. This is not always to be relied on, as students are apt to pick up and copy the ways of their teachers, but characteristic initials or monogram, if not the full name, and at least the year in which the work was finished, should be included somewhere in the design. The quilt on figure 160, is signed and dated 'Mary Lough, Jan. 1968'.

5 PATTERNS: FLAT, CORD AND STUFFED QUILTING

Patterns made by the three types of quilting included in this chapter have much in common. Sometimes two, or all three methods of working them have been used in one piece of work and although it has been said that all are 'purely decorative' and that none has any value for warmth, this is not entirely so. The term 'decorative' sometimes has carried almost an accusation of frivolity, as if the work was an unprofitable use of time, but all the methods provide a means of adding substance – and in some cases necessary stiffening (106) – and so a degree of protection and warmth to materials intended for purposes in which a thicker type of padding would have been too bulky and too warm.

Nowadays, with the popularity of commercial, machine-quilted outer garments and bed covers made of wadded quilting, it is easy to overlook the purposes in earlier fashion and furnishing, for which other kinds of quilting were more suitable and were used. Examples of appropriate uses for flat and corded quilting were the waistcoats for men and women and jackets for children, worn in the seventeenth and eighteenth centuries in Britain (102, 118, 120) and during the same period the embroidered or quilted caps for indoor wear, whether for adults, children or babies, were considered – despite the protests of the health cranks – to be indispensable as head covers against draughts, giving a certain comfort and protection at a time when living in a house was not many degrees warmer than living out of doors (106, 110, 111, 112, 115, 116). The Syrian children's coats, worn in the early part of this century, are other examples of the use of cord-quilted silk and cotton (154, 155 and p. 156).

As domestic work, the three types no doubt were made principally in the manor-house rather than in the cottage. The sewing of the fine patterns generally is done in back stitch, which is slower in practice and needs more working time than for the running stitch used in wadded quilting, which in England, Wales and America has such a long cottage tradition, but in the early days of domestic needlework in this country, when local girls and women were employed in the big house, regular time was given over to sewing in the daily routine of the household, and it is unlikely that anyone

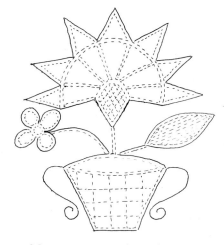

90   *Pot of flowers on an eighteenth-century waistcoat*

escaped doing her share of the work in hand, which would have included quilting from time to time.

The character of some patterns, especially the floral types, which are associated with flat, cord and stuffed quilting, appears also in wadded quilting – notably on petticoats – which was made during the eighteenth century, so even if the different methods of doing the work were considered to belong to different levels of society, the patterns were not so tied (60, 72,

91   *Pot or vase of flowers from an eighteenth-century wadded petticoat*

91). Husbands and sons employed in tailoring, and perhaps able to do some pattern-drawing, may have carried the influence of corded patterns from their places of work to wadded quilting in their homes; but many of the flat and corded patterns are not repetitive, so the general use of templates for them would have been ruled out, with the exception of those which are identical with wadded quilting such as shell, wineglass and diamond filling patterns. This would have been a handicap for the unskilled in freehand drawing, and would have called for the help of a professional who would have to be paid for his services, even if he was the village schoolmaster, like Mr Walter Gale. The fine silk, satin, cotton and linen materials and the silk and linen threads necessary for flat and cord quilting were costly and difficult to get, so generally speaking the work would have been out of reach of any but the well-to-do.

Although a remarkable amount of flat, cord and stuffed quilting has been preserved, apart from the work itself, there is no recorded or inherited tradition connected with any of them in the ways of marking and of working the patterns, which matches the detailed histories of wadded quilting which have been written in Britain and in America.

The identification of patterns by the use of local or family names such as those associated with wadded quilting, seems to have no place in flat, corded or stuffed work, but any pattern outline which is common to all quilting, for convenience may be referred to by the names attached to it in wadded work. The universal filling patterns, known as the 'square' and the 'long diamonds', the 'shell' and the 'wineglass' are examples, and they can be seen in work of all nationalities from an early age. There is no evidence either, as to the means by which the patterns were marked on to the materials, but as embroidery is so closely allied to all types of quilting in this chapter, it is possible and probable that the same methods were used for both.

The drawing of pencil lines to mark out patterns for sewing has disadvantages, and not the least is the risk of disfiguring the material. An early method of marking embroidery patterns which is less conspicuous than drawing and at the same time clear enough for guidance in sewing, was by pricking and pouncing, a method known and widely used at least from the sixteenth century. Of the early printed pattern books in use in the sixteenth and seventeenth centuries, few have survived the pricking of the patterns they contained, but those which have done so show clearly the origins of many from which quilting as well as embroidery patterns have developed (92, 93, 175, 176). The use of transfers, which is the solution to many problems facing the present-day worker, does not solve all those of quilting patterns, as appropriate patterns available for them are limited in their variety, but

92   *Seventeenth-century flower patterns for quilting and embroidery*

93   *Seventeenth-century 'spot' and filling patterns for quilting and embroidery*

good prickings can be made from tracings of illustrated designs, without the necessary destruction of pricking directly from them. This is as good a method as any for flat and cord quilting patterns, which are drawn on to the right side of the material and in any case, once a transfer has been used it is finished, but a good library of prickings can be built up if the originals are made on good paper (p. 182). Patterns for stuffed quilting can be marked by pencil lines or by transfer if a suitable pattern is available; both ways are equally satisfactory as the marking is done on the backing material (Appendix D). A method for pouncing with the use of template outlines advocated for American workers is given in Appendix A, but as templates are of little practical use for any of the types in this chapter, the procedure for the pricking of pattern outlines drawn or traced on to paper is given in Appendix B.

Flat Quilting

The purpose of this quilting is to join together two layers of material by means of sewing through them with a single line of back stitching along the outlines of patterns marked on the top layer. The bottom layer generally is of poorer material than that of the top, for which fine linen, silk or satin traditionally is used. The patterns are affected to some extent by the thickness of the backing; in work containing a linen of moderately heavy texture, for instance, the surface patterns appear to be slightly raised although no interlining is used in this work.

The designs consist of two kinds as in wadded quilting – major decorative patterns and small repetitive background fillings – but unlike the wadded work, all of the quilting in one piece of work may consist of a filling pattern, on which other decorative surface embroidery of a formal or floral character may or may not be added. Patterns of corded or stuffed quilting also may be worked with a flat-quilted ground but these are included later in the chapter (pp. 75 and 79).

The patterns are planned in much the same way as for other kinds of quilting and embroidery, often with a centre arrangement and a border to the work, and sometimes with smaller patterns set all over the background. The chief patterns usually are of a floral nature, more naturalistic than formal, and with long flowing stems carrying flower and leaf outlines in more detail than is possible in relief patterns, and the general appearance of the work is of fine and delicate workmanship.

Border patterns often are very simple; some have only two or three rows of back stitching on the edges of the work, others are rather more decorative, with a single line of small scallops; but in some pieces of work the border patterns almost take over in importance from the rest of the patterns. The pillow sham or cover, illustrated on figure 105, is an example of typical flat quilted patterns. It was made towards the end of the seventeenth century and is a classic illustration of the relationship between the patterns in all kinds of quilting. The fillings on the ground of the centre panel and in the border pattern are identical with those in wadded and cord patterns; the church-window border is similar to the several versions found in wadded quilting and occasionally it is worked with cord; the narrow cable or twist pattern in the small borders is common to quilting patterns of most ages and nationalities. The floral centre pattern also is typical of those in the coloured embroidery borders associated with flat quilting.

Another pattern, found sometimes with those in surface embroidery, is the background filling known as the 'meander', which is used with corded patterns also (21, 109), and a repetitive leaf-like pattern of much the same character as the meander was used as an all-over design on the early seventeenth-century quilted linen jacket, which is in the Middleton Collection of textiles on permanent loan to the Nottingham Castle Museum (94).

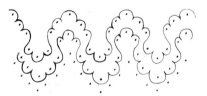

94   All-over ground pattern on
seventeenth-century jacket,
backstitched in red silk, with dots
in brown silk, on linen

95   Detail of feather pattern from figure 109

A jacket in the possession of the Victoria and Albert Museum, also of quilted linen, was made at the end of the same century and has patterns of curled feathers and small formal roses in a ground of scrolling (96).

Embroidered patterns in colour which are included with traditional flat quilting, were added to bed quilts and garments on which the quilting consisted of background fillings only. On large bed quilts the extra decoration is considerable, sometimes deep borders of heavily embroidered designs were worked over the quilted ground, as well as the usual centre and other arrangements, and in these cases it seems that the quilting had the definite function of reinforcing the materials to carry the embroidery. The account

96 *Detail of feather patterns and scrolling from a seventeenth-century linen jacket*

of the sixteenth-century 'quilte of crymson sattin . . . all lozenged over with silver twists' and with 'a cinquefoil within a garland of ragged staves, fringed about with a small fringe of crymson silke' (p. 87) gives an idea of the kind and amount of embroidery which was added to the quilted satin.

Not all bed quilts are heavily embroidered: many of the eighteenth-century examples are more restrained in the amount of surface embroidery, and a lighter sort of pattern sometimes is added to the spaces enclosed by the ground-work fillings; a well-known traditional arrangement to illustrate this is shown (175), in which small floral sprays are worked within the wine-glass filling. A woman's quilted waistcoat illustrated (102) shows the square diamond ground pattern with small flower patterns embroidered over the quilting. The border of the garment was embroidered on unquilted material, probably after the garment had been made up, and John Stilwell, 'the drawear', may have drawn the flower patterns on to the professionally quilted and tailored garment, for the customer to embroider at home. It is likely that this was the practice also with stomachers when they were in fashion, as a flat-quilted ground was used for some which were embroidered.

The large patterns worked on bed quilts have contained most of the stitches known to embroidery. Examples of couched and laid work can be found occasionally, and sometimes metal thread or wool have been used, but generally the embroidery is worked with silks, in satin, stem, long and short, split, back and chain stitches. The patterns may contain a variety of colours, or at times, the whole of a border and other patterns on a quilt may be worked in one colour only; red or crimson is not an uncommon choice. The only type of pattern which seems to have been linked traditionally with a certain kind of stitch is the small floral spray or any small-scale pattern of the kind, which always is worked in chain stitch (174).

Materials on which flat quilting has been worked in the past have included silk, satin, cotton and linen. In all work the bottom layer always has been more open in texture and of poorer quality than the fine materials used for the top, and almost invariably the bottom layer seems to have been on thin quality linen or scrim, even if the top has been of silk or satin. Most of the old work was lined after the quilting and embroidery were done, so it is not possible to verify the type of backing unless the outer lining is sufficiently dilapidated to show the back of the work. The majority of flat quilted garments have been made of linen throughout, but some women's pockets, jackets and waistcoats have been made of silk or satin.

The quilting itself commonly has been carried out in silk thread, but some examples of cotton or linen thread being used are known. Most flat quilting on linen has been worked with white, cream or yellow silk, although it is possible that, in some cases, the thread which appears to be white or cream may have begun as yellow and faded with use and age. Other coloured silks than yellow have been used, however; the early seventeenth-century jacket mentioned above was stitched with red and brown silk, and patterns worked in red occur from time to time. A small linen bag was flat quilted during the 1960s, in red and cream silk, with a pattern taken from an eighteenth-century cot quilt, worked with yellow silk (157).

A number of bed quilts have not been finished at the edges, the workers seemingly having had enough by the time the quilting was done and the work lined, but many of those with the necessary stamina or determination had also the feeling for that most elegant of finishes, a fringe. Some fringes may be as much as four inches long and when added to an embroidered quilt they are made of silk; fringes as a rule, though, are made of linen and are about two inches in length and mostly of coarse linen thread, but some are knotted and twisted in fine thread. The pillow sham (105) has a short linen fringe at the edges and the embroidered waistcoat on figure 102, was finished with a knotted fringe in natural-coloured silk. Otherwise, most edges were worked through the turned-in materials with one or more rows of back stitching, or bound with strips of linen or silk, according to which material had been used for the work.

Cord Quilting

More than in any other type of quilting, patterns which are padded with cord rely for their perfection on the skill and accuracy with which they are worked. Many of them are similar to the traditional patterns associated with wadded quilting, such as the feather, rose, shell and a number of borders and fillings which are common to all types, but whereas the padding is sewn into the work in one process in wadded quilting, two separate operations are needed to complete a corded pattern using two layers of material. The sewing is done first along two parallel lines with back stitch, and the cord is threaded between them and the layers of material. This is where the skill and accuracy are needed; unless the distance between the stitched lines is correctly spaced, the cord may fit too tightly and the pattern be pulled out of shape by puckering the material, or if the space is too wide for the cord, the pattern is not properly raised (181, 182). A second method of working can be used, by which the cord is sewn to a single layer of material in one operation, but this is found rarely in old work and is used hardly at all nowadays (178, 179). Details of working with both methods are given in Appendix C.

Other methods of quilting are combined with corded work in a design from time to time, although much of the work on large bed quilts and hangings which was done in England towards the end of the seventeenth century, was so closely covered with cord patterns that little space was available for ground pattern and even less for other additions to the general design. On later work where there was room, however, flat and stuffed quilting patterns were added, and also embroidery in white and coloured thread.

Most of the work which is available for study here dates from the seventeenth and eighteenth centuries, but examples of European work showing the use of cord in quilted patterns have survived from the sixteenth. A heavy linen quilt of German origin of this period is in the possession of the Victoria and Albert Museum. The design, which is back-stitched through two layers of linen, is of an all-over geometrical pattern of octagonal and square compartments, which are outlined with a double row of cord, and within each octagonal compartment is a secondary pattern of an unpadded eight-pointed star, outlined with two rows of back-stitched flat quilting. A four-lobed leaf shape is outlined within the outside angles of the star patterns, and inside each star a fabulous beast is worked in single outline; the animals vary in pattern, some are winged and others with a stag's head are equipped also with wings, the tail of a lion and clawed feet (97, 100). All the ground within the octagon is darned through both layers of linen and after this was done, the backing, which is of coarse open linen, was cut (but not cut away) between the lines of back stitching. The result of this is that the corded out-lines are emphasised, but the animal and leaf patterns appear to be lower than the level of the darned background. The square compartments are worked in the same way with small animal figures, but without the leaf patterns, and the quilt is finished at the edges with a fringe. The work is heavy and somewhat clumsy and perhaps a lighter quality material might be more successful.

97   *Winged beast with claws and a lion's tail, on a darned ground. Detail of figure 100*

A seventeenth-century Portuguese corded quilt, also in the collections of the Victoria and Albert Museum, no doubt is familiar already to students of quilting (108).[2] The outlines of several patterns are familiar also and a comparison of this work with the eighteenth-century English wadded quilt in the Museum of Costume, Bath, which is illustrated on the Frontispiece, shows the use of different methods and materials on almost identical patterns. The corded quilt is made of twilled cotton and padded with a thickish soft cord or thread, and the other is of fine silk, interlined with wool. In both, the sewing is done with running stitch, which is unusual in corded work. The alternating twist and plait borders appear twice in the same positions on both quilts; there are slight differences – two rows of cord separate these two patterns on the early quilt and only one on the other and the English worker was less confident of her ability to turn the patterns at the corners and filled them with a whorl pattern within a circular outline, which is similar to a larger version on the Portuguese quilt. There is a relationship in the formal tree and leaf patterns in both also, but the circular and corner leaf patterns on the middle panel of the English quilt are more common to other eighteenth-century work. This quilt seems to have a foot set in each century, but unfortunately it has no recorded history.

An early example of cord-quilted linen with a flat-quilted ground is a relatively small piece of work made about 1700, measuring $21\frac{1}{2} \times 29\frac{3}{4}$ inches, which was intended, supposedly, as a chalice cover. The central group of figures is a representation of The Last Supper in which the figures, table, chairs and so on, are worked in fine detail with quilted cord. The rest of the work contains more secular patterns of rose, feather, leaf and other patterns carried out with cord quilting, on a ground of flat-quilted meander pattern. The work was finished with a short fringe, to which a number of small tassels were added at intervals (95, 109).[3]

98   *Detail of rose and leaf patterns from figure 109*

Very large quilts and hangings of cord-quilted linen were fashionable as furnishings during the last half of the seventeenth and in the early eighteenth centuries in England, and a number of existing examples can be found – which in a few cases are in occasional use still – in private houses or in those which are open to the public, some of which are the property of the National Trust. Photographic illustrations do not do justice to the fine detail of their patterns, nearly all of which are floral in character. Large vase or basket shapes with a mass of realistic flower, leaf and branching stem patterns, are worked in outlines raised with fine cord but with no fillings added. Narrow borders sometimes separate the centre arrangement from wider borders containing repeats of the central patterns. A quilt from Great Tangley Manor, near Guildford, now in the collections at the Victoria and Albert Museum, contains some fine flower-basket patterns, which show great attention to detail in the patterns of recognisable rose, carnation, peony, daisy, marigold and other flower patterns; the quilt was worked in running and double running stitches and was made during the first half of the eighteenth century (129).[4] Similar patterns worked on quilted curtains, also of early eighteenth-century work, are illustrated in *English Secular Embroidery* by Margaret Jourdain, but in these there are no basket patterns; the floral sprays are continuous over the ground.[5] Other examples of what may have been made for curtains or hangings are to be found as bed quilts, which clearly have been cut from larger pieces of work and joined again to bed size.

Examples of cutting and rejoining pieces of eighteenth-century corded quilting are common. This is a natural kind of economy in work which had taken a long time and much labour to make in the first place, and numerous examples of it can be found in clothing during the century. In common with quilted garments of wadded work, those with cord patterns properly were worked on the linen or cotton materials in the piece, on which the outline shapes of sleeves, collars, pocket flaps and so on had been marked previously, with sufficient allowances made for cutting out and subsequent turnings. An example of the end of a sleeve is shown (117) with the quilting completed and ready for making up, and allowances for buttonholes having been made in the quilting patterns; it was made about 1750 and is said to have been intended for a page at the Court of George II.[6]

Caps for children and babies which were considered essential for their health (or even for their survival), have been treasured in their hundreds among family possessions up and down the country, made in all manner of different kinds of needlework, and among them the quilted caps contain a great variety of patterns. Some clearly have been quilted for the purpose, as the patterns fit the shapes of the caps or bonnets, and allowances made for the joining seams, but by far the greater number were cut down from larger pieces of work. Although the shapes varied, whether a cap or bonnet was being made, all of them consisted of three sections – two shaped side pieces and a straight strip which covered the top of the head, as shown on figure 113. When the three were joined the curved edges of the side pieces drew the middle section into the shape of the cap; in some, the edges of each section were bound with strips of cotton or linen, but mostly the joins were made by turning in the quilting until the patterns matched. Four caps are illustrated, showing a variety of patterns (115),[7] (116).[8] Quilted caps for adults are not common, and of the two illustrated, that on figure 106, is the earliest known example in England, made probably during that last ten years of the seventeenth century and quilted for the purpose. The patterns on the turned-up brim fit the curved shapes and the crown is made in two pieces, with seams at the back and front and short darts at the sides to shape the cap to the head. The second cap, of a more conventional shape (111), is composed of four pieces, each similar to one section of an unmade cap illustrated on figure 112,[9] which, with the other three sections, was quilted especially for the purpose, on a length of linen with allowances for making up. The completed cap, however, probably was cut from a larger piece of quilting, if we can judge from the disjointed patterns at the seams. Both caps are finished with a tassel on top of the crown to hide the joins and decorate the apex of the cap. The patterns on the lappets of the cap illustrated (110) clearly were quilted to the planned shape.[10] Nearly all caps are finished at the edges with a binding of cotton or fine linen but an occasional example can be found with stitching in keeping with the quilting pattern (116).

The baby's jacket on figure 120,[11] was cut in one section, probably from another garment; the patterns on the sleeves and on each side of the front do not show the deliberate matching which would be likely on a garment quilted especially for its shape. The same cannot be said, however, of the man's tailored waistcoat made during the second quarter of the eighteenth century (118, 119)[12] in which the matching detail is faultless and carries the mark of the professional and highly experienced worker. It illustrates also a traditional characteristic of cord quilting, in the addition of embroidery stitches worked in white linen thread. Some of the quilted formal flower and leaf patterns contain fillings of pulled stitches and others have fillings and small patterns worked in French knots, some packed tightly together to fill the spaces entirely and some in small groups or scroll patterns. Much the same treatment was given to the sleeve illustrated on figure 117, with the addition of Florentine stitch in the centre pattern. The child's cap on figure 115b, contains scattered holes, pricked and overcast, among the cord-quilted patterns, which include some leaf patterns in stuffed quilting and the centre of one flower worked with pulled stitches; another cap shown on figure 116, is worked with French knots filling some of the spaces between the quilted shapes, or in a square diamond pattern or small groups in others.

Dates and signatures rarely are found among the patterns of cord-quilted work, although in the few cases of their inclusion in quilts of flat or stuffed work, they have been carried out with cord as the padding (142).

The usual means of finishing caps or garments has been with a binding of cotton or linen, sometimes a braid or tape has been used, but a plain edge is most common for the patterns. For work other than garments, a fringe has made a more decorative finish (109, 142, 143).

Stuffed Quilting

Something of the character of patterns in all other kinds can be seen in those of stuffed quilting. Outlines are worked in back stitch or running stitch and the backgrounds with back stitch or with a darning kind of running stitch;

thread or cord is used for padding narrow lines – such as branching stems for the floral patterns – and for all other patterns the stuffing is cotton or wool, as for wadded quilting, but while the padding is spread evenly all over this work, that in stuffed patterns is controlled by the demand of each part of the design. Fruit and flower patterns are raised a little more than those of the leaves in some patterns and tapering points can be defined by regulating the amount of padding (143). Occasionally the stuffed patterns are so closely spaced that there is no room or necessity for background quilting and the ground material is left unquilted. Characteristic background patterns, which often are flat or cord-quilted, are the square diamond filling, close diagonal or parallel lines (142, 143), a wide chevron (100), and close lines of running or darning. Background darning gives a crêpe-like effect and is not necessarily worked to a definite pattern, but in some cases the lines run straight or diagonally in one direction over the work, and in others a series of short curved lines cover the ground between the raised patterns (112).

Most of the early work has been done on linen or cotton, which is better suited to the nature and appearance of the patterns, than present-day rayon or similar fabrics, which have not the yielding quality of linen and do not lend themselves to the work or improve its quality or good looks.

The early fifteenth-century Sicilian quilt (p. 13) could be looked upon as a vast sampler of patterns for stuffed quilting. The figures of men, horses and fishes, branching patterns of leaves, fruit and flowers, repetitive units of border pattern surrounding the rectangular compartments in which representations of incidents in the narrative of Tristram are enclosed, and the shapes of the letters in the inscriptions, are some examples of the variety of shapes and patterns contained in it. Pattern details of clothing and armour are worked with meticulous detail and many could be adapted to any kind of quilting. The sails of the ships are patterned (75), so also are the sides of the hulls in which is a repetitive pattern not unlike a mushroom (76) and the worker betrayed a certain humour in the features of fishes in the quilted 'water', with caricatured human expressions. Floral patterns are represented by nearly realistic flower, fruit and leaf shapes attached to running stems (9, 10), among them the vine pattern, which has been the most common of all patterns in stuffed quilting, up to the present time. Other recognisable floral and leaf patterns of equal importance with the vine in the Sicilian work are the rose, lily, ivy, acorn and oak, and some smaller vegetation includes a trefoil and a creeping plant like ground ivy.

The running vine pattern as a border, or smaller units, with a spray of leaves and fruit, are much in evidence in quilts which were made in the eighteenth and nineteenth centuries, especially in those in private and museum ownership in the United States of America.[13] A number of them, often referred to as 'all-white quilts', are illustrated in books on American quilting and show a diversity of style and pattern in which several contain wadded quilting patterns adapted to the process of stuffing, as well as those more common to the tradition.[14] Of the two quilts illustrated here (142, 143), one is dated and signed 'M W T 1821' within an oval garland of leaves, and the circular centre arrangement contains the American Eagle and other national emblems; the other quilt, although unsigned, belongs to the early nineteenth century also. In this the centre contains a cornucopia of fruit and flowers, and the borders are worked with palm-like leaves, and sprays of flowers and leaves fill the rest of the ground and the corners. Both are in the quilt collection of the American Museum at Bath.

Some patterns of stuffed quilting are included occasionally on other American quilts, which are made of pieced work or patchwork (148). Princess feather patterns on an eighteenth-century example in the home of George Washington, are worked alternately in applied work and stuffed quilting, to make a striking centre pattern.[15] On other quilts, the blocks alternately are of pieced work and stuffed quilting patterns, one of the latter contained subjects relating to the sea.[16] Among some pieced-work patterns, the piecing itself is stuffed; the trees on an American quilt of the Foundation Rose and Pinetree pattern (in private ownership in England) are stuffed, and a Cockscomb quilt contains small blue and orange cotton stuffed birds.[17]

In common with corded quilting, workers' signatures are more likely to be found among the patterns of stuffed quilts than in examples of wadded and flat quilting, although a certain amount of the letters may contain cord as padding. The finish of the quilts is similar to other types in this chapter, that is, by binding at the edges with strips of the same kind of material used for the quilt; or by running together at the edges (171) or by sewing on a fringe. Fringes used always to be handmade and often are quite elaborate, those on figures 142 and 143 being unusually long.

6   THE SIXTEENTH CENTURY

References in writings and other documents provide most of the evidence there is of the importance of quilting during the sixteenth century. Here and there, however, remainders of the work done within this period are to be found, and together with recorded descriptions and uses, these help to give a more detailed picture than is known for any earlier century. The character of the work seems to have changed during this time also, as trade with countries in the East which had a native tradition in quilting brought new life to European domestic work, which until then seems to have been of a rather sober nature. The use of coloured thread for the quilting stitches became common; until then, the only evidence of its use is the brown colour which outlines the major patterns in the Sicilian quilt, but this is made to appear mouse-coloured when compared with the brilliance of the original colours of the Indian work. Surface embroidery worked on a quilted ground was another attraction and there is evidence also which suggests that the same trading may have been responsible for introducing work in which the patterns were padded with cord; until about the end of the fifteenth century they appear to have contained soft wadding or stuffing.

Quilts made from silk and satin became more widespread – up to this time linen, cotton and wool had been commonly, but not exclusively used, as being hard wearing for most purposes – but probably the possession of them was confined to the wealthy. The Royal Wardrobe was well supplied at any rate, as Katherine Howard was given 23 quilts of sarsenet from it, as a mark of favour, in May 1540,[1] but quilted clothing of all kinds was worn throughout the century in England.

The subject of their health, then as now, was of earnest concern to many people and quite early in the century, Sir Thomas Elyot, a writer on education and politics and a translator of the classics, wrote also *The Castel of Helth*, published in 1541, wherein he gave symptoms and recommended cures for a long list of complaints, for a number of which he claimed first-hand experience.[2] He set out in 'The Forthe Boke', his own symptoms of a chronic cold which he had endured for four years – 'sores in the mouthe, tothe ache, pynne and webe in the eyes, dulnesse of heringe, quynces, frettinges of the bowelles with fires, moystness of brethe, griefe in the herte, palseyes, ache in the muscules and joyntes', for which he had taken advice from 'dyvers phisitions, to kepe my bed warme'; he had dosed himself with various preparations also. Then he happened to read 'the boke of Galene',[3] only to find that 'I had ben longe in errour, wherefore first I did throwe away my quylted cappe, and my other close bonettes, and only did lye in a thynne coyfe, which I have ever sens used both wynter and somer.' As he added a 'light bonet of velvet' to this, it seems unlikely that his head was much cooler, but he declared he was better, having taken various medicines and dietary remedies as well. Whether eventually, the cure turned out to be worse than the ill-effects of wearing his quilted nightcap is not recorded, but he survived the publication of his remedies for only five years and died in 1546, at the age of about 47.

More details are given on the making of quilted nightcaps in another book, published in the year following *The Castel of Helth*. Andrewe Borde (or Boorde), 'of Physick Doctor', wrote his own opinions on dealing with many aspects of diet, dress and behaviour affecting health, in a book with the title *Here foloweth a Compendyous Regyment or a Dietary of Helth, made in Moutpyliour*,[4] but he held views opposite to those of Sir Thomas Elyot on the necessity of warmth at night. 'The VIII Chapter doth shewe how man shulde ordre hymselfe in slepe and watche and in wearynge his apparell', in which he is convinced that 'To slepe on the back upryght is utterly to be abhorred, when you do slepe let not your neck nother your sholders, nother your handes, nor feete nor no other place of your bodye lye bare but is covered. . . . Let your nyght cap be of scarlet, and this I do advertyse you to cause to be made a good thick quylt of cotton or els of pure flockes or of cleane woole, and let the coverynge of it be of white fustyan, and lay it on the fetherbed that you do lye on and in your bed lye not to hote not to colde but in a temperance.' In addition, the windows of the house and especially those of the bed chamber had to be closed at night, at a time when those who could do so, slept within the drawn curtains of their beds also, in an attempt to defeat the draughts and cold in the unheated houses. Nevertheless, discounting the value and medical significance of his instructions Dr Borde gave reasonably clear ones on the materials which he thought were suitable for quilted nightcaps, and at a time when little has been written about the work at all, he shows that the difference of opinion which existed between himself and Sir Thomas Elyot on the subject of nightcaps, was not on whether they should or should not be worn, but whether they should be quilted. Little else is to be found about quilted night garments, but a single reference is made in the wardrobe inventory of the Habsburg, Charles V, to '16 quilted silken nightshirts' at the time when he went to live in Spain after his retirement in

1556.[5] It appears to be the only indication of quilted silk being used for garments other than for day-time wear.

Quilting on day clothes had not reached the level of fashion to which it was to come in the seventeenth and eighteenth centuries, but a reference in a wardrobe account towards the end of Henry VIII's reign mentions 'one pair of linen sleeves, paned with gold over the arm, quilted with black silk, and wrought with flowers between the panes and at the hands'. Sleeves were richly embroidered during the reigns of Henry VIII and Elizabeth I and it is probable that in this case the quilting was worked flat with back stitch.[6]

The making of fabric armour, such as the quilted jack, was listed among contemporary trades in Thomas Newbery's book, *Dives Pragmaticus, The Great Merchaunt Man*, which was published as a child's instruction book, the receipt for its printing being entered in the accounts of Stationers' Hall for 1562–63, 'Received of Alexander Lace for his lycense for pryntynge of a book intitled *Dives Pragmaticus* very pretye for children etc. . . . iiijd.' In the Preface the author calls up men of all trades and professions to come and buy from *Dives Pragmaticus* 'to the end that children may learn to read and write their designations, as well as their wares and implements', and in many pages of rhyming couplets these are listed exhaustively from 'fine Pomanders, fine Toothpikers and whistles' to 'Harnesse, Helmets, Mayle cotes and Jackes', as well as to tailors and quilters, who would be connected with these trades (see p. 41).

Descriptions and accounts of the wearing of fabric armour continued throughout the sixteenth century and from this period, two examples at least, are known to have survived. A German military skirt, with a quilted lining of heavy blue linen, thickly padded with flax and dating from about the first 30 years of the century, is in the collection of the Metropolitan Museum of New York.[7] An arming doublet, in private ownership also in New York, may have been made even earlier (99).[8] It has been attributed to the fifteenth century, but the owner, Mr C. O. von Kienbusch, believes it to be of sixteenth-century workmanship, but not later than a mid-century date. It will be seen that the quilting was done in horizontal lines, on chamois-leather sewn on canvas, with mail sleeves extending well over the breast and back; the fastening down the front originally had seven buttons. Half of the back (not shown) has been repaired with linen, and leather laces are sewn about waist-level for the purpose of attaching other garments. This example of fabric armour is said to be unique and the only one of its kind extant; it, too, is possibly of German origin. Other examples of quilted garments made during the century which have survived, include two sets of pink silk quilted doublets, breast, back and fald padded with cotton, which date from the end

99 *Arming doublet. The front of the garment showing chain mail over quilted chamois-leather. German, probably sixteenth century*

of the period and are in the collections of the Pitt–Rivers Museum at Oxford.[9]

A jack containing a metal not commonly sewn within the padding, bears an historical interest, according to John Proctor's contemporary account of Wyatt's Rebellion in 1554. After his desertion by many of his followers, Wyatt 'fell into so great extreme of anguish and sorrow, as writing a letter of expostulation to some of his familiars abroad in reprehension of their infidelity in that they sticked not to him so fast as they promised, he bedewed the paper whereupon he wrote with tears issuing so abundantly from his eyes as it would bear no ink. And so leaving to write, calling for a privy coat that he had quilted with angels not long afore, which might serve both for his defence, and a refuge for his necessity being in another country. . . . "For England", said he, "is no place for us to rest in."' There can be no doubt that the coat was made after the manner of a jack, with angels (a gold piece then worth the equivalent of about ten shillings) sewn into the padding in place of the usual metal or horn scales. His precautions of course came too late.[10]

Mention of the type of armour with which quilted fabric was worn can be found in fiction and in fact throughout the last half of the century, although not all of it proved to be effective protection in combat. The tale of Sir Walter Scott's *Lay of the Last Minstrel* was set in the Border country in the

middle of the 1500s and in the battle between Sir Richard Musgrave and the
heroic Lord Cranstoun –

> Cranstoun's lance, of more avail
> Pierced through like silk, the Borderer's mail;
> Through shield, and jack, and acton past,
> Deep in his bosom broke at last.[11]

The True Use of Armorie by William Wyrley, published in 1592, contains an
account of *The Honourable Life and Languishing Death of Sir John de Gratby
Capitall a Buz*, 'one of the Knights elected by the first founder of the Garter
into that noble order'. His life was spent fighting one battle after another, all
recounted with most bloodthirsty detail, and in fair combat Sir John usually
was the victor. But in one, in spite of his ability to shear through metal and
fabric armour, he was ambushed and outnumbered by 30 of his enemies –

> Th' instructed thirtie, found me where I deale
>   So huge and mighty bloes, as that no plate,
> No hardned steele, no quilt, nor warped meale
>   Could make resist, but yeelded open gate
> To my sharp axe, my bloes so hevie sate
>   But here these thirtie sease me in the fray
>   Any by fine force they bear me thence away.[12]

Padded and quilted garments were worn under tournament armour and
the quilted jack was included among items of Elizabethan military armour
for light troops. Sir John Smith's *Instructions, Observations and Ordres Militaires* for the years 1591 to 1595, include an order for archers – 'Archers should
weare either Ilet holed doublets that will resist the thrust of sword or dagger,
covered with some trim and gallant kind of coloured cloth to the liking of
the Captain . . . or else Jackes of maile quilted upon fustian.'[13] Some of his
later comments on military matters proved to be unacceptable and he was
committed to the Tower, but no exception was taken to his views on fabric
defences.

Descriptions of quilted armour were given in Spenser's *Faerie Queene* (pp.
9 and 12), and in his *View of the Present State of Ireland* written in 1596, he
describes a number of military garments and adds, 'All these that I have re-
hearsed unto you be not Irish garments but English; for the Quilted leather
jacke is English; for it was the proper weed of the horsemen, as ye may read
in Chaucer, where he describeth Sir Thopas his apparell and armoure, when
he went to fight agaynst the Gyant in his robe of shecklaton, which shecklaton

is a kind of guilded leather with which they used to embroider theyr Irish jackes.'[14]

Records of quilted garments, whether of domestic or military types, probably outnumber those of the bed quilt, but better than any record are the examples of some quilts which actually have survived. Of others which did not survive, however, records show that they were made of satin or silk, which would account for their lack of staying power, although the fate of one was decided not by wear and tear, but by explosion. A bedspread of 'quilted taffeta' was on Darnley's bed in the house in Kirk o'Fields, which was blown up and destroyed, and presumably the quilt with it, in 1567.[15] Other silk quilts appear among items in household inventories. A number of these, taken from old Welsh inventories, are mentioned in *Traditional Quilting*,[16] and some of the earliest are listed in 1551 among the household goods at Powys Castle of Edward, the last feudal Baron of Powys –

> In the New Chamber over ye Garden . . . Item a quylte of redd sylke
> In the Nursery . . . Item a quylte and a coverlet of dornes.

It may be that the nursery quilt was not of silk, as this is not mentioned especially. Other quilts are included in an inventory of goods belonging to Sir John Perrott at Carew Castle in 1592 and have their respective values attached also –

> Item ij old quiltes of yellowe sercnet, xxs.
> Item a changeable silke quilt, price xxs.
> Item an old black and white silke quilt for a bedd, price iijs.

For the last item to be priced so much lower than the others, it is likely that it was of earlier make, but worth less because it was worn, although there is no indication of the age of any of them. The fact that six quilts were entered as one item, suggests that they were of an ordinary type, probably for every-day use; although sarsenet was a silk material, it was in common use by the sixteenth century.

A much-quoted entry from the inventory at Kenilworth, of the goods of Robert Dudley, Earl of Leicester, in 1584, probably refers to a different kind of quilt altogether in – 'A faire quilte of crymson sattin, vi breadths iij yards 3 quarters naile deep, all lozenged over with silver twiste, in the midst a cinquefoil with a garland of ragged staves, fringed aboute with a small fringe of crymson silke, lined through with white fustian.'[17] Any quilt notable for its rich materials and embroidery of this kind, would be more appropriate for a day cover when the bed was not in use.

A remarkable quilt of Indian work has been preserved at Hardwick Hall in

Derbyshire, in which the quilting was done in back stitch, using red, blue, green and orange silk threads, through two layers of unbleached cotton, with a thin interlining of cotton wool. Its date is not recorded, but it has been suggested on good authority that it is of sixteenth-century workmanship, probably made in the Malda district in Bengal, and if so, it is likely to have been made before 1575. This provenance is based on the relationship between the quilt patterns and those with which the Islamic architecture in Malda was decorated, and a date previous to 1575 follows naturally on this reasoning, as the dynasty of Malda was destroyed in the year 1575 to 1576.

The general design of the quilt consists of a number of rectangular compartments, outlined by a series of patterned borders containing a great variety of geometrical, stylised and pictorial patterns, closely arranged on the ground. The close spacing of the quilted patterns all over the work, leaves very little to be seen of the woven material. Human and animal figures decorate some of the borders; men on horseback and on foot, armed with swords and shields and accompanied by dogs, are shown on one, and on another, men and women seated on chairs under trees are playing what appears to be a game of chess. Other figures include elephants, each having on its back a howdah and riders, with men on the ground between them. Tame birds and animals are shown, as well as the pattern of the Hindu peacock with a serpent in its beak. Formal flower and leaf patterns fill many of the geometrical outlines. The quilt is in a very fragile condition now, much of the cotton is discoloured and worn and the once brilliant silks have lost their lustre, but still it is possible to distinguish the fine workmanship through the glass top of the case in which it is kept. When fully spread the quilt measures ten feet eight inches long and seven feet three inches wide, and a section of one corner, measuring approximately 25×18 inches is illustrated in *Needlework Through the Ages*,[18] on which it is possible to see that a number of narrow straight and circular dividing borders are patterned with a small scrolling pattern, worked alternately in red and blue silk, which is very similar in arrangement to those seen in Welsh patterns (135, 144, 152).

Without the evidence of sixteenth-century inventories and other household records, it would be difficult to establish the existence of bed quilts made in England or Wales at the time, although even these records do not contain proof that they were so. The almost casual inclusion of them among other items, infers that they were not of unusual value, and so possibly they were made then, as it is known they were later, by the women of the household and used until they were worn out, with the same lack of concern as that shown by Sir Thomas Elyot towards his nightcap. Quilts of European and Indian make which are known to have survived, have done so to a great

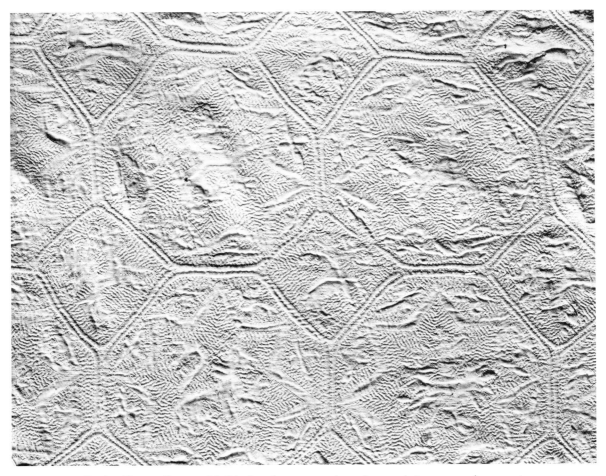

100   *Quilt of heavy linen, with fabulous beasts on a darned ground, in octagonal compartments with cord-padded borders. German, sixteenth century*

extent, because the linen and cotton of which most were made were unattractive to moth and were durable and of good quality. A German quilt, of
which detail is illustrated on figures 97 and 100, was made from two layers
of heavy linen, with the pattern outlines padded with firm cord and sewn
with back stitch. A flat quilted ground in darning stitch surrounds unpadded
animal, bird and leaf shapes, behind which the backing material has been cut
(see p. 76). The practice of cutting the lower layer of material does not seem
to have been a common one, but a difficult and similar process is described for
the making of a farthingale of later date (seventeenth century) in which the
quilted patterns were stuffed with cotton and combined with embroidery in
pulled work. After the embroidery was done, the coarse backing material
was cut away behind it.[19]

Human figures, animal and bird shapes and many others, as well as geo-metrical patterns were common to Indian and Portuguese quilting. An elaborate quilt in private ownership in Italy, is made of linen stitched with gold-coloured silk thread with patterns containing these kinds of features, although the main decoration is pictorial in character. A large centre panel shows a scene of ships on water (probably the sea, as waves are indicated) which are typical of mid-sixteenth-century Mediterranean galleys, and a tower shape, which could be a lighthouse or a small fortress. Among other patterns is a double-headed eagle, which is to be found in other Indo-Portuguese work, and figures in sarongs occupy the spaces in an arcaded border of arches supported by pillars worked with a spiral pattern.

By the end of the century, quilting was in common use on caps for night wear, for day wear and for armour. Bed quilts were common also, certainly in upper-class households, and probably others of a humbler type were among the possessions of most good housekeepers, of whatever social standing. In 1587, the price of a quilt belonging to William Jeneson of Newcastle was given as six shillings and eight pence,[20] a drop in value as compared with 20 shillings for one of the Powys Castle quilts, and although no indication is given as to the quality or condition of either, presumably both were new, or nearly so.

Perhaps it is appropriate for the records of the sixteenth century to end with a reference by Shakespeare in *Henry IV* (about 1597) in words spoken by Henry, Prince of Wales to the stout Sir John Falstaff – 'How now blown Jack! How now quilt!'[21] It is clear that by then the appearance of a padded quilt was familiar enough for the likeness to be understood readily by an audience, and appreciated as a joke against a portly figure. Was there, also, a double reference to his shape and his name, in likening him to a blown or over-stuffed jack?

7 THE SEVENTEENTH CENTURY

The seventeenth century saw a considerable rise in the popularity of quilting for clothing and bed furnishings in England and Wales, but a decline in its use as defensive armour. Items also appear in accounts for quilted padding for furniture, and padded and quilted linings for trunks and coffers in which clothes were kept, or carried when travelling.

Continuing trade with the East encouraged the use of colour and rich materials, as well as of surface embroidery, mostly in floral patterns worked with silk and metal threads, but fine linen was not supplanted by silk and satin, and towards the end of the century very fine quilting was worked on white cotton and linen in which the patterns were padded with thin cord. Thanks to the durable nature of the materials, a number of examples of this work have survived in a reasonable state of repair, most of the patterns reflecting the floral and informal character of those embroidered in colour on silk or satin. Embroidery in white cotton or linen thread was added to the cord patterns on garments but there seems to be little or no evidence of it on large quilts or curtains. There is little doubt that this work was done in, and for, the big houses and their occupants; examples of clothing which remain are of elaborate workmanship and fine-quality material, in which it would be impossible to do anything but live a leisured life, and the quilts and hangings were made on a scale which was suitable only for large beds and in high rooms.

Travellers from Europe to the East brought home stories of the peoples and their countries, in which the imported quilts and embroideries had been made, and the adventures of one of these, Edward Terry, a nephew of Sir Thomas Roe (founder of the West India Company), have been given in a clear and instructive account of all he saw in the early seventeenth century, including the uses of cotton from seed-sowing, to the quilting and embroidering of the woven material. Although the account of his journeys is added to those of an Italian, Pietro della Valle, and his name is omitted from the fly-leaf (he being described simply as 'A Relation of Sir Thomas Roe's.'), his descriptions of all he saw show him to have been an excellent observer. The voyage to the East Indies began on 'the third day of *February 1615*, when

101 *Linen coverlet with embroidered patterns in coloured silks on a flat quilted ground, finished with a knotted fringe. English, seventeenth century, 53 × 50 inches*

our Fleet fell down from *Graves-end* into *Tilbury-Hope*, where we continued till the eighth day following, an adverse wind forced our abode until the ninth of March, on which day it pleased God to send us, what we had much desired, a North-East wind which made us leave that weary Road, and set Sail for East-India.'; what he saw and related belonged to the early part of the century, although his writing of it was not published until 1665.[1]

After accounts of the growing of cotton and indigo and the processes of making, dyeing and printing the patterns on the cloth, he continued with a description of 'the Natives there [who] shew very much ingenuity in their Curious Manufactures; as in their silk-stuffs which they most artificially weave, some of them very neatly mingled either with Silver or Gold or both. As also in making excellent Quilts of their stained cloth, or of fresh coloured Taffata lined with their Pintadoet, or of their Sattin lined with Taffata, betwixt which they put Cotton-wooll, and work them together with Silk. Those Taffata or Sattin-quilts, are excellently stitched by them, being done as evenly and in as good order, as if they had been drawn out to them, for their direction.'[2] And in a further account of how people of 'better quality' travelled, he describes what he calls 'slight Coaches with two wheels, covered on the top and back-end but the fore-part and sides open, unless they carry women. These coaches will carry four persons besides the driver, but two may lie at ease and at length in them upon quilts, that lie in the body of them, upheld by girt-web, with which they are bottomed which makes them far more easie.'[3]

The travels of 'a noble Roman', Signor Pietro della Valle, covered the same country – 'East-India and Arabia Deserta' – and in a series of *Familiar Letters to his Friend Signor Mario Schipano*, one dated 'November the seventh 1623', tells of a visit to King Veuk-tapà Naeika. The King 'was seated upon a kind of porch on the opposite side of a small court, upon a Pavement somewhat rais'd from the Earth, covered with a Canopy like a square Tent, but was made of boards and gilded. The Floor was covered with a piece of Tapistry, something old, and the King sat after the manner of the East upon a little quilt on the outside of the Tent . . . having at his back two great Cushions of fine white silk.'[4] Neither Edward Terry nor Pietro della Valle recorded having seen any quilted garments on their travels, but Sir Thomas Herbert related in *Some Yeares Travels into divers parts of Asia and Afrique* – 'Their habit is a quilted coat of calico, tyed under the left arm.'[5]

Quilted garments were worn in England throughout the century, although regulations concerning armour contain fewer references to those worn as fabric defence. Gervase Markham remarked on the need for head protection in *Decades and Epistles of War* and in *Souldier's Accidence* (1625):

'The shot should have on his head a good and sufficient Spanish Morian well lined in the head with a quilted cap of strong linen and bound with linen ear plates';[6] and the Honourable Roger North in *Examen* mentions padded silk armour which was pistol proof.[7] It is likely also, that civilian caps and clothing often were reinforced with a quilted padding, as a reasonable precaution against attacks by the roaming ruffians of the time. Quilted garments similar to the arming doublet (99) still were worn under main armour but portraits painted at the latter end of the century show the gorget (padded with quilting and lined with silk) worn by then merely as a fashion.

Much more numerous are the records and examples of domestic quilting in many kinds of clothing and furnishing, which increased as a popular fashion throughout the 1600s. The use of embroidered patterns in colour, worked on a flat-quilted ground, and coloured thread for the quilting itself predominated. Quilted garments were fashionable for men as well as for women. Men's jackets and waistcoats of quilted silk and satin, with inter-linings of soft wadding, have been preserved, and a suit of white quilted satin doublet and breeches, worn about 1620 to 1630, is in the collections of the Victoria and Albert Museum.[8] Waistcoats of white linen with cord-quilted patterns were worn from the last part of the century for at least a hundred years.

Quilted waistcoats and bodices, with flower patterns worked in colour on the quilted ground, were fashionable for women's dress; the waistcoat illustrated on figure 102, was made during the 1680s and a jacket (also of English work), of about the same date and made of white cotton padded with wool, was quilted in chain stitch with blue silk thread. It is in the possession of the Nordiska Museet, Stockholm and is illustrated in *The Art of Embroidery*.[9] A jacket of even earlier date, made at the beginning of the century, has small dots of brownish silk, worked in the spaces between the quilted pattern in back-stitched red silk (pp. 71, 72 and figure 94). A number of other examples have been preserved and although similar in style and decoration, none is exactly alike.

Other kinds of quilted day clothes were worn by women. The farthingale mentioned in the previous chapter (p. 89) was of seventeenth-century work, and the elaborate kind of pattern, combining quilting and decorative embroidery stitches in white thread, is an early example of what was to become a rage in the eighteenth century, when this embroidery was equal in importance to the corded quilting.[10] Part of the skirt and the border of a linen robe (104)[11] shows a formal diaper pattern of quilted cord, and on the border, informal outlines of daffodil, tulip, carnation, convolvulus and other flower and leaf shapes, quilted in running stitch, can be recognised. This type

102 *Woman's linen waistcoat, with flowers embroidered in coloured silks on a flat quilted ground, finished with a knotted fringe. English, c. 1680*

103 *Woman's jacket with coloured floral patterns in red and green woven into the material before quilting. English, c. 1690*

104 *Part of a cord-quilted linen robe, with a diapered ground pattern and a border containing patterns of daffodil, carnation, convolvulus, tulip and leaf shapes. English, seventeenth century*

105 *Pillow sham with flat quilting on a linen ground. Lily and leaf patterns and surrounded with borders containing twist, church-window, fan and numerous filling patterns common to all types of quilting. English, late seventeenth century, 35 × 36 inches*

of naturalistic flower pattern, sometimes outlined with back stitch in flat quilting and sometimes with the outlines raised with cord, is a characteristic of much seventeenth-century quilting, which seems to have become less popular in the early years of the eighteenth century. The flowers resemble those which were worked in coloured silks, but it is more usual to find them on an unquilted ground, as they are on the border pattern of the robe, and later, on the elaborate eighteenth-century quilt from Great Tangley Manor (129).[12] A white quilt in private ownership in Somerset, similar in pattern to the Great Tangley quilt but with vases or urns of flowers in place of baskets, probably dates from the last quarter of the seventeenth century and appears to have been made, at some time, from hangings or curtains; there are a number of joins, and the quilting was done before the joins were made. The pillow sham illustrated on figure 105,[13] is an exception to the common method of quilting naturalistic flowers on an unquilted ground, and in this case the outlined flower shapes are worked on a ground of the simple square diamond pattern, all the work being done in flat quilting.

Other examples of naturalistic patterns can be found on some garments of wadded quilting, but in this type of work there is always a quilted ground pattern; the pot of flowers (90)[14] was worked on the corners of a border of running flower patterns on a man's white satin jacket. Women's petticoats were quilted, many of the patterns being raised with cord, or else flat quilted, as well as those padded with wadding. Although more concerned with the lace on petticoats, in *Tyrannus; or, The Mode* (1661), John Evelyn may have seen them of quilted red and white silk or of white material and the quilting done with red thread –

> Short under petticoats, pure, fine,
> Some of Japan stuff, some Chine,
> With knee-high galloon bottomed;
> Another quilted white and red,
> With broad Flanders lace below.[15]

In spite of the dire results threatened by the disapproving, to those who chose to defy them or ignore the warnings, a cap was considered to have distinct advantages –

> It's light for summer, and in cold it sits
> Close to the skull, a warm house for the wits;[16]

and so they continued to be worn. Women's and children's caps were quilted towards the end of the century, but as the fashion continued for some years into the eighteenth century, it is difficult to date any examples with certainty, unless some record or reliable history is attached to them. The quilting on the child's cap illustrated on figure 115b,[17] is in character with patterns worked in the seventeenth century, but as it appears to have been made from quilting done for another garment and cut to shape for the cap pieces, it may have been made up early in the eighteenth century from material quilted some years before. The method of making the caps is described later on p. 108 and illustrated on figures 113 and 114. The patterns shown on figure 115b are more widely spaced than in caps which are known to be of eighteenth-century date, and the pricked holes and pulled stitches allow for more ventilation than usual, which makes it a matter of speculation as to whether John Locke's arguments, on the inadvisability of head coverings, may have persuaded the mother of the wearer to compromise between tradition and the then revolutionary way of bringing up children. Mr Locke's ideas were well respected and to our eyes, commendably tough in many ways, and he recommended (in 1693) that if nature had so well covered a child's head with hair 'and strengthened it with a year or two's Age, that he can run about by Day, without a Cap, it is best by night that a Child should be also without one; there being nothing that more exposes to Head-ach, Colds, Catarrhs, Coughs and other diseases than keeping the *Head warm*'.[18]

Men wore day- and night-caps of embroidered linen, silk and satin, but quilted caps for them do not appear to have been popular, as there is no mention of them and so far, one only has come to light, which may have been worn at the end of the century. The unusual shape of the cap illustrated on figure 106, suggests that it may have been made during the 1690s, to accommodate the high horned wigs of this period (until about 1710) but it has no recorded history (p. 78).

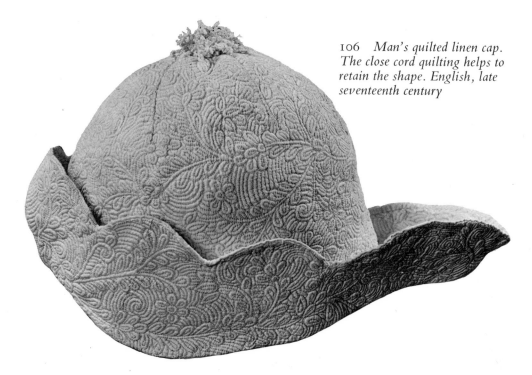

106   *Man's quilted linen cap. The close cord quilting helps to retain the shape. English, late seventeenth century*

By the end of the century, in one way or another, quilting was used on almost every kind of garment to which it could have been applied with reason, but there is evidence in plenty to show that the quilted bed cover was of even more importance, and must have been in use in every house of any consequence. Quilted pillow covers were made to match the quilts; pillows were kept on the outside of the cover during the day-time and when the pillow itself was not quilted a pillow sham or false cover was laid over it (105).

Written descriptions and accounts of quilts, as well as examples which have been preserved, leave no doubt as to the quality of the materials or of the fine needlework in them. Of the references to be found, most are among the possessions listed in inventories, wardrobe accounts and so on, of the rich and of those in upper-class society. It is probable that a number of them had been imported and sometimes this is mentioned, but others must have been made within the household for which the goods were listed. An inventory of the possessions of Sir Thomas Kyston of Hengrave was taken in 1603, and included 'One twilt of tauney taffata sarsenett embroydered all over wth twiste of yellow silk, wth the escutcheons of Sir Thomas Kyston's and my ladye's armes';[19] and a descriptive entry is included in the Wardrobe Accounts of King James I, on the occasion of the marriage of his daughter the Princess Elizabeth to the Elector Palatine in 1609 – 'Item. To John Baker, our upholsterer, for 3 quilts of fustian, lined with taffeta, filled with wool, and sewed with silk, and for 2 counterpoynts of plush, both sides alike, sewed with silk.'[20] Embroideries of great richness are listed among the items of the inventory made at the time of the death of Henry Howard, Earl of Northampton in 1614, and the description of 'a china quilt stiched in chequer worke with yealowe silke the ground white'[21] is typical of later and surviving work, which is quilted with diaper patterns on white linen and sewn with yellow silk thread.

The Company of Merchants Trading with the East (the East India Company) who began trading in 1600, were responsible for importing in quantity into Britain the coveted chintzes, embroideries and quilts. By their descriptions and enthusiasm for these things seen abroad, travellers like Edward Terry had prepared the ground at home, and the Royal Proclamation of Charles I in 1631 encouraged their entry into England by permitting their import, with many other goods, from the East Indies. Among the spices, sugar-candy and porcelain on the list, were also 'rich carpets of Persia and Cambaya, quilts of satin, taffaty, painted calicoes, benjamin, damasks, satin and taffaties of China, quilts of China embroidered with gold, quilts of Pitania embroidered with silk' – a delectable collection to back up the travellers' tales. It is possible that the 'carpets of Persia' may have included those which were quilted and embroidered, as some Persian prayer and bath mats were so made.[22]

A sidelight on the fashionable taste of the time, as well as the price of quilts in the trade, is given in a letter of the East India Company written in 1641 – 'The quilts of chintz being novelties, produced from £5 5s to £6 the pair; a further supply, therefore, is desired, and both as regards these and chintzes, more should be made with white grounds and the branches and flowers to be in colours, and not (as those last sent) all in general of deep red ground and other sadder colours.'[23] In the same year an entry, taken from a table concerning textiles made in connection with the Book of Rates, mentioned quilted materials sold by the length – 'Stript, tufted or quilted canvas with silk the piece containing 15 yards, iv^l.'[24]

Some quilts were made of silk with reversible patterns, and different colours on each side. Although padded with soft cord, the silks were of equal quality on each side and not, as for linen or cotton quilts, with a more coarsely woven material for the backing. Single cord was used for most of the patterns but where a thickening was needed, two or three strands were laid side by side but not stitched separately, which is customary for cord padding. Animal and bird patterns were common to Eastern work and when quilted, the use of two or more strands of cord is noticeable on the flanks and thicker parts of the bodies; the cord is tapered to a single strand where the pattern outlines narrow. Animal, bird (107) and stylised plant shapes, sometimes were enclosed in geometrically shaped compartments, similar to the type shown on figure 108, and this style possibly influenced the pattern of the sixteenth-century German quilt also (100).

107   *Bird patterns common to seventeenth-century work*

The furore created by the 'novelty' of the coloured quilts may have been the reason for the preservation of some others of the time, which may have been considered to be sad in appearance. Their monochrome colours, such

108 *Cotton quilt with bird and arboreal patterns enclosed in geometrical compartments. Surrounding borders contain similar shapes, also twist, plait and other patterns in running stitch. Portuguese, seventeenth century*

as indigo, dull yellow or drab, or a light coffee colour, would not have pleased the mood of the Restoration period and perhaps they were banished to the bottom of the linen chest, while the more favoured, with branches and flowers on a light ground, graced the beds. The quilt on figure 108 may owe its survival to the cotton covers being of a somewhat dull and neutral colour, but its value to the history of quilt patterns is that it contains several which are among those looked upon as traditional in England and Wales. Their relationship to some on the quilt shown on the Frontispiece, and to a host of others dating from the seventeenth to the twentieth centuries, is indisputable.

Records show that quilted upholstery was in use from the early days of the century. Although this work cannot rank as needlework, and cannot be compared, in pattern or appearance, with quilting that is sewn, nevertheless the principle of fastening together two layers of material with an interlining or a padding of soft stuffing between them, is the same as that for the other processes which are classed under the heading of quilting. The materials which were used, were chosen for their suitability for the job in hand and range from leather to silk, but whatever the kind of outer covering, or the stuffing, the method of fastening them together, as well as attaching the 'quilt' to whatever was being upholstered, was by quilt nails; these had flat heads which were large enough to hold down the layers of material without tearing. The nail heads sometimes were covered with the same material as that used for the top cover of the quilt, especially with the more delicate stuffs, such as silk. Boxes and coffers which were used for moving furniture and valuables were lined to protect the contents, and the linings often were quilted. The making of such coffers, which were of leather-covered wood, was controlled by the Leathersellers Company, whose ordinances of 1635 included fines for faulty workmanship; a paper lining, instead of one made with cloth, incurred a fine of two shillings and sixpence.[25]

Early in the century an item from an upholsterer's bill which was charged to the Royal Wardrobe Accounts for 1623 to 1624, included specific details of the materials which were used for upholstering some chairs –

> Oliver Brown and John Baker upholsterers . . . for making up six folding cheyres of crimson vel^{vt} and for fustian downe, spanish lether, girth-web, and sackcloth, quilt nails and plates of Iron quilt for them. £x . xi . x.[26]

John Baker probably was the same man who made the quilts of fustian for Princess Elizabeth in 1609, as an upholsterer to the Royal Household. A later workman, John Casbert, in 1674 made 'For his Mats Closet Whitehall, a chaire of Sky coloured Dammaske being round in the back and quilted with a bagg of Downe with borders and elboes stuffed and 2 stools suitable.'[27]

The linings of coffers and cabinets in which clothes were kept, especially women's garments, were lined with quilted silk and stuffed with scented padding; no doubt the reason for this was that many clothes were un-washable, due to the lavish embroidery and ornament with which they were decorated. In 1673, Richard Pigg charged £25 'for a large cabinet with nine drawers covered with Turkey leather: lined with sarsnett and quilted with perfumes: with ten locks and garnished with guilt nails'. In this case the nails mentioned had gilt heads and were used as a decoration on the outside of the cabinet; the nails used for the inside quilting, probably were covered with sarsenet to match the lining. In 1676 'ye Lady Beeling' had to pay £10 for 'a *Cabinet* with several drawers covered with Russian leather and lined with sarsnet and quilted with gilt nails ye locks and handles of the best sort with a twisted frame and a leather case'.[28] The linings of some coaches also were upholstered with leather or silk, quilted with covered nails.

By the end of the 1660s, in spite of the fashion for quilted garments and head wear, it was the bed quilt which was of the most importance, and once more we find quilting being considered in its effect upon health. This time it was by John Locke, who was concerned with the correct upbringing of a child – 'Let his *Bed* be *Hard*, and rather Quilts than Feathers. Hard Lodging strengthens the Parts; whereas being buried every Night in Feathers, melts and dissolves the Body, is often the Cause of Weakness, and the Fore-runner of an early Grave.'[29] But for those who had survived the dangers of this softness in their youth, the colourful materials and embroidery of the imported quilts were in welcome contrast to the period during the middle of the century when extravagance of any sort was under a cloud, and in consequence, the demand for them continued. With this rise in the demand and their popularity, it was only to be expected that the prices would rise too. The days of being able to purchase a pair of quilts for five or six pounds were over and in the Expense Book of John Hervey, first Earl of Bristol, the cost of one quilt showed how much the price for them had risen – on 30 August 1689 'Paid Mary Bishop for ye use and by order of Mrs Jane Harrison for an India quilt for a bed, £38.'[30]

8 THE EIGHTEENTH CENTURY

A change in the style, or pattern, or fashion of any kind of needlework, is not dependent on a change of date, nor even a change of century, and the period labelled '*c.* 1700' for instance, given as the date for a number of examples of quilting, may cover ten years or more on each side of the year 1700 (109). Quilted work bearing any date, unfortunately, is rare. By the beginning of the eighteenth century, life in Britain was more prosperous than it had been during the previous hundred years; there was less general need for economy, and as regards the development of quilting, the most noticeable feature was that there was more of it. More people could afford to keep up with the fashion in dress and furnishing, and the 'novelties' of the mid sixteenth century had stimulated the making of similar quilts here. In spite of the prosperity, however, economy did not go by the board entirely and a number of the surviving cord-quilted garments and bed covers, clearly were cut from larger pieces of work – bed quilts made from curtains, hangings or larger quilts, and small articles of clothing cut down from larger garments, such as petticoats. Steele's observation in *The Tatler* in the 'Case of the Petticoat', referring to a woollen petticoat of exceptional size, must have been influenced by a form of economy of which he had some knowledge – he was unlikely to have thought it out for himself – 'I ordered it to be folded up, and sent as a present to a widow gentlewoman, who has five daughters; desiring she would make each of them a petticoat out of it, and send me back the remainder, which I design to cut into stomachers, caps, facings of my waistcoat sleeves and other garnitures.'[1] Children's garments can be seen to have been cut down but there is little positive evidence of any 'other garnitures' in cut-down quilting.

The amount and variety of quilting that must have been made from the last part of the sixteenth century onwards, can be gauged to some extent, by the number of surviving examples, not only of bed quilts but of clothing such as caps, waistcoats, petticoats and dresses. The elaboration of the work on quilted petticoats caused a change of fashion about the middle of the century, when the style of dresses was altered to allow for the skirts to be open in front to show the quilted petticoat beneath. There is evidence also,

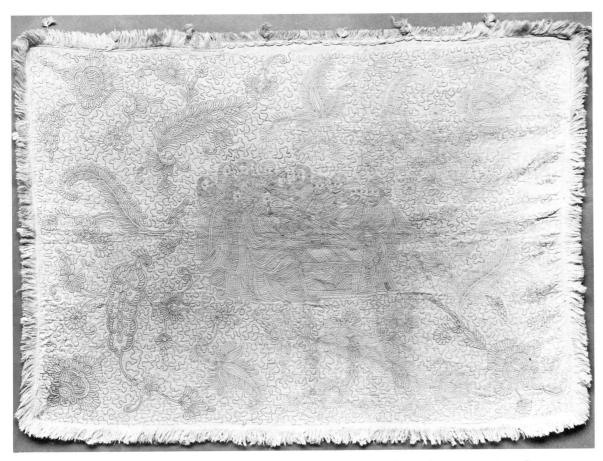

109 *Linen panel worked with flat quilted ground in back stitch, with representation of The Last Supper in cord quilting. Feather leaf and flower patterns are set on a ground worked in meander. Edges finished with linen fringe and tassels. The panel may have been intended as a chalice cover. English, c. 1700, 21½ × 29¾ inches*

to show that patchwork was known as a substitute for uncut lengths of material as the top layer of an interlined bed quilt.

Some garments, quilts and hangings of cord quilting which are attributed to the early part of the century, continued the style of the late seventeenth-century work, in which patterns were worked on an unquilted ground (104, 122) but fewer examples of this work have survived than have those in which the cord patterns were surrounded by flat unpadded quilting, worked either with back stitching in a close all-over pattern (109) or with darning in straight or curved lines, similar to the ground shown on figure 100. The comparative scarcity of surviving examples with an unquilted ground may have been due to the fact that it did not wear as well as more heavily quilted work and so more of it has perished, or that it was not as popular, and so less was made. The patterns always are fine and elegant in outline, and were worked equally well on cotton, linen and satin, and although large hangings, curtains,[2] and quilts (129) were quilted in this way, its lightness and detail seem to be more appropriate to clothing, especially caps. The lappet cap illustrated (122) shows the type of pattern clearly, and this cap of oyster-coloured satin lined with rose-pink silk, probably was made from another garment, perhaps a petticoat or the skirt of a dress; the scrolling stems of flower and leaf shapes can be seen to have been cut to shape for the front edge of the brim and lappets, and the base of the cap section has a drawstring threaded through worked loops to adjust the fitting.[3] Caps with long, hanging lappets were not common and the fashion for them must have covered a short period only, as examples and references to them are rare, but it is recorded in the thirty-sixth number of the *Connoisseur* in 1754 that 'of all the branches of female dress, no one has undergone more alterations than that of the head. The long lappets, the horseshoe cap, the Brussels head and the prudish mob pinned under the chin, have all of them had their day.' One other known example with long lappets, of the same period, has survived; it is made of fine cotton but the quilting in this case was done especially for the cap, the scrolling leaf and flower patterns being arranged symmetrically round a central carnation shape on the back of the cap section and ending at the base of each lappet round the same flower pattern.[4] The histories of the caps are unknown, but both appear to be of English work.

A man's cap with short lappets, illustrated on figure 110, shows patterns which had been planned to fit the shape in every detail, even to the stitching of the bound edges which are worked with back stitch along the middle of the binding, giving the appearance of a finish with a double row of quilted cord. The date of the cap is given as *c.* 1700, and it is shown as a protective lining to a Doge's cap or *berretta* of leather of an earlier date, which is attributed to the Doges Marco and Agostino Barbarigo, 1485–1501.[5] This cap was for day wear but a reference to a quilted nightcap also in 1700, can be found in *The Way of the World* which was published in that year – 'a quilted nightcap with one ear' – is among the collection of other tattered wares recommended by Lady Wishfort for Foible to set herself up in trade, in her famous outburst of 'boudoir Billingsgate' against her maid.[6] Another cap of early eighteenth-century work (111) shows a type of pattern popular at the time for cord quilting, which has been compared to the traditional 'wheel' pattern in smocking, said to indicate that the wearer was a carter or waggoner by trade. This kind of similarity occurs in many kinds of traditional needlework, where the patterns are related but not accompanied by

111 *Man's cord-quilted linen cap, lined with cotton. The crown is in four sections with an additional piece for the brim. English, early eighteenth century*

110 *Man's quilted cotton lappet cap, shown as a protective lining for an earlier fifteenth-century Doge's berretta. Cord quilted with running and back stitches with some French knots. Italian, eighteenth century*

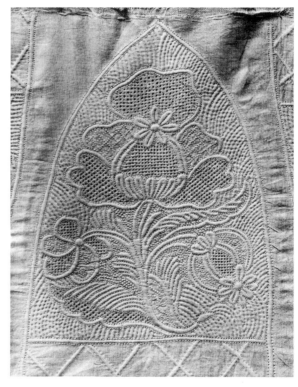

112 *One section of a man's linen cap, worked with linen thread in back, running and pulled stitches, with some French knots. Parts of other sections worked on same strip can be seen. English, mid-eighteenth century*

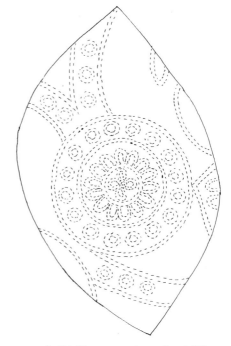

113 (left) *Centre section of a child's cap to cover back and crown of the head*

114 *One of a pair of side pieces to be attached to centre section*

the same significance; in this case it is unlikely to indicate any such activity of the wearer of the cap, nor of the baby whose cap pieces are shown in the drawings on figures 113 and 114, which are almost identical with those on the adult's cap. Caps for infants and children were not made in the four sections usually found in larger adult sizes but those of the bonnet shape were made with almost square side pieces; a very finely worked example of this type, contains heart patterns on the back of the cap and in the corners at the front, in which the outlines were made from strings of small hearts, very similar in arrangement to the pattern used sometimes for wadded quilting (63).[7]

A characteristic of much eighteenth-century quilting on garments is the use of embroidery stitches in white thread as fillings or ground patterns for cord quilting on white linen or cotton. French knots as fillings and ground work nearly always are among the stitches used; they may be worked solidly together or arranged in small patterns such as a trellis, scroll or circles, sometimes as the only embroidery other than the quilting (110, 116), and often with pulled, punched, Florentine and other stitches (115b, 112, 117, 118, 119). The more elaborate work of this kind generally was used for men's waistcoats (p. 108, and figures 117, 118, 119), but French knots with cord-quilted patterns were popular for babies' caps.

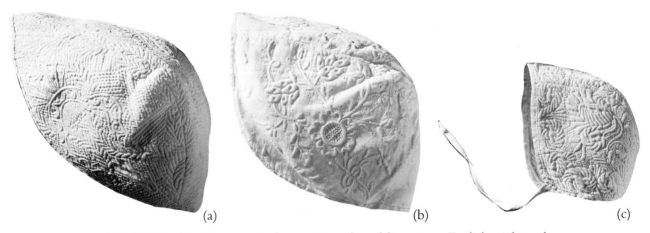

(a) (b) (c)

115 (a) *Child's white linen cap in three sections, bound linen tape. English, eighteenth century* (b) *Child's white linen cap in three sections. Drawn thread in flower centre, some leaves stuffed and ground pricked with overcast holes. English, early eighteenth century* (c) *Child's white linen cap in three sections. Edges bound linen tape, one tie missing. English, eighteenth century*

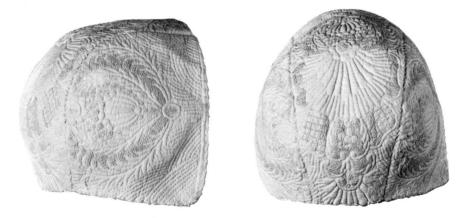

116 *Side and back of child's white cotton cap in three sections, worked back and running stitches, some French knots. Edges stitched. English, eighteenth century*

117 *Cuff of a linen coat sleeve. Cord-quilted patterns worked in back stitch, with embroidery in pulled work, Florentine stitch and French knots in linen thread. Spaces left for later working of buttonholes. English, mid-eighteenth century*

118 *Man's sleeved linen waistcoat. Cord-quilted patterns in back and running stitches with added embroidery in pulled stitches and French knots. English, eighteenth century*

119 *(opposite) Detail of figure 118, showing pocket flap and one corner of the waistcoat front*

Coats and jackets for infants were made of cord or wadded quilting throughout the century. The jacket on figure 120, is an example of a small garment which was made from a larger piece of cord quilting (p. 104); a sleeveless christening cloak of ivory satin, lined with white silk and thinly interlined with lamb's wool, was made for the purpose; the patterns match at the seams and fit the shape of the garment (89, 121). Its history is known also; it was worn by (and probably made for) Thomas Symner Mostyn Champeneys for his christening in 1769. Later he became Sir Thomas Champeneys and was the twenty-fifth in lineal descent from the first owner of Orchardleigh Manor near Frome in Somerset.[8]

Small items of dress for adults often were quilted and although it would have been practical for them to have been cut down from larger pieces as for children's clothes, this does not seem to be so. Perhaps it was an unwritten rule of fashion that this was not done in the best circles, as existing specimens appear to have been made for the purpose. Pear-shaped pockets worn under the skirt of a dress, made in pairs and tied round the waist with tapes attached to them, were embroidered over a flat-quilted ground; the quilting in this case lent a little necessary stiffness to the material and kept the pockets flat. Stomachers also, were quilted in the same way, or with fine corded patterns arranged to fit the V-shape of the garment, on linen, silk or satin. An example in the Gallery of English Costume in Manchester, is fitted with an inside pocket at the base. Cuffs of fine linen, flat quilted or raised with thin cord, some described as 'nurses cuffs', were made to slip over the cuffs of a dress, the quilting again providing a practical stiffening. Mittens for babies also were quilted. Little mention is made of quilted pin-cushions. A custom begun in the sixteenth century, for wearing a small pin-cushion hanging from the waist, lasted into the 1700s but none made of quilting has survived. Larger pin-cushions for keeping on the dressing-table were made and a reference to them in *Domestic Needlework* mentions 'large cushions of quilted linen with beautiful designs in yellow silk, in use in the late seventeenth and early eighteenth centuries'.[9] An example of this type still exists, which was made from two early eighteenth-century fragments of previously cord-quilted linen; the patterns are formally floral in character and the pin-cushion measures approximately eight inches long and six inches wide, with the edges finished with a fringe.

One of the most important fashions in quilting, however, was in its use on men's and women's waistcoats, and for jackets, petticoats and dresses, and many examples can be seen in museums and other collections of textiles and costume, which show the extent to which quilting was adapted to various changes of fashion during the century (102, 104, 118). Women's

120 Baby's cord-quilted jacket. White linen over coarser linen, edges bound linen tape. Made in one section with inset sleeves and three pairs of tape ties. English, late eighteenth century

121 Ivory satin christening long coat lined with white silk and padded with fine lamb's wool. Wadded quilting worked with running stitch in all-over reversible patterns. Length $29\frac{1}{2}$ inches, width between side seams $29\frac{1}{2}$ inches. English late eighteenth century

waistcoats, coats and jackets were quilted for warmth as much as for the decoration they added to costume. Some were made of wadded quilting, silk, satin, linen or cotton being used for the outer layers and thin interlinings of wool for the padding. Others, perhaps for summer wear, and certainly slimmer in line, were made of flat or cord quilting on white or natural-coloured linen, cotton or silk, and sewn with cream, white or yellow silk thread. Cord-quilted patterns were worked with flat-quilted grounds and when flat quilting only was used, flower and not formal patterns were worked over it. Occasionally the embroidery and the quilting were worked with the same coloured thread.

The fashion for quilting caused such a demand for it that not only could quilted garments and bed covers be bought, but quilted materials were on sale in the shops, in London at any rate, to be made up into clothing or quilts at home. The accounts of Lady Grisel Baillie of Jerviswood (although unaudited) show the extent to which these materials, as well as quilted clothing, were available and a worthwhile outlay for the money. On a visit to London in 1717, she bought quilting for herself and her daughters, which is entered for the first of January.

Account of my own cloathes.
For 27 yd white Indian quilting at 4s 6d and 5s 6d   £4 13s 6d

Account for my Grisie's Cloath.
For 11 yd quilting for coats at 5s 6d   £3   os 6d

Account of my Rachy's Cloath.
For 7 yerds Indian quilting at 5s 6d   £1 18s 6d
For a white satine quilted coat   £2 15s od
For a yellow pertian quilted coat   £1 15s od[10]

In 1718 she paid 30 shillings for 'quilting a goun' as an item entered 'for my Rachy's child's cloathes.' The only mention of caps in her accounts occurs for 'friday 20 October', while she was in Paris on a 'Foreign Tour', with an entry 'For caps quilted for dressing 4 of them. 0. 5s 0. sterling.' There is not an entry for the purchase of the caps abroad and they must have been part of her travelling wardrobe, but quilting was as fashionable in European countries as in England. Spanish quilts were among the items in inventories of Louis XIV[11] and other examples of quilting have been preserved in European museums. Swedish and German work containing elaborate patterns of quilting with white embroidery stitches which were common to English white quilting of the time – satin and pulled stitches, French knots and so on –

are illustrated in *The Art of Embroidery*, as also is the Venetian cap shown on figure 110.[12] A reference to a quilted garment, possibly French, made in the late seventeenth or early eighteenth century, can be found in the *Historical Memoirs* of the Duc de Saint-Simon; on a visit to Madame Voysin at Dinant in Flanders, Madame de Maintenon was provided by her hostess with a 'Sumptious dressing-gown, modestly cut and snugly quilted'; the lady had arrived just as 'the weather had changed suddenly from excessive heat to a damp chill' and had come unprepared with warm clothes.[13]

The quilted petticoat or underskirt of the eighteenth century, possibly is the best remembered of all petticoat fashions. *The Tatler* and *The Spectator* took especial delight in commenting upon any extravagances of feminine fashion and while the quilted petticoat was still worn out of sight at the beginning of the century, it did not escape their satire. A 'reply' to criticism in *The Tatler* in February 1709, took the form of

> *The humble petition of Deborah Hark, Sarah Threadpaper, and Rachel Thimble, spinsters and single women, commonly called waiting maids,*
>
> SHOWETH
> That your worship has been pleased to order and command that no person or persons shall presume to wear quilted petticoats, on forfeiture of the said petticoats, on penalty of wearing ruffs, after the seventeenth instant now expired. . . . Your petitioners there fore most humbly pray that your worship would please to allow that all gentlewomen's gentlewomen may be allowed to wear the said dress, or to repair the loss of such perquisite in such a manner as your worship shall think fit.[14]

The size of hoop petticoats at the time drew the critical remarks of Addison and Steele and quilted petticoats also, did not escape. 'A quilted petticoat of the largest size' was among the goods supposed to have been stolen by Bridget Howd'ye from Lady Fardingale,[15] and they flattered themselves that their words had been taken to heart in a letter in *The Spectator* on 16 August 1711.

> *Mr* SPECTATOR
> I and several others of your Female Readers, have conformed ourselves to your Rules, even to our very Dress. There is not one of us but has reduced our outward Petticoat to its ancient Sizeable Circumference, tho' indeed we retain still a Quilted one underneath, which makes us not altogether uncomfortable to the Fashion.[16]

Seventeenth-century ideas on warm underclothing continued into the

eighteenth century. Linen, satin or silk were used for the top layers of petticoats, usually backed with coarse linen, calico or callamanca and interlined
with wool; sometimes the wool was dyed blue (Chapter 2, p. 22).

Petticoats were tied at the waist with tapes or drawstrings and in some the
quilted part was attached to an unquilted top. Usually this was in a straight
piece, about 12 to 15 inches deep and acted as an unshaped yoke, sometimes
set into a band at the top, and seems always to have been of different material
from that used for the quilted part of the garment. A silk taffeta petticoat,
quilted during the first quarter of the century, was attached to a calico top,
lined with glazed calico and padded with wool; other examples of about the
same period which had calico tops, were made of white satin lined with
linen scrim, cream silk lined with a similar linen, a satin petticoat was lined
with callamanca, and a pink satin one, lined with coarse linen, was attached
to a cotton twill top. A length of quilted blue silk illustrated in *Traditional
Quilting* appears to have been intended for a petticoat which would have
been attached to a plain top.[17] Some petticoats have no interlining, the
linen backing probably being considered sufficient to raise the patterns and
perhaps, like flat-quilted jackets, they may have been intended for summer
wear; but with or without padding, it is clear that care had been taken to
make some lie as smoothly as possible, while others must have been bundled
up at the waist. Perhaps some of these had been 'handed down' to a smaller
member of the family; one petticoat is on record as having a waist measurement of 41 inches and not many figures would have attained as comfortable
a size as that.

The fashion for quilted petticoats was universal in Europe during the
eighteenth century and one which was followed in America also. A quilted
callamanca petticoat is kept in the collections at Old Stourbridge Village in
Massachusetts and many others can be seen in most textile collections in
America. A full-rigged sailing ship with attendant sea-birds was worked on
a petticoat in the possession of the Museum of the Daughters of the American
Revolution, but the conventional feather, vine and similar patterns are more
common. Examples of them have been preserved in museums in that
country, but little seems to have been written about the making of them, the
work on quilted bed covers having received most of the attention, but
possibly the garments which were worn there early in the century, had been
taken over from the countries from which the women had come. An
advertisement from the Boston *Newsletter* in October 1707 is quoted in
Needlework Through the Ages, and reads – 'A tall, lusty Carolina Indian
woman named Kesiah Wampun had on a striped, red blue and white Homespun Jacket, and a Red One, Black and quilted White Silk Crape Petticoat,

122 Woman's lappet cap. Oyster-grey satin, lined with rose-pink silk and cord-quilted patterns on a plain ground. Drawstring through worked loops at the base of the hood for adjustment. English, early eighteenth century

123 The front of a quilted petticoat. Wadded quilting in running stitch on natural coloured satin, interlined with thin wool and lined with worsted. Diaper pattern with leaf, spiral, square diamond and other fillings. English, early eighteenth century

a White Shift and also a blue with her and a mixt Blue and White linsey Apron.'[18] A description (written in 1915) of clothing worn by immigrant Dutch settlers of the seventeenth century, mentions the petticoats which were 'the pride and joy of these transplanted Hollanders'. They were thickly padded with wool and quilted, and worn short enough to show their home-knitted hose. 'The tucked-up panniers worn by the women displayed to the best advantage the quilted petticoats. Red, blue, black and white were the favourite and predominating colours and the different materials included fine woollen cloth, camlet, grosgrain silk and satin.'[19]

More recently, in *Five Centuries of American Costume*, two references are made to eighteenth-century quilted petticoats – 'The hoop or "Panier" was the frame work worn under the dress. Quilted, wadded or embroidered petticoats were also worn to bolster out the floating gown', and later, 'a dress of apricot-coloured silk – lawn fichu and undersleeves – muslin apron with bib covering quilted petticoat' is illustrated.[20]

Towards the middle of the century in England, elaborate patterns in the quilting encouraged – or were encouraged by – the fashion in which the skirt of the dress was made so that it was worn open from the waistline to the hem in front, to show part of the quilted petticoat or underskirt. Although a separate garment, the petticoat was part of the dress but was interchangeable – one dress could be worn with a number of different petticoats, or a change of dress could be worn over the same petticoat. The colours of petticoat materials were varied from white or cream to every shade of blue, pink, rose and red to dark browns and greens. Collections of English costume contain many examples of quilted petticoats as worn with the appropriate dresses, notably in the Gallery of English Costume in Manchester, Snowshill Manor (a National Trust property in Oxfordshire) and the Museum of Costume in Bath (123).

The amount of quilted pattern varied. Some patterns extended a considerable way up from the hemline and usually they were of realistic flower and leaf patterns, such as those shown in the cornucopia on figure 83. Others were worked to make a deep border with swags and festoons of ribbon, cord and tassel, and feather patterns, many of which may have been the source for those on quilts designed by Joseph Hedley and George Gardener (pp. 42, 43 and figures 22, 23, 58, 151). One mid-century petticoat border consisting of a running flower and leaf pattern, in which the flowers were of the Tudor rose type, had a number of small filling patterns in the centres of the flowers (124). Other patterns were of long sprays of flower or leaf shapes – the lily and tulip were much favoured – rising from the hem nearly to the waist. The borders on some other petticoats were geometrical in type,

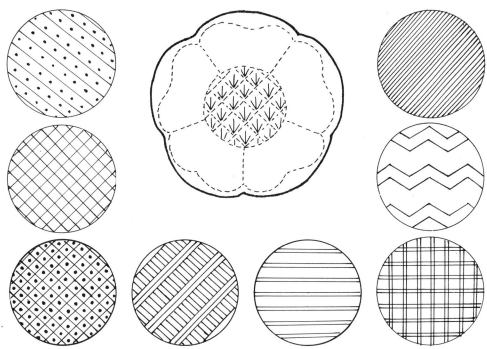

124 *Tudor-rose pattern from a running rose and leaf pattern on a satin petticoat; each flower has a different filling. English, eighteenth century*

125 *Detail of a filled feather pattern from figure 151*

126 *(right) Diaper pattern common to quilts and petticoats*

and they rose nearly half-way to the waist in diaper patterns with different fillings similar or identical with a number to be found on quilts (88, 124, 126).

The top part of a petticoat with these patterns, was usually quilted with a simple filling such as the square diamond (123); floral borders also were finished off with the same type of ground pattern but more often rows of a single, wavy or chevron line were used (127, 128). Thin lines of a realistic cord-and-tassel pattern were worked above the cornucopia and occasionally, lines resembling the hammock pattern filled in the top.

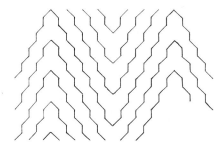

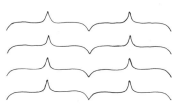

127   *Chevron type of ground pattern for petticoats*

128   *Typical ground pattern for petticoats*

   Quilted petticoats, like bed quilts, could be made professionally and were sold in the shops of tailors and outfitters. Among the goods supplied by James Cutt, coat-seller of the Ape on Horseback in Henrietta Street, Covent Garden, were hose, shoes and quilted petticoats[21] and Jane Ellis of Chancery Lane was a maker of quilted petticoats in 1710.[22] During the period of high fashion for the quilted petticoat, the *London Tradesman* in 1747, noted that – 'quilted petticoats are made mostly by Women, and some Men, who are employed by the Shops but earn little. They quilt likewise Quilts for Beds for the upholder. This they make more of than the Petticoats, but nothing to get rich by, unless they are able to purchase the materials and sell them finished to the Shops which few of them do. They rarely take on apprentices, and the Women they employ to help them, earn Three to Four shillings a Week and their Diet.'[23]

   There is no doubt that quilting for petticoats was done at home too, as they had been earlier in the century by the industrious aunt of two gadabout nieces, whose habits (according to *The Spectator*) had her disapproval – 'Their Dress, their Tea and their Visits, take up all their Time, and they go to bed as tired with doing nothing, as I am after quilting a whole underpetticoat.'[24] However, another change in fashion caused the petticoat to vanish from view again. By the last quarter of the century skirts were reduced in circumference and no longer worn open, and dresses were made as a single garment, although the really slender line did not come in until the 1800s and quilted petticoats were worn for warmth for some years after their fashionable heyday.

The fashion in bed quilts was more enduring than the several kinds of garments in which the style was affected by the use of quilting, and a number of examples of English and imported quilts have survived to testify to their variety through the century. Many of them, carrying on the seventeenth-century style in patterns, were embroidered with coloured silks on flat-quilted grounds and although a variety of stitches was used, according to the style of the embroidery (101, 134), often the patterns were worked in chain stitch only, in the manner of the imported work. In some, red and dark green were the only colours used; a cot quilt made early in the century was worked on linen with red and green wools, with a flat-quilted ground.[25] Cord-quilted patterns often enclosed areas of embroidery in colour; sometimes it was worked over flat quilting, but where the spaces within the quilting were small, no ground stitching was done (175). Cord quilting without embroidery or ground pattern, already mentioned in connection with seventeenth-century work and eighteenth-century clothing, can be found on early eighteenth-century quilts also, but it appears to have died out by the middle of the century.

The use of pillow cases and pillow shams (105) continued from the seventeenth century; although they were made to match the quilts, single pillow cases have survived in greater numbers than matching sets,[26] but some sets have survived and one quilt, in the possession of the Victoria and Albert Museum, has three matching pillow cases in the set. Other bed furnishings – valances and hangings – were quilted also; some have the patterns raised with cord (129) and others have a thin layer of padding. A complete set of furnishings at Levens Hall in Kendal is notable for being the earliest known example of quilted patchwork, having been made about 1708. Until this time, so far as is known, all quilts had been made from measured lengths of material, unless of course pieces had been joined for repairing purposes, but the top layer of this quilt is composed of pieces cut to shape to make a pattern – presumably from leftover scraps – of the cherished imported Indian prints.[27] The quilting, in a simple square diamond pattern, was carried out in red thread with running stitch. Mrs Delany is known to have made a set of linen bed furnishings as a wedding gift for her niece, which she quilted and embroidered entirely with yellow silk,[28] and Celia Fiennes, who died in 1741, left 'stitch pillows and a quilt' as a bequest in her will.[29] An inventory of the goods of William Wogan of Llanstinan in Pembrokeshire, taken in 1710 included 'a quilt with pillows' as part of the furnishings of the 'Great Parlour'.[30]

Other eighteenth-century inventories list quilts under various descriptions; some mention the kind of material of which they were made, others

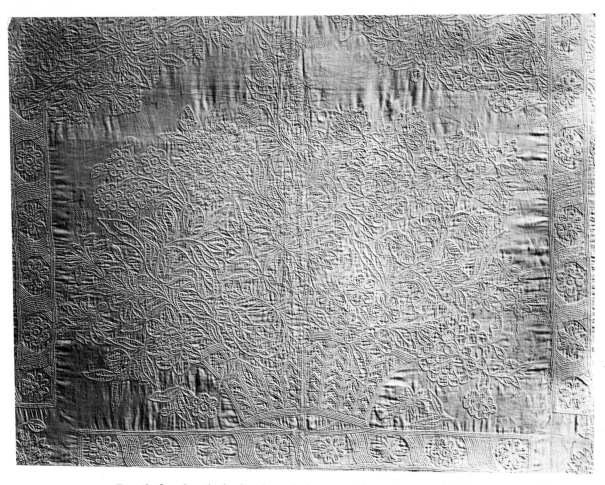

129 *Detail of cord-quilted white linen bed-cover with running and double running stitches in cotton thread. Patterns of a basket of realistic roses, carnations, lilies and leaves on a plain ground. From Great Tangley Manor, Guildford. English, early eighteenth century*

make note of the colour. Bed furnishings in the London house of the Duke of Bedford included a 'linen quilt' and 'a lindsey back quilt' with implied social distinction between them, as the first was in the Clerk of the Kitchen's bedchamber and the second in the kitchen-maid's room, but both servants slept in four-post beds. Early in the century in 1701 the young wife of the second Duke bought 'India calico quilts' from James Rudyerd and John Jesse at The Three Kings within Ludgate according to one of the accounts, and in a list of the contents from the 'yellow nursery' in Southampton House, bought by Rachel, Lady Russell in 1711, were furnishings which included 'one Tristram quilt' and 'a calico quilt'. Nothing descriptive is given of the Tristram quilt; presumably the patterns contained scenes or figures from the legend of Tristram but it is not possible to know from this entry whether it was an English-made version of the stuffed quilts from the Sicilian school (p. 15) or an original which had been bought during the Duke's travels in Europe. A later inventory (1771) of the same household included 'a small white quilt'[31] and 'For a calico twilt to the blew bed', Lady Grisel Baillie paid 25 shillings in 1715.[32]

Were it not for the numbers of surviving examples of white quilts, written observations on quilts in the eighteenth century might lead to a supposition that nearly all were embroidered. Understandably, the coloured patterns caught the eye more readily than the fine and highly skilled work of the white quilting but unquilted bed covers were embroidered with patterns of the same colours and character, as the ones worked in combination with quilting; and further to confuse observers without enough knowledge of needlework to distinguish between the two kinds of work, some quilts contained ground patterns (such as the small shell and the wineglass) which, although they resembled the types used for quilting, were in fact made by couching coloured or metal thread. As this confusion seems still to exist in some descriptions of these covers, it is possible that the misleading use of the word 'quilt' originated from this period, and cautious reliance should be put on references to them, unless they were made with some knowledge of needlework. In the section dated 1753, *The Travel Letters of Lady Mary Wortley Montagu* contain an account of her daily activities at home – 'I generally rise at six, and as soon as I have breakfasted, put myself at the head of my needlewomen and work till nine.' And of her travels in Turkey in 1718, in a letter to the Countess of Mar, she gives a description of quilting which she saw on a visit to Fatima, wife of the Deputy Grand Vizier – 'Her house was magnificently furnished and very well fancied; her winter rooms being furnished with figured velvet, on gold grounds, and those for summer with fine Indian quilting, embroidered with gold.'[33] But whether George Farquhar's observations were as knowledgeable is not so sure. In *The Beaux' Stratagem* (1707), his character Francis Archer uses the richness of a half-seen embroidery as an excuse for entering Mrs Sullen's room, saying 'There's the finest bed in that room, Madam. I suppose 'tis your ladyship's bed-chamber? . . . I think the quilt is the richest that ever I saw. I can't at this distance, Madam, distinguish the figures of the embroidery, will you give me leave, Madam?'[34]

Of the eighteenth-century quilts illustrated (129, 134, 135), that on figure 134, is dated and signed. Among the border patterns, the compartment on the right of the centre at the bottom, bears the initials E.S. under a shield of arms, and below, also quilted in, is the date 1703. Each of the compartments on the surrounding borders contains a pattern of heraldic characters; figures of a mermaid, a merman, and a woman clearly wearing a quilted skirt, are represented; also to be seen are a sailing ship, two buildings, a tree in leaf, a lion, a horse, a camel, small animals which appear to be rabbits or hares, some birds including a duck, and two fishes. A narrow inner border of geometric pattern is shown in detail on figure 130. Although the worker had a straighter eye and skill for quilting than embroidery, the work is different from others of the period, in which the quilting pattern is subservient to the embroidery. The bed cover of quilted yellow silk on the Frontispiece has no embroidery, nor has it any known history, except that it is English and of eighteenth-century work, but the similarity of the patterns to those on an earlier quilt (108) known to have been made in the seventeenth century, suggests that it may not be of later date than the 1750s.

A later and also undocumented quilt of Welsh origin is thought to have been made about 1770, by a member of a Pembrokeshire family whose Christian name was Elizabeth; since then it has been bequeathed to succeeding Elizabeths of the same family. The quilt is made of cotton, with a block-printed floral chintz as a lining; this lining is of a nineteenth-century print and so it appears that the quilt must have been relined at some stage. The fine patterns and quilting are in the best tradition of Welsh work and several are shown in detail on figures 69, 131, 132, 133, 135.

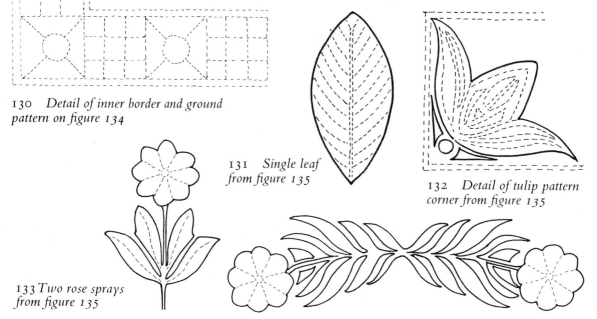

130   Detail of inner border and ground
pattern on figure 134

131   Single leaf
from figure 135

132   Detail of tulip pattern
corner from figure 135

133 Two rose sprays
from figure 135

134　*Linen quilt with embroidered patterns. Quilting worked with cotton thread in back and running stitches through thin interlining. Embroidery worked with polychrome silk threads in stem, satin, split and chain stitches, with some bullion work. Border compartments contain patterns of gryphon, mermaid, merman, fishes, a duck, 3-masted ship, castle, camel, hound with flower, rabbits, birds, a tree, woman wearing a quilted underskirt, and beneath a heraldic shield the initials E.S. 1703. English, early eighteenth century*

Quilts with a combination of embroidered and quilted patterns became less popular after the middle of the century, with a corresponding decrease in the amount of cord quilting which was done, although the character of both cord and embroidery patterns was retained in a number of wadded quilt patterns, especially the floral types (91), and some of the finer border patterns (146). To compensate no doubt for the lack of embroidered colour, more use was made of patchwork in coloured materials for the top layers of quilts, and examples of those so made, have survived from the middle of the century onwards. A quilt of white silk, made in Devonshire about 1750, had a border of quilted white and green silk triangular patches[35] and Joseph Hedley is known to have quilted patch tops which he had made.[36]

Eighteenth-century quilts which have survived in America, are those made during the second half of the period. Instruction in quilting is known to have been given in teaching establishments by 1716, and by mid-century, material and furnishings could be marked out with patterns by a professional, ready for quilting at home (p. 44), but quilted materials were not on sale by the yard as in England, and many of the materials of which the early quilts were made were of European or English manufacture, taken out by emigrants. The use of patchwork for the tops was a popular economy for quilt-makers and, as in England also, took the place of the earlier embroidery, which in turn, had been supplanted by colour-printed cotton and linen. Many of the quilted bed covers made during the later 1700s can be seen in museum collections in America, and the patchwork tops, as well as the quilting, show patterns which reflect the same traditional background as those in Britain.

Quilted upholstery for coaches and furniture continued to be made. 'In the room above the kitchen . . . a quilted chair' was among the effects of Robert Jones of Plas Brith, in an inventory taken about 1742,[37] and the strength of quilted material and the protective virtue of quilted linings for boxes and chests, were impressed on the observant mind of Jonathan Swift according to the number of times he referred to them in *Gullivers Travels to Lilliput and Brobdingnag* (1726). During his stay in Lilliput, 'Two hundred semptresses were employed to make me Shirts, and Linnen for my Bed and Table, all of the strongest and coarsest kind they could get; which, however, they were forced to quilt together in several Folds; for the thickest was some Degrees finer than Lawn.' Likewise 'Five hundred Workmen were employed to make two Sails to my boat according to my Direction, by quilting thirteen fold of their strongest Linnen together.' When he was in Brobdingnag, the first box in which he was carried about, had a quilt from a doll's bed for him to lie on and a later and larger box in which he was to be exhibited, was lined throughout with soft cloth 'well quilted underneath'. A more elaborate affair was a wooden box made by the Queen's cabinet-maker with a door and windows which he called his closet, 'was quilted on all Sides, as well as the Floor and the Cieling to prevent any Accident from the Carelessness of those who carried me'. The hangings were of quilted silk and cotton which, to Gulliver's disappointment, were stripped off by the rescuing sailors at the end of his adventure.[38]

Quilting received another bad mark on the grounds of its effect on health from James Cook, when he related in his *Voyages* that 'The chamber in which they slept breathes the richest and purest of all odours, unalloyed by the fumes which cannot but arise where the sleeper lies under two or three blankets and a quilt,'[39] but another traveller of about the same time, Marie Sophie von la Roche, commended in her diary, the arrangement and furnishing of the cabin on the packet-boat, in which she crossed from Holland to Harwich on 1 September 1786 – 'The berths are ranged along the side walls in two rows like theatre boxes, one above the other; they have thoroughly good mattresses, white quilted covers and on a ledge is the chamber made of English china, used in case of sickness.' In more elevated surroundings when she went to Leonard's Hill, the seat of Lord Harcourt, she noted the furnishings of a bedroom which 'displayed yet another aspect of the Countess's industry and good taste. It is hung with a delicate pale-blue chintz, with a border of the sweetest flower garlands embroidered in blue of the same shade on a white ground, similarly the curtains, quilts on both the beds, and chair covers.'[40]

9 THE NINETEENTH CENTURY

The popularity of quilting at the beginning of the 1800s was in distinct contrast to that it had had one hundred years earlier. After the fashion for quilted petticoats had died out about 1770, the virtual disappearance of quilting for all fashionable upper-class clothing was hastened by new styles in which thin materials were used for straight, high-waisted dresses, and any thick or bulky undergarment, such as a quilted petticoat was out of the question. Rows of cord were inserted sometimes, on such things as the bottom of petticoats and sunbonnet brims when a little stiffening was necessary, but except that the method for doing this was the same, there was little resemblance to the cord-quilting patterns of the eighteenth century.

Quilted bed covers were outmoded by coverlets made of colour-printed cotton, once imported and expensive, but by this time being manufactured in England and so within the reach of many who had not been able to afford them before. Another 'enemy' of quilting was the growing popularity of applied work and patchwork for bedspreads, especially in the well-to-do houses. Pieces of the prints used for dress and furnishings, valued too much to be thrown away, were collected and re-used for patchwork bed covers which bore some resemblance to the fashionable coverlets. The printed patterns and the patchwork shapes were not as accommodating as embroidery in conjunction with quilting; embroidery could be added to quilting without taking anything from the pattern of either, but the delicate outlines of quilting were lost among the distractions of coloured patterns and seams. Cord-quilted bed covers seem to have died out altogether and the latest examples which have survived, are dated as having been made not later than the end of the eighteenth century.

Many of the coverlets either were unlined, or had a thin lining attached only at the edges, with no attempt at lining. There is some evidence that about the end of the eighteenth century quilted bed covers were made from very large squares or rectangular pieces of cotton print and were intended to go under the thin day-time covers, the quilting being carried out in simple patterns. A number of patchwork quilts made during the first 20 or 30 years of the nineteenth century have survived and show that they were well

135   *Cotton quilt, interlined wool and lined with nineteenth-century cotton print. Finely quilted in running stitch with leaf, tulip, rose, fan, scroll, twist patterns and small and large square diamond fillings. Welsh. Said to have been made by Elizabeth Griffith in 1770*

quilted, albeit with simple patterns. The influence of patchwork on the patterns of quilt-making has been shown in Chapter 4, but although it disrupted the traditional style, it brought out the strength of the tradition which took the disruption in its stride and turned it to good effect, especially in the so-called 'block and strip quilts' (147, 150).

The use of quilted materials for clothing was not dropped altogether, and although none of it inspired any romantic outpourings from nineteenth-century writers and poets, in the way their predecessors had been overcome by the quilted petticoat, nevertheless its practical value of warmth for petticoats was still appreciated. There is little doubt that they were worn mostly in country districts with a harder way of living than in the towns, and where flimsy garments, however modish, had little attraction. Evidence points to these country districts being where quilting had become a customary household occupation, and which are known to have included parts of Yorkshire (especially in the North and East Ridings), counties of Durham, Northumberland, Cumberland and Westmorland in the North, Somerset, Wiltshire, Devonshire and Cornwall in the South and in the counties of South Wales. It had been thought that quilting was confined to areas in which mining was the chief industry, but the fact that highly skilled work was done in the South and West of England shows it was more widespread than that, although it is possible that in the first place its popularity in these southern counties had spread from South Wales.

Not many of the petticoats which were everyday wear have survived, and although they were still being worn within the last hundred years, less is known about them than the ones of silk and satin in the previous century. Working petticoats were made of stout materials suitable for outdoor wear on farms and in the fields, such as homespun woollen stuffs which turn the wet to some degree; others for light work were less cumbersome, and cotton (both white and colour printed), flannel, satin and silk, were used for the outer layers over a thin padding. Locally manufactured materials, such as cotton in the North and flannel in Wales, seem to have been used most, but not all went to the length of making it a local fashion, as did the women of Llangwn in South Wales, who were partial to two layers of quilted flannel for their petticoats, one of red and the other black, which everyone wore.[1] Another custom followed in South Wales was for quilting petticoats of black satin, merino or alpaca, in which it was 'the ambition of every respectable woman to be buried'.[2]

As a rule, nineteenth-century quilted petticoats were severely practical, and the amount of pattern was restricted to a border pattern above the bottom hemline and a simple filling pattern (such as the square diamond) up to the waistband, into which the quilting was put with gathers or flat pleats. Some were quilted with wider and more elaborate patterns, similar to those used for quilt borders (p. 118) and some had scalloped edges.[3] Petti-coats usually were made at home and looked upon as part of the household dressmaking, and some girls learned to quilt them, before they graduated to bed quilts. Information for quilting petticoats is given in Caulfeild and Saward's *Dictionary of Needlework*, but in the context, refers only to machined stitching, as it was of their opinion that 'no hand-quilting comes up to machine work'. The best and thickest wadding is recommended so that 'when Petticoats are to be quilted, the Runnings should be well in-dented and the satin or silk set up puffily. . . . Mantles, opera cloaks and babies' cloaks that are wadded for warmth, should not be so puffy as petticoats, or they would set clumsily.'

Quilted skirts seem to have been worn as much as petticoats, as examples of them have survived, and it is known that they were worn for working on the Yorkshire Wold farms and by north-east coast fisherwomen. An illus-tration in *Traditional Quilting* shows women gathering mussels on the foreshore at Runswick in 1870, with quilted skirts turned up over heavy petticoats, and pinned at the back to keep them from the salt water,[4] and as late as about 1910 Northumbrian women hawking fish in the near coastal villages, wore dark-coloured quilted skirts, covered by a clean apron, to protect them from the heavy baskets they carried on each arm. Softer materials were used when skirts were intended for wear in a less rugged kind of life and these were worn in other parts of the country besides the North. Evidence has been found of silk skirts being worn in the South-west (136,

136   *Oak leaf and acorn pattern taken from a black silk dress made in Devonshire, 1868*

137   Circular pattern of hearts, acorns, oak and ivy leaves, with square diamond filling, from the same skirt as figure 136. 1868

137)[5] and in 1860 a cotton skirt in red Paisley patterned print was produced commercially, lined with plain red but padded with down instead of wadding; it was machine-quilted in a square diamond pattern. The fastening was at the back by means of a button and tapes on the waistband, and it carried a label –

BOOTH & FOX

ARCTIC GOOSE DOWN

SKIRTS

36 inches pattern

FAST COLOURS

Wash with Down in. Shake

when drying.[6]

Hand-quilted petticoats were worn in America, where the fashion for them, quilted with elaborate patterns on silk and satin, continued into the nineteenth century. Harder wearing materials also were used.[7]

Other items of dress for women were roomy hoods of quilted taffeta lined with silk for evening wear, which could be worn without disarranging the hair unduly and were something like the traditional sunbonnet in style but with a narrow frill round the face, and another to cover the neck at the back. A warm garment in the Gallery of English Costume in Manchester, also for evening wear, is a hooded jacket of diamond quilted satin, with an added border of scrolling pattern, next to the flounced edges of the hood, cuffs and jacket.

Women's stays contained rows of fine quilted cord, as a means of adding firmness to the materials which lay between the main armour of cane or whalebone supports. The example illustrated on figure 138, dated as worn between 1815 and 1825, was made of white cotton satin, laced up at the back and with a wide busk inserted in the front panel.[8] The cording on this and similar stays – some made in fawn, red or black – show a quality of decoration worthy of an outer garment. Children's quilted stays and bodices were

138 *White cotton satin stays, reinforced stiffening of quilted cord, in addition to whalebone busk and strips. Nineteenth century*

made at home as a rule and often were quilted by machine through two or three layers of material without added padding or stiffening. The bodices were short, sleeveless garments of quilted twill or flannel according to the season, and considered indispensable for boys and girls alike when young. They were worn to cover the chest and back, over a warm wool vest (generally hand knitted) and under two petticoats, one of flannel and the other cotton or calico. Small replicas of the bodices were made also for dressed dolls, many of which have been preserved in collections of children's toys.

Of other clothing, as compared with that of the eighteenth century, bonnets with tie-strings replaced the closer fitting caps, and cord quilting was no longer used, the only padding being that of cotton or lamb's wool. A popular kind of garment for babies' outdoor wear was a long carrying cloak. This was made with a short cape or shawl collar attached, and when the cloak was made of light woollen material, such as flannel, the cape usually was of quilted silk or satin; facings down the front and round the hem also were quilted, but the pattern seems always to have been a plain cross diamond and the stitching was done by machine. The demand for this fashion in infant wear is indicated by an advertisement in the *Daily Chronicle* for 30 April 1879 which appealed for 'Quilters for infants' cloaks'.

A minor fashion in men's clothing in the nineteenth century was for coat and jacket linings to be of quilted satin, which was repeated on turned-back collars and cuffs and as facings for lapels, and it was the mode for the dandies of the day to wear the coats open and held back to show off the quilted linings. A photograph of Charles Dickens shows him wearing a three-quarter-length coat with a quilted lining, turned back at the cuffs and on the front, to show the quilting done in feather and circle patterns. Dickens paid a visit to America in 1842 and his clothes appear to have made a great impression, as he is said to have 'dressed to knock his provincial audience cold in admiration of his elegance'. An American fashion for men in the late 1850s was for turned-down shirt collars 'elaborately patterned over cord'.[9] Men's wear of a different kind was worn early in the century. Describing conditions in England after the fall of Napoleon, various kinds of clothing common to different trades and classes are described by Sir Arthur Bryant in *Protestant Island*. 'Most Englishmen at their callings dressed in clothes of stoutest quality; . . . brewers in quilted coats of immense thickness; . . . firemen in horse-hide lined with leather, quilted with wool and strengthened with metal', which must have equalled the wearing of plate armour and a jack for discomfort.[10] Quilted clothing worn for fire-fighting in Japan, a suit of which is illustrated (139), was less unwieldy. Here the garments were made

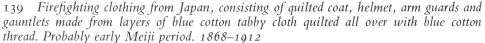

139 *Firefighting clothing from Japan, consisting of quilted coat, helmet, arm guards and gauntlets made from layers of blue cotton tabby cloth quilted all over with blue cotton thread. Probably early Meiji period. 1868–1912*

from several layers of closely quilted blue cotton tabby. The patterns were resist dyed on the material, indicated the ownership of the fire-fighting company, the name of the operator, a man called Oh-no, and the size of the items of the outfit, which consisted of tunic, helmet, leg pieces and gloves.

Quilted dressing-gowns or those with quilting as a lining, or only on collars and cuffs, had become commonplace everywhere. In 1852, Tolstoy recalled memories of his tutor, Karl Ivanych 'in his bright coloured quilted dressing gown, with a belt of the same material round the waist, a red knitted cap with a tassel on his head, and soft goat skin boots on his feet, [he] continued to walk around the room smacking at the flies on the wall'.[11]

   Quilted linings and upholstery were carried out by the same means as before in the trade. Furniture had quilted coverings of satin and other suitable materials, fastened with the customary quilting nails, the heads covered with a matching fabric; an example of finely quilted upholstery is illustrated on figure 140, in the lining of the cradle made for Napoleon's son, the King of Rome, in 1811. An assortment of smaller objects to be made at home for which quilting was recommended were illustrated in the *Dictionary of Needlework*; the pockets of a 'Wall Pocket for a Dressing-room' were to be lined with quilted blue alpaca, a clothes-basket had quilted satin and bands and frill of Breton lace for the lining of the lid; wicker work-baskets, plush-covered trinket-boxes, egg-cosies, 'a serviette for eggs', bed-pockets, and needlebooks, all had quilted linings, most of which were done by machine, but some were fastened with covered nails, and a wall-bracket of dark blue satin was finished with tufts of silk where the lines of quilting crossed; probably this was the only process that needed hand sewing.

The *Dictionary* was the first book of its kind and was much thought of from the time it was published, but although it set out to make certain that it contained 'information on every point in connection with needlework', little interest and even less guidance is given to the making of bed quilts. Information on quilting is scattered under various other headings and is not easy to find, while paragraphs in length and detail are devoted to crochet, patchwork and other kinds of work suitable for making bedspreads. The same can be said for other books on needlework which followed the *Dictionary*. Instructions for 'quilts' dealt with making geometric patterns of patchwork but were followed by no mention of subsequent quilting. It is small wonder that quilt-making proper became forgotten among followers of needlework magazines.

Neither fashion nor the needlework books changed the ways of quilting done in country districts. The girls learned to quilt without the sight of a book, being set to it from an early age, often by threading the needles for the women at the frames as a beginning, and later, whether they liked it or not, having to take their turn at the work on hand. Wages were low and often the families were large, and quilting filled a need for which there was little money to spare. It was accepted as part of the daily routine, especially in the mining districts of the northern counties and South Wales where 'making quilts was as necessary as making bread and therefore time had to be found for it'.[12] Making for household use was not the only call on the quilter's time; daughters (and sometimes sons) had to have their complement of quilts when they married. Included among them would be the best marriage quilt, often with the 'true lover's knot' or hearts among the patterns (144, 145, 159). Other work was taken on, such as helping out with a neighbour's quilting or making up material for someone who was unable to quilt but prepared to pay for having one made.

Some women quilted for a living. The work was done at home, and if possible a room was kept especially for it, so that the frame could be left as it was when other household work interfered with the sewing. If the living-room was the only one available, the half-made quilt and the frame had to be rolled and set aside for meals and other interruptions. This problem was universal, and whenever mention is made of quilting and how it is made, the space needed for the frame has been of concern. Keeping it attached to a pulley from the ceiling sometimes has been found practical both in England and in America, but only so when the room was of sufficient height, and this is of rare occurrence.

In a number of North Country villages in England, especially in mining districts, women ran Quilt Clubs, which others could join and have quilts

141 *Quilt on beige-coloured cotton typical of work done in South Wales. Heart, pear, leaf, fan corners, and church window patterns. Made by Mrs Irene Morgan. Welsh, second quarter twentieth century*

made for them from their own materials, paying meanwhile in regular instalments. The payments usually were small, not more than a shilling or two weekly, but a good and industrious worker could be sure of regular money, and the success of the clubs was such that they continued well into the twentieth century. The charges for making a quilt other than for a club member varied somewhat, depending on the part of the country and the quality of the work; a quick worker was able to earn more than a slow one – Mary Jones of Panteg, is said to have worked equally well with either hand – but a fair average was about five shillings for making up a customer's own material.[13]

In South Wales professional quilters went the round of the countryside, planning the patterns and making the quilts for the houses in which they lodged, while they did the work in return for their board and a small sum of money, which varied from sixpence to about one shilling a day. In north Devon one quilter is recorded as having charged three shillings and six-pence for quilting the patchwork tops made by her neighbours, as compared with the prices of ten to twenty shillings for elaborately patterned quilts in parts of Cornwall; probably this included the materials as well as the sewing.[14] The village dressmaker also included quilting in the work she did for her living, whether she did it in her own home or in the houses where she went to sew for the family. She was responsible too, for many of the nineteenth-century quilts of patchwork, made from the left-over pieces of her trade, but women who looked upon themselves as skilled quilters were somewhat ashamed of the patchwork side of any quilt they made, and never made them with patchwork on both sides. The 'right side' of a quilt was the one made from plain lengths of material where the patterns showed clearly, and the patchwork was used for the bottom layer of backing.

The professional pattern-makers and markers also did their work for payment, although for some it was a sideline to another job, such as Mr Gale's school-teaching and the shopkeeping of Mr Gardiner. Most of them took apprentices and some made quilts as well (149, 150, 151 and p. 42), with the apprentices working alongside their masters – sometimes for as long as one or two years – before they were considered to be trained and worthy of their teachers. Many of the apprentices became noted in their turn, handing on their knowledge to another generation. The payment for apprenticeship varied. Some apprentices lived in, helping with the housework and quilting in return for tuition; sometimes a sum of money was paid by a girl's parents towards her board. Others lodged with their teachers by the week, providing their own food; they went home at the weekends, returning on Monday morning stocked up for another week. As they became proficient, some earned a small sum of money each week, quilting with their teachers, and in South Wales, some apprentices went round with an itinerant quilter to help with the work.[15]

Quilts in America during the nineteenth century were also looked upon as necessities in a well-run house, but the ways in which the women set about making them was influenced to some extent by the popularity of patchwork. This grew out of a greater need for economy in manufactured materials than in England, and the practice of making patchwork tops during the winter months culminated in the well-known gathering held in the Spring, known as the 'Quilting Bee'. This was as much a social occasion as a means of getting help with the work of quilting, and American social history would not be complete without the 'bee' which was held in connection with many tasks, such as spinning, husking and so on, as well as with quilting the winter's patchwork. Rivalry in the originality and skill of the patchwork was keen, but no less so than in the ability to sew well enough to receive an invitation to help with another's quilt. Men attended the quilting bees, although none is recorded as having helped with the sewing, but enough women were invited on occasions to enable the work to be done in relays. Early in the century, Ruth Henshaw Bascomb of Gerry in New Hampshire entered in her diary: 'This afternoon 21 young ladies paid us a visit and assisted us in quilting' – this was for the purpose of quilting a petticoat and for a patchwork quilt, which took three days to quilt – 'a large number of gentlemen' came one evening but probably not to sew. Mrs Bascomb accounted for all her activities, which included spinning, weaving, knitting and dyeing both flax and wool for household requirements and, as Ruth Henshaw before she married, she did dressmaking and furnishings for her family, including the handmade trimmings for all of it. She was good at millinery also and mentions one of her bonnets, which she altered by adding 'a leghorn forpart and pink sarsnet quilted crown and binding'. She died in 1847, after what truly can be called a 'full' life.[16]

The part played by quilting in the life of country people in America probably was of greater social importance than in England and Wales. There were many similarities, in that the work flourished in communities which were the most isolated, and where bed quilts were a necessity, for economy as much as for warmth. The industry, pride in the work and rivalry were equally matched in quilters of both countries, as also was the fame of the individual for excellence in one or other aspects of her work.

Accounts of nineteenth-century American quilting make no mention of any equivalent of the quilt clubs in northern England, nor has the quilting bee, as such, had any recognised part in the quilting tradition on this side of

142   White linen bed cover of stuffed and cord-quilted patterns on a finely quilted ground. American eagle, 17 stars, figure with flag, fruit and leaf patterns, finished on three sides with a fringe. Made by Mrs Mary Waldron Thompson. American. Signed and dated M.W.T. 1821, 86 × 106 inches

the Atlantic. One or two records do exist, however, of districts in which neighbours were invited to help with quilting on occasions, and were rewarded with a party or feast when the work was done. In the area round Almondbury and Huddersfield in the West Riding of Yorkshire, quilting feasts were known in the nineteenth century. 'When a woman had patched a bed-quilt, she invited her neighbours to help to quilt it', and refreshments of 'tea and cakes were given; formerly a cold posset consisting of new milk, sugar, currants and rum (or beer)'.[17] Quilting parties also were held in Northern Ireland, where neighbours worked on a quilt in relays of six at a time. 'No quilting session was complete without the customary party, the

143   *White linen bedspread of stuffed quilting on a closely quilted ground. Cornucopia with fruit and flowers, sprays of flowers and leaves. Finished on three sides with an exceptionally long fringe. American, early nineteenth century, 96 × 98 inches*

accepted return for expenditure of time and effort. The menfolk of the district gathered when the quilt had been finished, and the dancing, singing and general merriment continued until the small hours of the morning.'[18] All attempts to find the words of the song 'McCaughey's Quilting', which was sung in celebration of such an event, have not been successful, but it appears that it featured a number of local people and those who remembered the song were unwilling to sing or recite it. A custom in Cushendall in the Glens of Antrim, was that after a quilt was completed, 'the girl was kissed under it'.

Songs and stories have been written in America about quilting parties, all relating to the same kind of jollification. 'The Quilting Party' written by Stephen Collins Foster, probably is the best known and dates from about 1856.[19] The words are simple and in the style of a folk-song, with a repetitive chorus after every two lines of verse.

1. In the sky the bright stars glittered,
   On the bank the pale moon shone;
   And t'was from Aunt Dinah's quilting party
   I was seeing Nellie home
   I was seeing Nellie home
   I was seeing Nellie home
   And t'was from Aunt Dinah's quilting party
   I was seeing Nellie home.

2. On my arm a soft hand rested,
   Rested light as ocean foam;
   (chorus)

3. On my lips a whisper trembled,
   Trembled till it dared to come;
   (chorus)

4. On my life new hopes were dawning,
   And those hopes have liv'd and grown.
   (chorus)

It is surprising that quilting songs are not more numerous, as certainly there is something to sing about when a quilt has been completed.

English and Welsh quilts of the nineteenth century show an increasing use of patchwork for one of the outer covers as time went on, and these quilts make up the majority of the ones that have survived; examples of plain quilts are not so numerous, but of those which remain many are remarkable for the fine quality of the work. The quilt on figure 149, is one of these;

144 *Cotton quilt interlined with wool and lined with large patchwork pieces, finished with a pleated frill. Hearts, fans, pear, spiral, twist, and shell and diamond filling patterns worked in running stitch. Corner patterns repeat the centre circle in smaller scale. Probably a marriage quilt. Welsh, nineteenth century 90 × 96 inches*

marked out by Miss Sanderson and worked by a Northumbrian quilter, it is an example of the value of a small-scale ground pattern, as a setting for the elaborate centre and border patterns. Two other North Country quilts, showing the influence of patchwork on the arrangement of the quilting patterns, have been mentioned already (pp. 60, 62 and figures 147 and 150); the Welsh quilt on figure 144, has a patchwork backing, but the pieces, made from buff- and blue-coloured floral prints, are large, and had little or no effect on the quilting. This may have been a marriage quilt as it contains a large heart pattern as a centre, but as a rule marriage quilts were too important to show any sign of economy, and the best materials were kept for it. The quilt shown on figure 145, which has a number of heart patterns, is known to have been a marriage quilt and was made by Miss Rosamund Lewis of Tallwyd for her marriage to Mr William Mendus in Treffymion Chapel in March 1886; it is in daily use still by one of her descendants. It was made from lengths of cream cotton, with a wool interlining and has a pink and green sprigged floral cotton on a cream ground for the backing.

145 *Cream cotton marriage quilt, interlined with wool and lined with floral cotton. Heart patterns with various fillings, wave, chevron, leaf, rose, star, spiral and church window patterns in running stitch. Made by Miss Rosamund Lewis. Welsh, c. 1885*

146 *White linen quilt, lined with linen. Rose, leaf, running feather, square diamond and several individual patterns. The fine border pattern shows the influence of eighteenth-century cord quilting. Made in Somerset, 1807*

White materials were considered the most desirable for quilts, as there was nothing to draw the eye from the perfection of the quilting, but with the decline of cord quilting, it is likely that any mention of white quilting was of the wadded type. One probable exception to this is the work of the voluble and industrious Miss Catherine Hutton, a rival in output to Mrs Ruth Bascomb, who wrote out for a friend – Markham John Thorpe, of the State Paper Office – an account of all the different kinds of work and occupations with which she had filled her life up to the age of 89. Among them she had made 'quilted counterpanes and chest covers in fine white linen, in various patterns of my own invention', which may have been quilted with cord padding as she had lived through the period when this work was popular. She took a pride in having been 'never one moment unemployed when it was possible to be doing something', so it is most likely that she knew how to do it. She died in 1846.[20]

147   *Cotton strip quilt made from lengths coloured red and buff, lined with calico and seen on the reverse side to show the quilting patterns. Lined hammock, scroll, twist and wineglass patterns in running stitch. Made in County Durham. English, late nineteenth century, 82 × 90 inches*

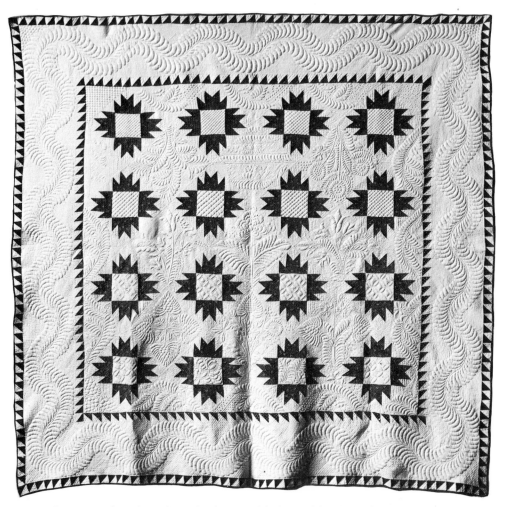

148 *Cotton patchwork quilt with alternate blocks and borders of patchwork in red and white. White squares quilted with bouquet, leaf, feather, square, diamond and teacup patterns, with very fine running-feather border. Made in Indiana by Mrs Mary Lawson Ruth McCrea. Quilted date and initials, M.L.Mc May 18th 1866, American*

In America, however, there is much evidence of the numbers of white quilts made during the nineteenth century and those with patterns of stuffed quilting have no rivals in English or Welsh quilting of the same period. Beautiful examples can be seen in George Washington's home, in the collections of the Mount Vernon Ladies' Association at Mount Vernon, and at David Townsend House, Chester County Historical Society, West Chester, Pennsylvania. Two which can be seen in England have been described already (p. 81 and figures 142 and 143), and an example of an American block quilt with patchwork, in the possession of the Smithsonian Institution, is shown on figure 148, in which patterns on the quilted blocks and the border have been stuffed. The ground is quilted with close, fine lines of running and the work is an object lesson in the value of different surface textures achieved by sewing without the help of added embroidery, and in quilting as an art. The quilt was made by Mrs Mary Lawson Ruth McCrea and finished in May 1866; her initials M.L.Mc and the date, are quilted into the middle block between the top rows of patchwork blocks. Patterns on some white quilts of American origin in the nineteenth century were padded with candlewick cotton; the same material was used also for tufted patterns on candlewick bedspreads, many of which were similar to those used for quilting.

Quilting by machine was introduced towards the end of the eighteenth century for some commercial purposes, and although it was advocated for work done at home by the writers of the *Dictionary of Needlework*, none has survived, so it could not have been successful in competition with hand quilting. A type of machine-made bedspread, known as a Marseilles (or Marsala, Marsyle or Marcella) quilt became popular from about the middle of the nineteenth century. It was woven on a loom with patterns made to resemble hand quilting and had been known since the eighteenth century, when it had been used for waistcoats as well as bed covers. It could be bought by the yard for making up at home, sometimes in colour ('yellow Marcella' was bought by the Reverend James Woodforde for a waistcoat).[21] The nineteenth-century bed covers were of a coarser weave than would have been possible for garments, but they were very hard wearing and many have survived. They began as bedspreads or 'quilts' on the best bed, travelled to the maid's room and the night nursery, dragging out a socially descending existence into the twentieth century, to the dust-sheet cupboard and the jumble sale, still defying old age.

Looking over the nineteenth-century development of quilting from a distance, it seems that the work did not so much go out of fashion, as that the fashion shifted from the town to the country, especially in the districts where the work was done regularly. Here, the possession of a number of quilts or petticoats, or both, or the reputation for making or marking out the patterns, conferred a social distinction on an individual. It was a matter of pride to be renowned as a skilled quilter and a great thing to have a pattern drawn by a master hand, who was looked up to and respected. It was something near to disgrace not to have a proper supply of quilts in the house but a mark of respectability to be buried in a quilted black petticoat.

10 THE TWENTIETH CENTURY

In spite of the fact that commercially produced goods were more easily come by in the villages by the year 1900, the custom of quilt-making in many country districts continued much as it had done for the last 20 or 30 years of the nineteenth century. A number of surviving quilts were made during that period and in the early part of the present century, but the general taste in furnishing had changed considerably since the beginning of the 1800s. Marcella or Marseilles bedspreads were fashionable, and wool blankets had increased in popularity, with machine-made 'quilts', filled with down or

149   *Cotton quilt marked by Miss Elizabeth Sanderson in patterns characteristic of the style of Mr George Gardiner. Quilted by a Miss Hall of Northumberland. Leaf scroll, rose and square diamond patterns, with an unusual twist border. English, c. 1900*

150 *Cotton quilt of pink and white patchwork basket pattern made by Miss Elizabeth Sanderson. The quilting has been adapted to fit the patchwork on the reverse of the side shown. Flower, leaf, scroll, twist, square diamond and chain type of border pattern. Made in Rookhope, County Durham. English, early twentieth century, 83 × 94 inches*

feathers, being used for additional bed covers in the winter. The best filling for them was down taken from the eider duck, which gave the name 'eiderdown quilt' to this type of cover; it became known eventually as an 'eiderdown', whether or not it contained eider duck down. More commonly these quilts were filled with stripped feathers, which made them comparatively cheap to buy or to make, and making or remaking them by hand took the place of traditional quilting in the dressmaker's or home furnisher's work.

Of the traditional quilts which are known to have been made during the first 15 years or so of this century, there is little to distinguish them from any made in the previous 50 years. Figure 149 illustrates one in the collection at the Bowes Museum, which was made in Northumberland in 1900 from a top marked by Miss Sanderson, and the basket-pattern quilt (150), marked by her also, was made in Rookhope, County Durham in 1912. A third quilt

151　*Cream sateen quilt, lined white cotton, said to have come from Allenheads. Rose, leaf, filled feather, hammock with chain or twist filling and lily finial and other patterns in the style of Mr George Gardiner. English, 1903, 84 × 108 inches*

(151), also in the Bowes Museum, which was made in 1903, is supposed to have come from Allenheads (not far from Rookhope), the one-time Allendale home of George Gardiner. Detail from the patterns of this quilt is shown on figures 25, 58 and 125.

Hand sewing of all kinds suffered from the inevitable neglect, caused by the shortages of materials and war-time conditions of the years from 1914 onwards, and quilting was no exception. More tops were made of patchwork because of its economy, but even so, quilts which are known to have been made between 1914 and 1920 are few. Funds for a War Memorial in a Northumbrian village were raised by a communal quilt-making and sale in 1918, for which one hundred quilts were made, but this was exceptional,[1] and by the 1920s quilting seems to have been almost forgotten except by those who had been brought up to it. The disruption of the war years, also had changed the outlook of the generation who might have carried on the work and only a few went back to a daily routine which included quilt-making. It is difficult to find a quilt made about this time and the only one illustrated here is not representative of the period, as it was marked originally by George Gardiner in 1898 as a wedding-present but not quilted until about 1920.

During the late 1920s, several, and almost simultaneous signs of renewed interest in quilting appeared. A North Country woman, Miss Alice Armes was appointed as organiser for handcrafts to the National Federation of Women's Institutes in 1924. She was born in County Durham and had first-hand knowledge and appreciation of the quilting in her home countryside, although she herself was not a quilter, and within a few years, quilting was among the subjects being taught in Women's Institutes in England and Wales. Quilters from the northern counties and South Wales were teaching in Midland and southern county villages, where a quilting frame probably had not been seen in use for 200 years. Most of the teachers came from South Wales and County Durham, and the fact that many were qualified to do so, was the result of research which had been carried out by Mrs Mavis Fitz-Randolph for the Rural Industries Bureau[2] from 1928 until 1939.

The work began as an investigation into the possibility of creating a home industry for women during the depression in the coal-mining districts, and so bringing in some financial help for their families from outside the mining areas. Quilting was an obvious choice of work, but the need for the quality of it to be high if it was to be offered for sale, was met by organised classes to instruct young women who showed ability, and refresh the skill of the older workers. The classes were financed by grants from various funds[3] and eventually the quilting which resulted reached selected retailers in London, and private customers. There was a good demand and the work sold well, and continued to do so until, once more, war broke out in 1939. The value of this revival of quilting can be seen still in the evidence of some of the quilts made at the time, of which two are illustrated (141, 152).

Early in the 1930s an independent research was made by Mrs Elizabeth Hake, into the existence of a quilting tradition with a character of its own in the south-west of England covering the counties of Wiltshire, Somerset, Dorset, Devonshire and Cornwall. The research was justified and showed that such a tradition had been active up to the end of the nineteenth century, but no evidence was found that it had survived to any extent later than that. Quilters with first-hand experience or recollections were traced and quilts were found which were of good workmanship, equal to those in the North and in South Wales. The patterns showed characteristics of work in other quilting areas, but there was a larger proportion of floral patterns, and both these and the more formal types had a strong tendency to naturalistic and freehand outlines. A number of the quilts of wadded, cord and flat quilting were illustrated, with the results of the research, in Mrs Hake's book *English Quilting*, and a few of the line illustrations from it are reproduced in this book on figures 27, 39, 40, 136, 137.

In 1948, certain authorities in South Wales who had an interest in the tradition of Welsh quilting,[4] put in hand a scheme whereby a record of all that was known of this work should be made, and approached Mrs Fitz-Randolph to carry out the work. The Rural Industries Bureau undertook to finance the scheme, which was enlarged eventually to include quilting done in the North of England as well. The results of the survey were published in 1954 as a book – *Traditional Quilting* – in which Mrs FitzRandolph set down a valuable record of wadded quilting, covering the nineteenth century and the first 50 years of the twentieth, which otherwise might have been lost.[5] Information on quilt-making methods and pattern development, and the importance of the work in the housekeeping of the countryside in the nineteenth century came to light as a result of the work done by the writers of both books.

The revival of quilt-making and subsequent interest in its use for other purposes, brought about also a revival of the work as applied to clothing. Garments such as dressing- and house-gowns were quilted, as well as smaller jackets suitable for indoor wear, and others, in still smaller scale, for infants and babies (153). The pattern used for the short jacket illustrated was adapted from that on the Champeney christening cloak (121). The quilted bodice for children continued to be thought indispensable, and quilted collars and cuffs were added to woollen dressing-gowns. Two cord-quilted

152   Beige cotton quilt with a good example of matching centre and fan corners, several arrangements of spirals, long diamond, shell (double outline) and wineglass patterns. Edges finished with two rows of running stitch. Made by Mrs Edgell. Monmouthshire. Welsh, second quarter twentieth century

153   Christening jacket of cream silk, interlined lamb's wool. Reversible patterns in running stitch adapted from figure 121 and show a wineglass pattern with square diamond filling. Twist pattern border and edges finished with silk-covered piping cord. Made for Oliver Edwards by Mrs Douglas Edwards. English, 1955

154 *Child's quilted long coat of apricot silk, lined with white. Reversible patterns of cord quilting, worked in running stitch, of straight lines in chevron arrangements. Pocket slits in side seams but no pockets. Probably made in Damascus. Late nineteenth/early twentieth century*

155 *Child's quilted long coat of light pink cotton, lined with white. Reversible patterns of cord quilting, worked in running stitch, mostly of straight lines in chevron arrangements and some triangular sections of square diamond filling. Probably made in Damascus. Late nineteenth/early twentieth century*

coats which were worn as dressing-gowns by a family of English children early this century, were brought from Beirut about 1901 and probably had been made in Damascus. One is made of apricot-coloured silk with a cream lining (154) and the other, which is of cotton, is light pink, lined with white (155). The patterns of both are reversible and show characteristics which are familiar to cord quilting in England and Wales. They were everyday wear for Arab children; made with no fastenings, they have pocket slits at each side but no pockets.

Small furnishings, such as cushion covers, became popular, especially as subjects for the amateur to test her ability before taking on a larger piece of work, such as a quilt. Others made by the practised quilter were worthy of being collector's pieces as examples of the best in twentieth-century quilting (156). Cord and flat quilting reappeared also, but it was used for making small pieces of work – cot, cushion and teapot covers being the most popular – which were equal in quality to work of the eighteenth century. Especially good cord quilting was done in Warwickshire by a group of workers who had an outlet for the sale of their work through a marketing scheme for needlework in Warwick, organised by the Women's Institutes of the county. Handwork of all kinds was selected for quality, and although much of it was made and sold, examples of the quilting are hard to find as the shop is no longer in operation.

Cord quilting was done by many individual workers too, and although this and flat quilting were not included in the organised schemes for wadded quilting, most of the needlework societies and other organisations with similar interests, such as the Royal School of Needlework, the Embroiderers' Guild and the National Federation of Women's Institutes, included the subject among those offered to their students and members, and the teaching samplers shown on figures 157, 175, 176, 178, 179, 180, 181, illustrate the high quality of the work being taught.

During the 1930s and after the end of Hitler's war in 1945, when materials were no longer rationed, wadded quilting was included among the subjects

156 *Cushion cover of cream Tussore silk, interlined wool. Welsh heart, two small units based on wineglass, and square diamond patterns worked in back stitch with buttonhole twist. Made by Mrs R. A. Burtt. English, 1959*

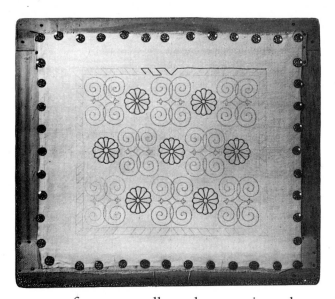

157 *Linen panel set up on the back of a picture frame, with partly worked patterns in flat quilting. Rose and scroll patterns in back stitch with red and cream buttonhole twist*

of some needlework magazines, but probably because of commercial interests, many of the instructions ignored the necessity for choosing materials which lent themselves to the work, and recommended, rather than discouraged, the use of taffeta, rayon, artificial silk and synthetic fabrics. The need for a frame was discounted and the sewing methods were described as 'easy', 'simple' or 'quick', none of which is applicable to quilting. Much the same instructions were given for the so-called 'Italian quilting', and the use of thick soft wool thread instead of firm cord was recommended for raising the pattern outline, which resulted in the eventual collapse of the padding after a period of wear and washing. A decorative kind of needlework known as 'shadow' quilting was popular during the first half of this century, in which the sewing method was the same as for cord quilting on two layers of material (p. 186), but the materials were thin, semi-transparent and usually white, such as fine silk or muslin. Thick strands of soft wool in different colours were threaded between the lines of stitching (182), which gave muted colour to the raised patterns. In more recent years stranded wool has been used occasionally for hand-quilted collars, cuffs and facings of dressing-gowns on coloured, but not transparent, materials; the patterns have been freehand in type and only for decoration.

In order partly to counteract the use of the term 'Italian quilting' but more to encourage the use of good materials, cord quilting was identified as 'linen quilting' and taught as such, in courses of practical instruction organised by the Women's Institutes. This description was not wholly accurate either, as the use of silk and cotton had been established since before the introduction of cord quilting into this country, but the technical instruction was excellent and the restrictive and compulsory use of linen in the practical examinations held by the National Federation of Women's Institutes, produced work which did much to revive this kind of quilting. Flat quilting also came within the description of linen quilting, for which transfers based on many traditional patterns were used by workers who were not able to make their own patterns. These transfers were unobtainable in shops which supplied other needlework materials, but the Embroiderers' Guild had a number of them made which could be used for flat and cord quilting, a selection of which is illustrated (48, 92, 93). The Guild collections of needlework contain several fine examples of cord quilting, some of which show the traditional use of coloured embroidery patterns, and pulled stitches in white or natural thread, which have been made in England and other countries in the present century.

By the middle of the century, quilting had been taken up commercially by the furnishing trade, and lengths of ready-quilted, machine-stitched silk and cotton fabrics were produced, which were intended for making up into all kinds of bed furnishings. 'Quilted' floral chintzes, sold by the yard, were padded with cotton wadding and the printed patterns outlined with machine stitches, so that they appeared as flowered blisters on the surface. Silk and satin materials, also padded with wadding but of a lighter quality and thickness, were sold for making or lining garments; it was used also for cot quilts and the linings of teapot and other covers, such as those for hot-water bottles. The patterns invariably were simple; often variations of the diamond or small shell filling patterns were used. From about 1960, quilted bedspreads in a number of different materials, have been produced in large quantities and of varying quality. Satin quilts, padded with synthetic wadding and stitched with silk thread in all-over repetitive patterns of complicated outline, have been advertised for sale at 30 guineas;[6] cheaper quilts with terylene or nylon outer covers over synthetic padding and patterned, almost invariably with square diamonds, can be bought from about 50 or 60 shillings each, according to the size. Bedroom furniture, such as wardrobe cupboards, chests of drawers, head-boards of beds and chair seats, of which the outer surfaces were covered with quilted material, appeared at the end of 1969 in an advertisement for the furnishing section of a large department store in the West End of London.

Not only is quilting put to this kind of misuse in trade, but 'quilted' is the description given to many small patterns of the kind used traditionally for fillings, especially variations of the diamond or small shell, which have been impressed on the surface of materials which are unsuitable for stitching.

These include stiff plastics used for inexpensive upholstery, and some sheet aluminium foil used for cooking purposes, described as 'quilted' cooking foil, has an impressed pattern of a small diamond shape.

The production of sewing-machines, designed to carry out technical processes of embroidery, has encouraged experiments in machine-stitched quilting by individual workers who are skilled with this tool for sewing, but except for carrying out the function of sewing together several layers of material, the results cannot be said to be as successful in other ways as compared with hand quilting. The patterns are heavier in appearance, as the solid line of stitching, instead of the broken one produced by hand sewing, compresses the materials, and without the elasticity and softness of the hand-sewn running stitch, the finished work loses much of its character. In recent years, needlework magazines containing instructions for quilting as applied to small furnishings such as cushion covers, seem to have recognised this, and have advocated hand sewing for the work. The use of traditional sources for the patterns has been appreciated also and illustrations of some finished pieces of work have shown this.

Hand-sewn quilts with traditional patterns are still made in the North of England by a small number of quilters, but in South Wales there seems to be a handful of workers only who make for their own needs. Quilting classes are held in villages from time to time, with resulting small pieces of work being finished but little continuance after that. One young Welsh woman gave as a reason for making nothing more than a cushion cover she had begun at the classes, that quilting was too slow and that there were more interesting things to do, but another student from the same course of tuition had gone on to make a pair of silk quilts for her own use. In County Durham quilting seems to attract more interest, and it is still possible to find a young quilter who has learned from an older member of her family or another quilter in her village, but even these are decreasing in numbers. For one reason or another, women who are skilled are not able to continue with their quilting. Marriage and its added responsibilities, the alternative of television and radio entertainment with which to occupy the afternoon and evening at home, the need for earning more money more quickly than can be done by quilting for selling, are among the reasons given by young women who are able to quilt but are not prepared to do so, except for their own use. There are one or two exceptions, of workers who will take an order for a quilt occasionally, but it takes some time for the order to be completed, and until the price compares with that for commercial work, hand quilting is not likely to attract skilled workers. A small bed quilt, measuring five by four feet and intended to cover the top of the bed only, costs in the

158 *Cotton poplin quilt, blue and pink reverse sides, interlined cotton wadding. Typical North Country patterns of a feather pattern known as goose-wing and half-roses predominating. Large and small square diamond fillings in running stitch, some with double lines. Made by Mrs Jack Fletcher. English, 1958, 67 × 92 inches*

region of eight pounds ten shillings, the worker charging only five shillings a square foot for her work. The cost varies with the type of material and it is usual for a quilter to charge more for working on silk, but for a small quilt (measuring five feet by four) made of cotton poplin the approximate details work out at –

	£	s	d
7 yards cotton poplin at 6s 11d (sufficient for both sides)	2	8	5
Courtelle wadding at 2s 6d		6	6
Thread		4	6
Designing and marking	1	10	0
Quilting at 5s a square foot	4	0	0
	£8	9	5

159 *Pink shantung marriage quilt, interlined Courtelle wadding. Patterns typical of North Country work in scroll, rose and leaf, true lover's knot at centre, sides and corners and square diamond filling in running stitch. Edges finished with two lines of running. Made by Mrs Mary Lough for her grand-daughter's wedding. English, 1966, 100 × 96 inches*

The working life of such a quilt in daily use, probably would be at least five or six times as long as one of machined satin.

Three of the quilts illustrated were made between 1958 and 1968, and all are of North Country work. The outer covers of two are made from cotton poplin; figure 158 shows a single-bed quilt which is in two colours, one side pink and the other blue, and was made in 1958; the smaller quilt, also in two colours, of cream and pale yellow, is signed and dated 'Mary Lough. Jan. 1968' (160). Figure 159 illustrates a full-sized quilt for a double bed and measures 96 × 100 inches; it was made as a wedding-present for the maker's grand-daughter. The materials on both sides are rose-pink shantung silk and the traditional true lover's knot is included seven times among the centre and border arrangements; several of the other traditional

160   *Cream and pale yellow cotton poplin quilt. Rose, feather, scroll lined twist, feather twist and square diamond patterns worked in running stitch. Signed and dated, Mary Lough. Jan. 1968. English, 60 × 54 inches*

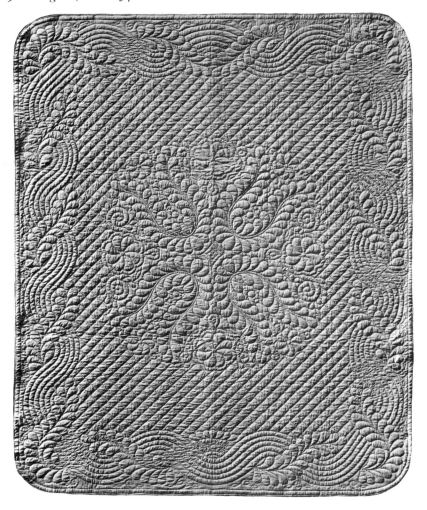

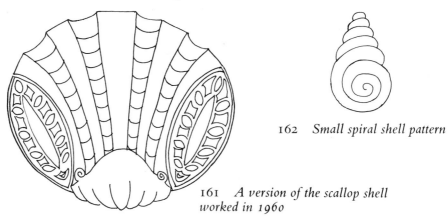

162   *Small spiral shell pattern*

161   *A version of the scallop shell worked in 1960*

patterns used for this quilt are shown in detail (26, 36, 37). Some individual versions of the shell pattern on the small quilt made in 1960 (161, 162) were used with one of the sea-wave border patterns (46) by a quilter who lives in Sussex. Other twentieth-century examples of recent date include the cushion cover already mentioned (156), which was made in 1960 and the baby's short jacket (153). Both pieces of work were made by quilters who live outside the districts usually associated with traditional wadded quilting, but it is clear that both were interested in the traditional type of pattern as applied to contemporary work, which was revived during the 1930s.

In spite of the virtual disappearance of the single-minded quilter, who did the work as a means of earning a livelihood, nowadays there seems to be a number of embroiderers who are able to quilt well, but look on the work as another skill to add to their accomplishments, with a smouldering rather than a burning interest in it. Nevertheless, there is a demand still for hand-made bed quilts, as the narrowing circle of skilled workers can testify, and there is no evidence that the demand is an artificial one.

Present-day American quilters are more faithful to the traditional work, and although nearly always the quilts are made with one side of patchwork or applied work, there is a refreshing enthusiasm for quilting also. Neither are the uses of cord and stuffed quilting overlooked, and American publications within the last ten years, have included instructions for carrying out work using both these methods.[7]

Since about 1965 in Britain, some interest has been shown for hand-quilted finishes on some garments. Collars, cuffs, hems and facings on women's jackets and dresses are among those which have been suggested, but up to now this has been for individual workers only, and not for the fashion trade. The methods which have been advocated are those used in wadded quilting, but in keeping with present-day ideas in embroidery generally, patterns which are not traditional in character are suggested. Some of these, of an all-over geometrical kind, would fulfil the function of keeping the layers of material in place, while others, often irregular, free-hand and thinly spread, give the work the appearance of being incomplete, as they are left without any unifying ground filling. Much of the work is experimental at present, with new materials as well as patterns being tried out, and the time to assess its value to the tradition of quilting lies in the future. Some of the geometrical patterns which are repetitive would be practical and give encouragement to the beginner, as a template or a ruler could be used to mark them on to the material.

Quilting applied to garments is worn nowadays to a greater extent than at any time since the eighteenth century, but with the difference that today the elegance and decoration are gone, the quilting is done by machine, and the garments are commercially produced. The present vogue for quilted coats and jackets is comparable only to the rage for the quilted petticoat of the earlier period, but as there is little room for a petticoat as an under-garment at all in present-day fashion, the petticoat itself has almost disappeared. However, garments which are intended to be worn in or out of doors, either are quilted all-over for complete warmth, or have quilted material attached at the neck and sleeves, to provide warm collars and cuffs. Quilted linings are common to many kinds of coats and jackets. Overcoats, mackintoshes and raincoats are made with quilted linings, some of which can be detached from the outer part of the garment, so that it can be adapted to a change in weather conditions. Evening jackets for men made of cloth in a variety of sober shades of brown, plum colour, dark red or green and so on, have revers or wide collars and turned-back cuffs of a matching satin, quilted inevitably, with square diamond pattern. Women's dressing-gowns, dressing-jackets and soft slippers, also can be bought, made from quilted material – usually silk or satin – or of soft woollen material, with quilted collars and cuffs of satin.

For women's outdoor wear, especially for winter activities such as ski-ing, short quilted jackets of synthetic, waterproof materials, have been made with patterns other than the diamond, and variations of the small shell have shown some welcome change. There have been signs of escape from the diamond too, in the ubiquitous, classless garment, the anorak. This short, padded and quilted jacket, often with a detachable hood, is made from weatherproof material and closed to the neck with a zip-fastener. The quilted patterns tend to be variations of the diamond but there are many variations, as well as hexagonal shapes and zigzag lines. The garment is made in all sizes and can be bought small enough to fit children who are too young to walk, up to those suitable for large men. They have been described as 'about the nearest thing we have to a National Dress'.[8]

All the domestic quilting of the twentieth century, however, seems to be rather ordinary work, when it is held against one example of a tougher sort which has a place in the history of quilting, and was equalled in its vital necessity, only by that of fabric armour. During the account of his last expedition to the South Pole covering the years 1910 to 1912, Captain Scott (later Sir Robert Scott) described in his journal, the construction of the hut in which the members of the expedition were to spend so much of their time. He said – 'It should be remarkably warm and comfortable, for in addition to this double coating of insulation, dry seaweed in quilted sacking, I propose to stack the pony fodder around it.[9] In an account written some years later and published in *The Worst Journey in the World* in 1922, Apsley Cherry-Garrard also gave details of the hut, in which the principle of using quilted padding for warmth, probably was put to its severest test ever. 'The hut was a roomy place, 50 feet long, by 25 feet wide, and 9 feet to the eaves. The insulation, which was very satisfactory, was seaweed, sewn up in the form of a quilt. The sides have double [match-] boarding inside and outside the frames, with a layer of our excellent quilted seaweed insulation between each pair of boardings.' The roof and floor had the same insulation built into them and the result was that 'during the winter, with 20 men living there, and the cooking range going, and perhaps the stove at the other end, the hut not infrequently became fuggy, big though it was'.[10]

11 GATHERED PATCHWORK

During the middle of the nineteenth century a type of work which had a certain popularity, was that of gathered patchwork. This showed a combination of quilting and patchwork which was done as the work progressed, and not in two separate processes, as in the conventional way of making a patchwork top and then quilting it. In the gathered work, each patch is composed of three layers – a base patch (generally calico) which corresponds to the lining in quilting, a small pad of cotton wadding or carded sheep's wool as in interlining and a second patch of material, which corresponds to the top of a quilt proper. The three layers are seamed and then quilted together to make one patch, which eventually is joined to other similar patches by seaming on the wrong side; this is the conventional method for geometrical patchwork.

In this way a full-sized quilt can be made from what amounts to a series of small quilts and although it is, in fact, the ultimate defeat for the attempt to differentiate between patchwork and traditional quilting, it cannot be ignored as a method of quilting and so, details of its construction are given. The process sounds somewhat tedious and involved, and it takes more time than the making of a bedspread of patchwork only, but by the time the work is complete, it is undoubtedly quicker than doing the patchwork and quilting in two separate operations, and the result is a bed cover that is both light and warm. These quilts rarely are lined, as each patch has its own lining and where unpadded patches are included, a lining is added to them as well as the gathered ones.

In existing quilts, the materials invariably are of cotton or calico, and usually are in plain colours. White or unbleached calico and Turkey twill were used in the North Country, the strong contrast of scarlet and white being suited to the work, but some all-white bedspreads of gathered work are not unattractive. Cotton and poplin shirting and pale-coloured dress prints were used in work done during the last 20 years or so of the nineteenth century. Unpadded patches often were included; diamond shapes without interlining heightened the effect of the gathered hexagons, and quilts with this combination undoubtedly have more interest, as part of the

163   *Quilt of gathered patchwork in black and white precale, white calico and black and green printed cotton. Padded with cotton wadding, edges finished with black cotton fringe. English, dated 1967*

pattern however simple, is in relief. In some nineteenth-century specimens the patches were gathered and quilted without a padded interlining but these were not successful; although pretty enough when new, no doubt, after washing and ironing the material collapsed without the support inside, leaving the quilts depressed and wrinkled wrecks. The padding or interlining in the patches is essential to make the work worth while and it will stand up to normal washing and ironing, especially if sheep or lamb's wool is used. It should be emphasised, though, that natural wool must be well washed and rinsed before it is used, and properly prepared as for the conventional wadded quilting (see p. 170).

Hexagon shapes, sometimes with the addition of diamond and triangular patches, are the most common, but there seems to be no reason why other shapes – say large squares, or large octagons and squares together – could not be used, but whatever the shape a large size is the most effective for quilts. In the quilt illustrated (163) and in the cot quilt shown in Mrs Fitz-Randolph's book *Traditional Quilting* on figure 41, the hexagons are almost four inches across, each of the six sides measuring two and a quarter inches, but for less ambitious work and using proportionately smaller patches, gathered patchwork can be used for tea-cosies and so on, as the small quilted areas help to retain heat. The method of making is exactly the same for all sizes of patch (Appendix E).

164   *Detail of figure 163*

Appendix A
NOTES ON WADDED QUILTING

Preparation of Materials

In order to make a quilt, all the layers of material should be cut to the same length and width as each other, and for a large piece of work, this will entail joining materials which are too narrow for the width required for the top and backing. A central seam should not be made as it spoils the good appearance of the centre pattern; to avoid this, one full width should be used down the middle of the quilt and joined to two half widths (or whatever measurement is needed) as side pieces (165). Hand-sewn seams for this, undoubtedly, give the best result and although seams may be machine sewn, usually they are noticeably alien among the hand-sewn patterns of the quilting. If the quilting is done by machine, this method of seaming is immaterial.

half width | full width | half width

165   *Diagram for joining quilt materials*

In all cases the selvedge should be cut off, and the seams sewn on the wrong side.

When the measurements are being reckoned, turnings of approximately one inch should be allowed for the seams and a good allowance be made on each side of what is reckoned to be the finished size of the quilt. Proportionately less may be left for turnings on smaller pieces of work, but as the quilting takes up some of the material in working, enough must be allowed for this as well as for turnings.

The seams of strip quilts, when they are made from uncut lengths of material, should be treated in the same way. Sometimes the strips are made alternately of uncut material and patchwork, and in these, the uneven patches should be turned in to make a straight edge which can be seamed to the uncut strips before the quilting is done. The same thing applies to 'block' quilts, when the squares usually are joined before quilting.

All seams should be opened and pressed on the wrong side with a warm iron. Materials for the top and backing also should be pressed before the work is begun, to remove all fold creases.

Carded sheep's wool, cotton wool and cotton wadding will handle more easily if they are warmed a little before using. It is advisable that this is done in a cylinder- or airing-cupboard or near a central-heating radiator and *not in front of any kind of fire*, coal, gas or electric, as most of these paddings are inflammable when exposed to direct heat or flame.

All wadding and woven materials sold by length, such as domette, cotton or synthetic waddings, blanket or flannel, to be used as padding, can be cut to the same size as the top and backing materials but cotton wool and sheep's wool must be added as it is needed.

Planning the Design

The marking of the patterns is done on the right side of the top material. After this has been cut to size and joined, the centre point should be found by folding lightly, first lengthways and then from side to side, and the centre marked with a X in a thread of a contrasting colour. Tacking threads of this colour, running through the centre point from the middle of both ends and sides, so that the material is marked into four quarters, are useful guidelines.

The next stage should be to mark out important measurements. Presuming that the pattern units have been chosen and the general layout of the design decided, appropriate measurements should be marked with long tacking stitches to show the boundaries of the centre arrangement and surrounding borders and corners. It is possible to become sufficiently familiar with the pattern units that, in time, a worker can know how many repeats of a unit will be needed for any given length or area, but a beginner will benefit from making a plan to scale on paper, corresponding with one-quarter of the quilt area marked by tacking. Using the actual pattern unit templates within this area, and drawing the outlines of each in position on the plan, all that is needed is to repeat the section four times when marking the material, according to the full-scale plan.

Planning patterns for strip, block and patchwork quilt tops is governed by the boundaries imposed by the joining seams. The type of pattern used for quilt borders is suitable for strip quilts and often the sort of shape which makes a good centre pattern will fit well into the square block shape. Quilts of patchwork only are often quilted in lines which follow those of the patchwork shapes, and no special plan is needed (166).

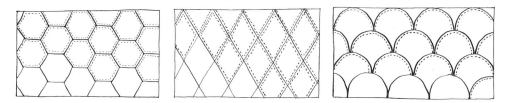

166   *Quilting stitches following the outlines of patchwork*

Designs for smaller things, such as cushion and teapot covers, can be worked out with great accuracy on a paper pattern in the actual size of the work. Dressmaking patterns used for dressing-jackets and dressing-gowns, and other garments, should be laid on the material while in the piece and outlined with tacking stitches; the cutting out of the garment is done after the quilting is completed on the length of material.

The choice of pattern units should be made always with an eye for their proportion to the size of the work to be quilted. A study of patterns in the quilts illustrated, emphasises the quality in the use of simple shapes for building up a well-balanced design, especially as a beginning to more ambitious work.

Marking the Patterns

Marking is done by outlining the template shapes on to the right side of the material intended for the top. There are several methods used by quilters nowadays, after the material has been prepared.

1 Two methods advocated for workers in America involve pricking round the pattern outlines which have been traced on to paper and the material marked through the holes:

(a) by the point of a pencil, leaving the shapes marked by dotted pencil lines, or

(b) by pouncing through the holes, dry powders such as cocoa, cinnamon or a mixture of one part of ultramarine to four parts of corn starch, the dotted lines being traced afterwards by a soft lead pencil. The use of lead pencil for marking is discouraged by English teachers of this type of quilting.

2 A method of marking taught in Britain in the 1930s was by outlining the templates with tailor's chalk and filling in details by hand, also with chalk. While chalk is still useful for some marking, it is liable to become smudged, or to rub off with handling. Workers who have been accustomed to marking the patterns as the quilting proceeds, while the work is in the frame, general use chalk but this practice seems to be dying out. It is not easy to follow a chalk line with accuracy, without a well-practised eye and hand. Some pattern details may be chalked in, but unless the worker is sure of her ability, it is advisable to mark with a needle.

3 The use of a rug or yarn needle to outline the patterns results in a clear indentation, which does no harm to the material and is sufficiently permanent to last until the sewing is finished. The needle should be held almost parallel to the work surface and a slight but steady pressure kept on the pointed end. If a short length of tape or thick wool is threaded through the eye of the needle, it gives an extra purchase to the worker's hold on the needle.

It is an advantage if the marking is done before the top material is put into the frame, especially for a beginner, so that the whole design can be planned and checked first as a safeguard against mistakes or change of mind. Marking should be done with the material spread on a firm table covered with some thick soft material such as felt or closely woven blanket or cloth. As the areas of the design will have been measured and marked out with tacking as given on p. 171, the templates or paper patterns can be placed in position and the marking-out done. After the template outlines have been drawn, the filling in of detail within the outline is done freehand, as a rule. This needs some practice for accuracy, but a piece of card, cut to the necessary curve for feather patterns or a saucer, can make a reliable guide for these and for the hammock pattern and so on. Coins can be used for smaller circular or semicircular patterns. Filling-in lines which need to be straight are best marked along the edge of a ruler; a clear plastic one will be found useful.

Most workers begin by drawing out the centre arrangement for a quilt; then the borders, corners and the background fillings are done last. It is important that these are accurate and straight. The shell or wineglass template is notched as a guide to accuracy (73); diamond fillings of all kinds should be measured and marked at regular intervals, so that the crossing points are evenly spaced. Whatever filling is used for background, the lines of the patterns, whether straight or diagonal, should be continuous, broken only by the large pattern units when they occur, and they should be worked right up to the outlines of each, as well as to the outside edges of the work when it is made up and finished.

Setting Up

The process of putting the materials into a frame preparatory to quilting them together is known as 'setting up'. The method may vary in small details according to the habit of the worker but it is a straightforward business, whatever the method, if the objects of the setting up are understood. These are:

1 That the layers of material should lie smoothly without wrinkling and be kept that way throughout.

2 That an easy, even tension should be maintained all over the work so that it is sufficiently 'springy' to enable the sewing to be done with even stitches. If the materials are too tightly stretched, it is impossible to take up the right amount of material in each stitch. As a large piece of work proceeds it is necessary to move on the quilted part from time to time so readjustments to the tension also must be made, but the means by which this is done is not difficult to master. A small cradle, cushion or teapot cover may need little or no moving at all once the setting up is done, and all are good subjects for the beginner.

The setting up is done in stages:

1 The first layer of material is the backing and this should be cut on the straight on all cut edges. Both ends of the material are fastened to the frame by oversewing to the webbing on the two runners.

2 The backing is then wound on to one runner, keeping the runner underneath the material, until about 18 inches, or any convenient amount, is left unrolled for working (167). Some American workers consider that 12 inches is enough, but the important consideration is the comfort of the worker, in which the amount of reach allowed by arm length plays the greatest part.

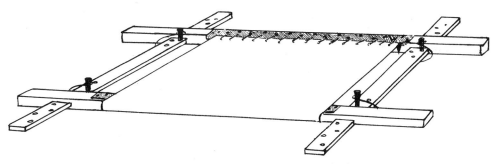

167   *Frame set up with backing attached and rolled on one runner, and stretched ready for padding to be laid over*

3 The stretchers can now be put through the slots in the runners and the four pegs inserted in the holes, so that the material is kept flat. It is by moving the pegs into the appropriate holes in the stretchers that the correct working tension is achieved (167); this should be firm enough to prevent the material from sagging, but not so tight as to make it impossible to sew through all the layers with short even stitches. The first stages of the setting up are best done with the parts of the frame spread on a firm table, but at this point, with the stretchers pegged to the runners, it can be laid across the chair backs or trestles or whatever support is being used, as it is more manageable for the next stages, when it is convenient, sometimes, to have one hand under the frame.

4 The padding is then laid over the backing in an even layer. If carded wool is used it must be teased out and spread as evenly as possible and free from lumps, covering the unrolled surface of the backing. If woven materials such as blanket, flannel or domette, or lengths of wadding, either of cotton or synthetic material, are being used, they should be cut into the length and width equal to those of the other materials, and all that is needed is to see that whichever is chosen lies smoothly on the unrolled backing, with the extra length hanging over the rolled end. In the event of carded wool or cotton wool being used, more must be added each time the frame is readjusted.

5 The third layer, or top material, can now be attached by firm tacking stitches through the three layers as close to the webbing as possible, on one side of the frame (168). The remainder of the top can be left to hang over the rolled end of the frame with the extra length of padding, or folded loosely and fastened up, so that it does not lie on the floor; a row of short needles should be put in close to the rolled part of the work, securing the three layers in position while the quilting is being done. Needles may be put in the materials at other places in the unquilted area if the worker feels they are necessary.

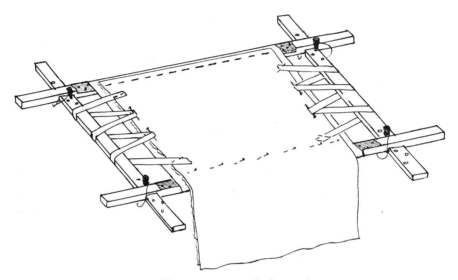

168   *Frame set up ready for working*

6 The materials should now be taped to the side stretchers to complete the setting up. A tape, approximately one inch wide is advisable, is attached by means of a pin or needle through the three layers as near to the webbing as possible; the tape length is then taken over and under the stretcher and attached again at an interval of not more than three inches. This is repeated until the rolled portion is reached and again along the other side of the frame, care being taken not to put a strain on the materials but to keep an even tension for working. It is important that all the layers are fastened through at each fold of the tape (168).

7 The materials are now ready for quilting but before coming to the methods used for this, details for readjustment of the frame as the work proceeds may be given here. When the pattern on the unrolled portion is completed,

this part must be rolled up to bring forward further material to be quilted. The first step is to remove the tape from the sides by unfastening it and then the pegs should be taken out to enable the stretchers to be removed from the slots. The quilted part of the work should then be wound on to the near runner, while the appropriate amount is unwound from the other. When this is done, the stretchers and pegs are replaced, and the needling and taping of unquilted material is done as before. This is repeated when necessary until the work is completed.

The Quilting

Quilting is the action of sewing together the layers of material for which the preceding preparations have been made, and for wadded quilting there are two recognised methods by which the sewing is done:

1   Back stitch
2   Running stitch

1 Back stitch is practicable only when a thin layer of padding is used between the top and backing and when the reverse side of the work is not seen, such as cushion and teapot covers (156). The sewing usually is done with a matching silk thread, or buttonhole twist, whether the material is of silk or linen, as it is softer than cotton or linen thread and lends itself to the work. A short, between needle, no. 9, is the most practical for this stitch.

(a) The thread should be fastened, without a knot, by making a back stitch on the wrong side of the work and bringing the needle up through the materials at the starting-point of the pattern.

(b) Stitches should be short and exactly even. Beginning with one running stitch, a back stitch should be made by inserting the needle into the point at which the thread was brought through for the preceding stitch, and out again two stitch lengths ahead (169). This back stitching is repeated throughout the work. To end off the thread, it should be run back on the wrong side, through the backs of the last six or eight stitches, and cut off.

169   *Back stitch*

2 Running stitch is commonly used for bed quilts, garments, or anything for which a fairly substantial layer of padding for warmth is needed. The sewing is done with a white or coloured no. 40 cotton which matches in colour the top of the quilt, even if the reverse side is of a different colour. If the materials are silk, a matching silk thread should be used. Nylon, or other synthetic thread, and mercerised threads are not suitable for hand quilting. As for back stitching, a no. 9 between needle is used. The chief difference in quilting done by running stitch and other types, is that this work is reversible. Each stitch, and the space between it and the next, should be of equal length on both sides of the quilt, so that the pattern is identical on each side.

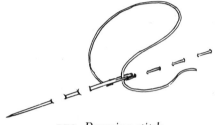

170 *Running stitch*

To do the work the worker sits at one end of the supported frame throughout the quilting and uses both hands, one on top and one held underneath, to help the upward and downward movements of the needle. (a) The thread can be fastened by two means. Some workers begin by making a small single knot, and with the needle inserted on a line of the pattern a little way from the starting-point, the thread is drawn through into the padding, and a slight tug given to bring the knot through from the surface material. The knot will catch in the padding and the puncture made by the knot disappears in working. A back stitch is made before the running is begun.

To begin the thread without a knot, it may be fastened by running the needle into the padding a little way from the starting-point of the pattern, and coming out at this point, drawing through all but an inch or two of the thread which is left in the padding. A back stitch is then made and repeated by inserting the needle into the first hole of the stitch but bringing it out a stitch length further on than the end of the preceding stitch. This will secure the thread.

(b) To do the quilting, the needle should be inserted as upright as possible, from the front to the back of the work, and helped up again to the front by the first or second finger of the hand which is held under the frame. Throughout the work, several stitches – at least two and three if possible

– should be made before the thread is drawn through except on a difficult turn or corner, when single stitches can be made. As the sewing is done from one side of the frame, it will be necessary for some stitches to be made running away from the worker; in these cases, the needle can be helped by pushing with the inside of the thumb-nail, instead of the thimble. To ensure continuity in the pattern, especially in the straight lines of filling patterns, it is an advantage to have a number of threaded needles carrying on different parts of the design. Each needle can be taken a short distance to keep the advance line evenly across the work, rather than have any one section built up ahead of the rest.

(c) To finish off a thread, it should be taken back through the padding for some way, until it is 'lost' there. A new thread should be started as for the beginning of the work, care being taken not to break the continuity of the pattern.

Making Up and Finishing

When the quilting is completed, the work is taken out of the frame, and all that remains to be done to a quilt, is that the edges should be finished off by one of three methods.

1 The edges may be turned in, and ensuring that the padding comes to the edge also, the layers are run together as near to their edges as practicable. A second line of running should then be made about half an inch inside the first, the stitches in both lots of running being equal to those in the rest of the quilt (152, 171).

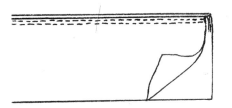

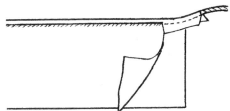

171   *Edges joined with two rows of running stitch*

172   *Edges joined by insertion of covered piping cord*

2 The edges may be finished by turning in and inserting a covered piping cord between them. The cord should be covered with strips of the material used for the top; they should be cut on the bias and be wide enough for an ample allowance of material. The covered cord may be sewn to the backing with running stitch and then slip stitched or hemmed to the other side (172).

Alternatively the piping may be attached by hemming on both sides and many workers prefer this. Whichever method is used, care should be taken at the corners, to see that the piping is eased round so that the quilt material is not puckered.

The piping cord finish is advisable for anything which may be subjected to wear at the edges, garments, cushion and teapot covers and so on, as the piping acts as a protection for the quilting and can be replaced when it is worn.

3 A finish which is common in American quilts is done by binding the edges with a bias-cut strip of the material used for the top. This may be turned in and hemmed over the raw edges of the quilt materials.

When the quilted material intended for a garment is taken out of the frame, the pieces – sleeves and back and front – should be cut out with allowances for seam turnings and made up with the usual dressmaking processes, except that it is advisable to join the seams by hand.

Appendix B
NOTES ON FLAT QUILTING

The kind of frame used for wadded quilting is suitable for flat-quilted bed-spreads and other large pieces of work; cushion and teapot covers, work bags and so on, can be made on one of smaller proportions, or on a standing frame, which leaves both hands free for working (13). It is possible to quilt smaller pieces of work on a circular, or double-ring hand-frame if the materials are well tacked together beforehand and the work adjusted to ensure there is no wrinkling or stretching (14). A small rectangular, rigid frame can be made of wood at home, if the corners are mortised or dove-tailed and the surfaces are well-prepared and smooth; the back of a picture-frame of this type can be adapted. Webbing or braid should be tacked along two sides or ends, to which the material can be attached. The work illustrated (157) shows this type of frame in use, with a small panel for a bag secured to the frame with brass drawing-pins, spaced at frequent intervals. This is a practical method, if the work is to remain in the frame for a short time only and if the pins can be put in on a more than adequate allowance for turnings. Drawing-pins should not be left in for any length of time.

Two layers of material only are needed for flat quilting. The top layer should be of fine-quality cotton, linen or silk; mercerised cotton, rayon, and materials other than those made from natural fibres, do not lend themselves to hand quilting. The backing material should match the kind used for the front of the work, although the quality should not be as good; the difference in quality can be seen by comparing the back and front of the panel illustrated on figures 175 and 176.

The sewing thread can be of silk, cotton or linen, but silk thread or buttonhole twist are smoother than any other for working, and the ex-perience of present-day workers is backed by the use of silk in so much of the work in the past. Flat quilting invariably has been carried out in back stitch, although some patchwork quilts, in which there is no interlining, have been quilted flat to the lining by running stitch.

Unlike wadded quilting, patterns in flat quilting are not reversible. They are marked on to the right side of the top layer of material, by means of transfers, tracings, freehand drawing or pouncing. As the patterns are worked in outline, many embroidery designs could be adapted, but for workers who prefer traditional patterns, a small selection of them on transfers is kept by the Embroiderers' Guild, some of which are illustrated (48, 92, 93).

Tracings can be taken from illustrations of any suitable patterns, by placing over them a sheet of greaseproof- or tracing-paper, and marking with a clear pencil outline. These can be transferred from the tracing to the surface of the material by means of carbon-paper, which is obtainable in blue for marking on light colours, or in yellow for full or dark shades. Patterns on figures 175, 178 and 180, were marked in this way; unworked parts of the pattern on figure 157, can be seen on most of the border and one partly worked motif.

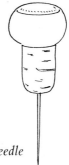

173   *Pricker made by inserting needle into glass-topped cork*

Pouncing is done by making a tracing in the same way and then pricking the pattern outlines with a series of holes at intervals of from one-eighth to a quarter of an inch, according to the material to be used; the coarser the material, the wider the spaces between the holes. A stout darning-needle, with the eye end inserted in a metal- or glass-topped cork, makes a practical homemade tool for pricking, which is comfortable to use (173). It should be held in an upright position in use. To transfer the pricking to the material, the paper should be laid on it in position and weighted to prevent any movement, and a pouncing powder (usually a mixture of powdered charcoal and chalk, obtained from a good chemist) spread over the holes; it should be brushed through with a small brush or pad of cloth, until the pattern is marked on the material by a line of dots. Some workers connect the dots with a thin line of watercolour paint but a fine pencil marks more easily and the line is covered completely (or should be) by the subsequent back stitches. The methods of tracing and pouncing are not as laborious as they appear and patterns made by either can be kept for future use if they are made on good paper in the first instance. Whatever method is used, ample allowance for turnings should be made round the edges.

To prepare and work the quilting:

(a) The patterns should be marked on the right side of the top layer of material.

(b) The top layer and backing should be cut to the same measurements and sewn along one edge to that of the webbing on one runner, with the same procedure as for wadded quilting. With the materials so attached, they should be laid flat on a work table and tacked together in two directions unless the work is small, in which case one direction may be enough. Both layers should be smooth and without wrinkles.

(c) The unattached ends should then be sewn to the webbing on the other runner.

(d) If the frame is adjustable, the stretchers and pegs are put in as for wadded quilting (167) or the screws adjusted on a standing frame (13), until the materials are firm and flat but not tightly stretched. If a small rigid frame is used, the adjustments should be made as the materials are being attached to the frame.

(e) Unless fixed to the sides of a rigid frame, the other two edges should be taped to the stretchers (168).

(f) Working on the right side of the work, the quilting is done with back stitching, through both layers of material, with short, even stitches along the marked pattern outlines (169). The work illustrated (175) shows the right side of an example of flat quilting in the wineglass pattern quilted with buttonhole twist on fine linen; figure 176, shows the same piece of work on the other side, with the backing also of linen but of a more open weave. The method of beginning and ending of the threads by running in along the backs of the stitches can be seen also. The floral sprays were worked in chain stitch (174) with a single strand of silk in colours of blue, pink and green; the patterns on figure 157 were worked in back stitch, with cream and red buttonhole twist.

(g) When the quilting is completed, the work should be taken out of the frame and the tacking stitches removed.

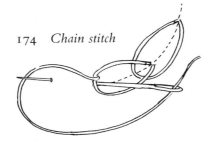

174   *Chain stitch*

175 *Sampler showing flat quilting in back stitch of wineglass pattern enclosing flowers embroidered in chain stitch. This pattern can be worked with cord outlines and embroidery done before the cord is inserted*

(h) Flat-quilted work needs the addition of a lining, unless the back is protected, as it would be in a cushion or teapot cover attached to the padding. Lining material generally matches the kind used for the quilting, linen with linen, cotton with cotton, silk with silk, but consideration

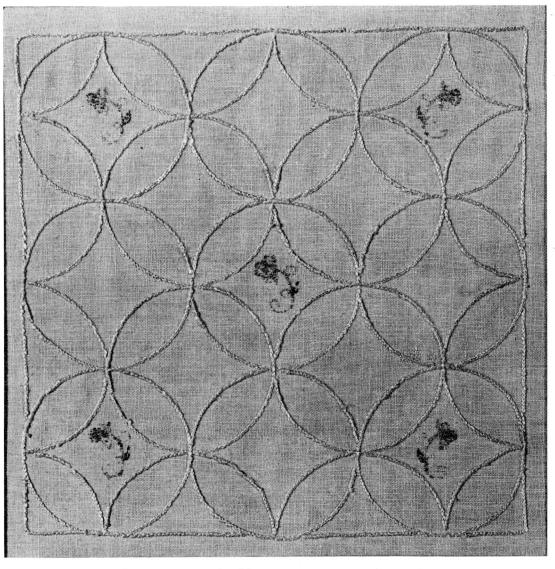

176 *Sampler showing reverse side of figure 175*

should be given to the purpose of the work; small bags for example, may call for a silk lining.

Traditional finishes for the edges of flat-quilted work are by binding with strips of whatever material has been used, or with a fringe (105), but a covered piping cord would be a practical method of attaching a lining, and of finishing the edges. Alternatively, the edges could be turned in and run together as for wadded quilting (171).

Appendix C
NOTES ON CORD QUILTING

Cord-quilting patterns may be worked by either of two methods, one in which the cord is quilted to one layer of material in one operation (Method I) and the other, by quilting two layers of material and inserting the cord after the sewing is completed (Method II). For each method the use of a frame is advisable, the kind being determined by the size of the work, but unless the pattern units are small and spaced some distance apart, quilting done on one layer of material cannot be worked in a double-ring frame; either of the adjustable types or a rigid frame are practical (13, 16, 157). Nowadays cord quilting is used for small pieces of work, the fashion for bed quilts of this kind having died out – for the time being at any rate – and the world of high fashion having ignored, so far, its elegant possibilities so much appreciated by this trade in the eighteenth century.

Almost inevitably, the material used has been of linen of the same quality as that for flat quilting – fine and closely woven for the top layer and a loosely woven backing, for which linen scrim is the most appropriate. Rayon, mercerised cotton and materials containing any but natural fibres are wholly unsuited to cord quilting.

Cotton cord is used for the padding and this can be bought especially for the purpose and according to the thickness needed (p. 24). Fine silk or good-quality muslin has been used as a top layer for some twentieth-century work, with a backing of butter muslin; a soft padding such as wool thread is inserted between the layers, as done in Method II, and this is coloured sometimes, when a semi-transparent material is used for the top.

A silk thread or buttonhole twist, or linen or cotton thread may be used according to the choice of the worker, but those with experience find that silk thread or buttonhole twist lend themselves well to all materials and to the back stitch with which the quilting is done.

Patterns are marked on the right side of the top layer of material, by the method given for flat quilting (p. 181), with the exception of freehand drawing which is not recommended for everyone, as evenly spaced double lines are essential. Transfers printed especially for cord quilting can be bought and although single line patterns can be adapted by practised workers, those with only a slight working knowledge of this type of quilting will appreciate the help of transfers for the necessary double tracks (178).

All creases should be pressed out of the material before the patterns are marked. Marking should be done before the material is put into the frame, with the material spread on a slightly padded flat surface when traced or pricked patterns are being marked (p. 182). Planning the layout of the patterns is as important as in any other type, and the centre and borders should be measured and marked with a X for the centre and lines of tacking for other important areas, such as borders, leaving adequate turnings for making up the work.

New piping cord should be well shrunk before being used. This prevents shrinkage after the work is finished and makes the cord more pliable for quilting.

To prepare the work for quilting with Method I:

(i) With the patterns marked on the right side of the single layer of material, this should be oversewn on two sides to the webbing on the runners of the frame.

(ii) With the material so attached, the other two edges are taped to the stretchers or sides, as for flat quilting (p. 176) and if a rigid frame is being used, the material should be adjusted as it is being attached to the frame.

(iii) Working on the right side, the cord is then attached to the back of the work with back stitch, in which the stitches are made alternately on the parallel lines, carrying the thread across from side to side. The cord meanwhile is held in position by one hand (kept under the frame), while the sewing thread is passed under it, so securing the cord by the crossing thread (177, 179).

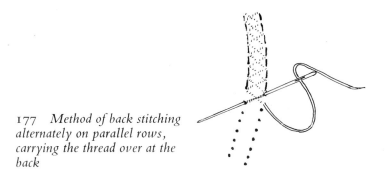

177 *Method of back stitching alternately on parallel rows, carrying the thread over at the back*

(iv) Long lines of cord can be left uncut for straight borders, but for intersections of curved or short lines in the pattern it is necessary to cut the

178　*Sampler of quilting with cord (Method I). Back stitch worked as on figure 177, with buttonhole twist on linen*

cord at some points where the intersections occur. Examples of this can be seen clearly on figure 179, and the front of the same piece of work is shown on figure 178.

(v) This kind of quilting needs a lining to protect the back of the work and the kinds of material and methods of finishing are the same as those used for flat-quilted work (p. 184).

179   *Reverse side of figure 178*

To prepare the work for quilting with Method II:
  (i) With the patterns marked on the right side of the top layer, this and
  the bottom layer, which must be open in weave, are attached to the
  webbing on the frame as for flat quilting. The taping of the remaining
  edges should be carried out in the same way also, ensuring that both layers
  lie smoothly but are not unduly stretched.

180   *Sampler of quilting with cord (Method II). Pattern outline*
back stitched with buttonhole twist on linen

(ii) Working on the right side of the work, the quilting is done with back stitch in short, even stitches, along the pattern outlines, through both layers of material, until the pattern is completed.
(iii) The work is then taken out of the frame and the tacking threads removed.
(iv) Working from the back of the work, the pattern is then padded with

181 *Reverse side of figure 180*

cord by threading it in behind the layer of scrim and between the lines of quilting. A needle with a blunt end and a large eye is needed and if the cord is stranded (untwisted) first, it can be drawn more easily through the narrow channel. To insert the needle, the strands of.the scrim should be parted, and the needle run along for about an inch or so, before emerging again and drawing the cord through. This threading should be repeated, with the needle re-entering the scrim through the exit hole, continuing to follow the pattern and coming out at short intervals. It is important, however, that the cord is not pulled through to the full extent of its

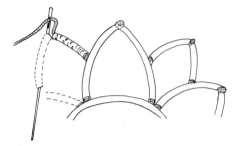

182   *Detail of figure 181, indicating points of entry and exit for the cord*

length each time, but that a small loop is left at each exit point; this guards against puckering the material and the loops will flatten out by degrees (181). Puckering is caused also by threading too long a length of cord into the needle at one time, and by the cord being too thick for the channel allowed for it. It is necessary to cut the cord at intersections of the pattern lines but with due consideration for the appearance of the work on the right side. Strategic exit points for the cord during threading (182) can be seen on figure 181, by the partings in the scrim at various places in the pattern. The well-planned cutting of the cord is shown also, with the result of it on the pattern on the right side (180).

(v) It is usual to line this type of quilting, in order to protect the back of the work, with material which corresponds with that on which the quilting has been done. The finishes at the edges are those most commonly used for the types dealt with in Chapter 9 and described on p. 179.

Appendix D
NOTES ON STUFFED QUILTING

Stuffed quilting is done more satisfactorily if it is worked in a frame. Small pieces can be made in a circular hand-frame, but an adjustable embroidery frame which will stand on a table, or on the floor, is very suitable for such things as cushion covers, tea-cosies and so on, for which soft, lightweight materials can be used (13). Larger and heavier work, such as bed covers, needs the type of frame used for wadding quilting (16).

To prepare and work the quilting in an adjustable frame:
    (i) The pattern should be drawn or transferred on to the *backing material*, whether this is muslin or scrim.
    (ii) The materials for the top and backing are both attached to the webbing at each end of the frame, with the *backing uppermost*. Although the materials may be pinned to the webbing, it is advisable to tack them (167).
    (iii) With both layers attached to the webbing, the frame should be adjusted to achieve the required tension, and the sides of the materials taped to the sides of the frame (168). Pins may be used to hold the tape in position but in the case of fine materials, it is advisable to use needles, and so reduce the risk of marking.
    (iv) Both layers should now be tacked together to hold them until the quilting stitches are done, but it is important that the tacking is not done over the outlines of the pattern; it should run through the background spaces only.
    (v) Working from the wrong side of the work – that is, along the outlines marked on the backing – the whole design is worked with fine, even, running or back stitches through both layers of material (183).
    (vi) The stuffing is then inserted. To do this the threads of the muslin or scrim backing are parted (but not cut) at convenient places in the design, and small pieces of soft wool or cotton wool are eased in with the help of a smooth stuffing-stick or some other suitable tool (a thick blunt-ended needle is useful for small areas), until the space between the lines of stitching are padded (184). It is important not to over-stuff the work; the pattern should stand up from its background on the right side but not be so fully packed as to stretch the material and distort the design.

183 (below) Patterns for stuffed quilting marked on the muslin backing of the work and sewn with running stitch

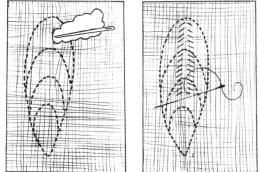

184 (above left) Stuffing of wool inserted with a blunt needle, through the parted threads of the muslin ·

185 (above right) Threads laced together after stuffing

(vii) When the stuffing is completed, the parted threads of the backing materials should be drawn together gently with a lacing stitch, so that the stuffing cannot escape (185). This is especially important with muslin but is advisable with whatever is used for backing.

The tacking threads are now removed and the work taken from the frame for making up. The example illustrated shows one-quarter of a design for a silk cushion cover, and the traditional finish for the edges of this would be the insertion of a piping cord, covered with the same silk, between the two layers, as for wadded quilting (172).

Stuffed quilting has been used frequently with corded quilting in designs for linen bed covers (142, 143, 148) and generally a thin lining on the wrong side is added. These quilts often are finished by running together the turned-in edges of top and lining as for wadded quilting (171), but many quilts in the eighteenth and early nineteenth centuries were finished with a cotton or linen fringe.

Appendix E
NOTES ON GATHERED PATCHWORK

1 A number of paper shapes are cut from a basic template of whatever shape and size is chosen.

2 A number of calico shapes are cut from a template approximately half an inch longer on each side than that used for the papers, to allow for turnings.

3 The papers are then covered with the calico pieces, by tacking them together as shown (186) to form the bases.

4 A number of pieces are cut from whatever material is chosen for the top patch, at least half an inch longer on each side than the base patch. A narrow turning is then made on each side of the patch, creasing it into position on the wrong side, and a gathering thread run evenly just inside the fold (187).

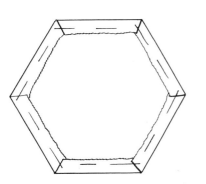

186   *Paper and calico tacked together for base patch*

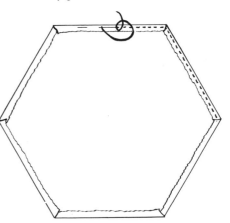

187   *Narrow turning on the top patch with running stitches for gathering*

5 The gathering thread is then drawn up, until the side measurements of the top patch equal those of the base.

6 As the prepared patches should now be the same in side measurements, they are placed together with the turnings *inside*, pinned at each corner and, making sure that the gathers are evenly spaced, they are joined along five sides to begin with, by oversewing the edges (188).

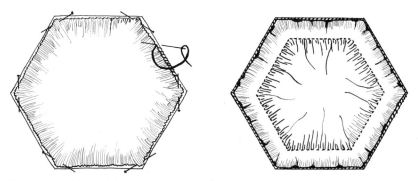

188   *Gathered patch being oversewn to the base patch*

189   *Top patch with running round centre*

7 Before joining the sixth side, the tacking and paper are removed from the base patch and whatever padding is chosen is then put in, being careful to spread it evenly in the *middle* of the space between the outer layers. The joining of the last side can be done. Care should be taken not to overfill each patch or the result will be more suitable for a pin-cushion than a quilt. One thickness of cotton wadding of average thickness with the skin removed from the top side, as for wadded quilting, should be enough, and a number of suitably sized pads can be cut in advance, to make sure that the same amount is put into each patch. If sheep's wool is chosen the amount will be governed by the quality – if it is coarse and springy, less will be needed than if it is fine and soft – but it is most important that it is properly prepared before it is used.

8 The area taken up by the padding varies according to the worker's preference, but as a rule, a space or border of from half to one inch round the edges of each patch is left unpadded. To make this border, the padding is kept in place by a running stitch which joins top and base patches about half an inch or more from each edge, taking up the fullness of the material little by little with each stitch (189). In some gathered patches two rows of running are made about a quarter of an inch apart and the same distance from the edges, leaving a smaller area of padding in the middle.

9 There remains now a balloon-like area of unstitched material over the padding. This is disposed of by stab stitching through the three layers, beginning on the outside of the area and working inwards, *keeping the needle*

vertical on each down and up stitch. The spacing of the stitches should be even, with a short stitch (about an average running stitch) on the top, catching down a very small amount of the balloon with the downward needle (190). With the needle below and having moved it in a clockwise direction for about a quarter of an inch, still held vertically, the return stitch is made and this is repeated in a spiral direction, gradually working towards the middle of the patch with each journey round. Each stitch from the top should make a small pucker in the balloon between it and the last stitch, so that by degrees the material is taken up and an effect of quilting is achieved, not unlike the *meander* pattern of flat quilting, but in relief (164, 191).

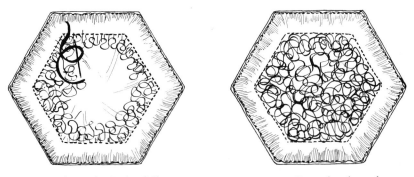

190   *Stab stitching the fullness
in the centre of the patch*

191   *Completed patch*

10 The completed patches are joined by seaming on the wrong side in whatever arrangement is planned, and the edges of the work are finished in any of the methods used for a traditional wadded quilt, and usually they are straightened by using half patches, where necessary, to do this.

Appendix F
LIST OF TEMPLATE DRAWINGS

Q.3   Borders

Q.6   Bell pattern: various uses

Q.7   Use of circle templates

Q.9   Border patterns

Q.10a Working drawings of ordinary quilting frame

Q.10b Working drawings of quilting frame with ratchet for turning the work

Q.11   Feather patterns, including border and corner feathers, square and curved feathers, feather wreath, pine feather and horseshoe.

Q.12   Feather patterns continued, including trailing fern (Welsh), Allendale feather border, running feather (Durham) and straight feather (Northumberland).

Q.13   Leaf patterns, flower-pot, tree used as border, fleur-de-lis, ivy, fern, little flourish, Welsh leaf and Welsh heart.

Q.14   Patterns based on the circle, including rose, shell, Tudor rose, feather circle, Weardale wheel, snail creep, true lovers' knot and fan.

Q.15   Various North Country patterns: ram's horn, flat-iron (Durham), scissors, goose wing, sheaf of corn, feather rose, paisley flower, banana, paisley pear (North), fleur-de-lis.

Q.16   Leaves, hearts and flower patterns, flat-iron (Welsh), tulip, paisley pear, heart (North), chestnut, thistle and Welsh heart.

Q.17   Diamonds: square, double, long, Scotch, chained; basket, wine-glass on diagonal and perpendicular axes, shells and fancy shells.

Q.18   Borders: heart, worm, plait, chain, feather hammock, cord and tassel, beehives, Welsh border, tulip, tree.

Q.19   Cable and twist variations: dog trail, Weardale chain, feather twist, trail (Welsh), lined twist and plait.

Q.20   Bellows and star templates and strip patterns.

These drawings of traditional pattern units for quilting have been copied from North Country and Welsh quilts and templates, both old and recent.

They can be obtained from The Council for Small Industries in Rural Areas, 35 Camp Road, Wimbledon Common, London SW19.

NOTES

Chapter 1

1 *Concise Oxford Dictionary*
2 *ibid.*
3 Also illustrated, *Needlework Through the Ages*, plate IV, fig. 2
4 *ibid.*, p. 39
5 *ibid.*, p. 40
6 *ibid.*, plate IX, fig. 1
7 *ibid.*, p. 82
8 *The Armourer and his Craft*, p. 90
9 *ibid.*, p. 49 (ref. *Historia Anglicana*, Walsingham Rolls Series, p. 457)
10 *The Faerie Queene*, VI Booke, Canto VII, v. 43
11 *Marmion*, v, iii
12 *The Habsburgs*, p. 49
13 *The Faerie Queene*, the III Booke, Canto III, v. 57
14 *ibid.*, the v Booke, Canto v, vv. 1, 2
15 *The Armourer and his Craft*, p. 85
16 *ibid.*, p. 86
17 *Canterbury Tales*, *The Prologue*, p. 2
18 *ibid.*, *The Tale of Sir Thopas*, p. 173
19 *The Armourer and his Craft*, p. 90 (ref. *Instructions, Observations and Ordres Militaires*, Sir John Smith, p. 185)
20 *ibid.*, p. 94
21 *Oxford Dictionary* (Quilt 1. S. Eng. Leg. 188/125)
22 *ibid.* (*Body and Soul*, MS. Laud 108, attributed to Walter Map. ed. T. Wright, Camden Society, No. xvi. 1941)
23 *ibid.*, (MS. A)
24 *Arthurian Legends in Mediaeval Art*, pp. 63 *et seq.*, plates 118, 119
25 *ibid.*, p. 65
26 *Country Life Annual*, 1956, p. 168
27 *Oxford Dictionary*, (Quilt 1. Merlin, 539)
28 *Tudor Cornwall*, p. 74

Chapter 2

1 *The Draper's Dictionary*, qu. p. 81
2 *The Armourer and his Craft*, p. 92

3 *Historia Naturalis*, Vol. VIII (Book XXIX), IX

4 *The Armourer and his Craft*, pp. 85, 86

5 *ibid.*, p. 88

6 *ibid.*, p. 87

7 *The Draper's Dictionary*, qu. p. 350

8 *Archaelogia*, Vol. XXI. qu. *The Draper's Dictionary*, p. 248

9 *Maid of Honour*, Philip Massinger, 1632, qu. *The Draper's Dictionary*, p. 153

10 *Traditional Quilting*, p. 88

11 *Old Patchwork Quilts*, p. 134

12 *Women's Day Book of American Needlework*, p. 116

13 From Mrs Mary Allen, Turnditch, Derbyshire

14 *Quilting as a Hobby*, pp. 10 *et seq. Woman's Day Book of American Needlework*, p. 120

15 *Canterbury Tales, The Prologue*, p. 12

16 *Animadversions on Speght's Chaucer*, Thynne, 1598, qu. *The Draper's Dictionary*, p. 61

17 *The Diary of a Country Parson*, Vol. I, pp. 162–3

18 *Reminiscences of a Gentlewoman*, p. 21

19 *Traditional Quilting*, fig. 3

20 *Notes on Quilting in the Isle of Man*

21 'Quilting in Glenlark, County Tyrone', *Ulster Folk Life*, Vol. 5, 1959, p. 62

Chapter 3

1 *Old Patchwork Quilts and the Women who Made Them*, pp. 43–4

2 *Traditional Quilting*, p. 59

3 *English Quilting, Old and New*, pp. 3, 4

4 *Quilts. Their Story and how to make Them*, facing p. 9

5 *The Romance of the Patchwork Quilt*, plate LVII

6 *Traditional Quilting*, fig. 8

7 The Council for Small Industries in Rural Areas. (COSIRA) 35 Camp Road, London SW19

8 *Samplers*, illustrated on frontispiece

9 *Traditional Quilting*, fig. 8

10 *Old Patchwork Quilts and the Women who Made Them*, p. 43

11 *ibid.*, p. 43

12 *American Quilts and Coverlets*, p. 60

13 *Traditional Quilting*, p. 74

14 See note 7

15 *Quilting. Traditional Methods and Design*, p. 9

Chapter 4

1 *The Household Book of Lady Grisel Baillie*, p. xxvi
2 *The Russells in Bloomsbury*, pp. 273–4
3 *Sussex Archaeological Collections*, Vol. IX, 1857, qu. *English Quilting*, p. 6
4 *Traditional Quilting*, Appendix II, p. 158
5 *ibid.*, p. 161
6 *ibid.*, p. 39
7 *ibid.*, p. 34
8 *Old Patchwork Quilts*, p. 20
9 *ibid.*, p. 142
10 *Traditional Quilting*, p. 119
11 *American Quilts and Coverlets*, p. 29
12 *Traditional Quilting*, fig. 39
13 *Patchwork Quilts*, p. 75
14 *Traditional Quilting*, p. 45
15 *Patchwork*, figs. 173, 174
16 *Traditional Quilting*, fig. 10
17 *English Quilting*, p. 3

Chapter 5

1 Victoria and Albert Museum, negative no. 66907
2 *Notes on Quilting*, plate 1, Victoria and Albert Museum ref. T. 121–1916, neg. no. 63885
3 *ibid.*, plate 8, Victoria and Albert Museum ref. T. 272–1927, neg. no. 59388
4 *ibid.*, plate 14, Victoria and Albert Museum ref. 1376–1904, neg. no. 17392
5 *English Secular Embroidery*, plates facing pp. 137, 138
6 The Victoria and Albert Museum ref. 359b–1887, neg. no. FH 888
7 City of Manchester Art Gallery neg. no. 3318, fig. a, ref. M.8467; fig. b, ref. 1922–2073; fig. c, ref. 1947–1865
8 The Victoria and Albert Museum ref. 233–1906; back, neg. no. FH 886; side, neg. no. 887
9 Victoria and Albert Museum neg. no. 72885
10 Civici Musei Veneziani D'Arte e di Storia, Venice, neg. M.N.9867
11 City of Manchester Art Gallery ref. 1947–1885, neg. no. 3320
12 Victoria and Albert Museum ref. T. 120–1934, neg. no. FH 889; detail, neg. no. FH 890
13 *The Romance of the Patchwork Quilt*, part 2, plates CXIV, CXV, CXVII; part 3, plate VII
   Old Patchwork Quilts and the Women who Made Them, plate 75
   Women's Day Book of American Needlework, pp. 116, 121

14 *The Romance of the Patchwork Quilt*, part 2, plates CVIII, CXVIII

15 *Woman's Day Book of American Needlework*, p. 110

16 *Catalogue of Pieced Work and Appliqué Quilts at Shelburne Museum*, pp. 20, 21

17 *Old Patchwork Quilts and the Women who Made Them*, plate 70

Chapter 6

1 *English Secular Embroidery*, p. 136

2 *The Castel of Helth*, p. 79

3 Galen – Claudius Galenus, *c.* AD 130–201: a Greek physician born at Pergamo. 'A voluminous writer on medical and physiological subjects'. He studied in Rome for some years and died in Sicily

4 *A Compendyous Regyment or a Dietary of Helth*

5 *The Habsburgs*, p. 115

6 *The Draper's Dictionary*, qu. p. 318

7 *Embroidery*, Vol. 16, no. 4, Winter 1965, p. 113 and illustration. Ref. *Metropolitan Museum Bulletin*, V, 1922, pp. 29, 30, 31

8 *Kretschen von Kienbusch Collection of Arms and Armour* (catalogue), fig. 142

9 *The Armourer and his Craft*, p. 84

10 *The History of Wyat's Rebellion, An English Garner*, p. 66

11 *The Lay of the Last Minstrel*, Canto Third, v. VI

12 *The True Use of Armorie*, p. 127

13 *The Armourer and his Craft*, p. 90

14 *The Draper's Dictionary*, qu. p. 62

15 *James I*, p. 15

16 *Traditional Quilting*, p. 156

17 *Notes on Quilting*, p. 5

18 *Needlework Through the Ages*, plate XLIX, 1

19 *ibid.*, plate LXXII, 3

20 *Country Life Annual* 1956, p. 168

21 *Henry IV*, part 1, IV, ii

Chapter 7

1 *A Voyage to East-India*, p. 325

2 *ibid.*, section V, p. 377

3 *ibid.*, Section VI, p. 384

4 *The Travels of Pietro della Valle*, ch. XI, p. 124

5 *The Draper's Dictionary*, qu. p. 288

6 *The Armourer and His Craft*, p. 90

7 *ibid.*, p. 94

8 *Country Life Annual*, 1956, fig. 3, p. 169

9 *The Art of Embroidery*, fig. 399, p. 248

10 *Needlework Through the Ages*, plate LXXII, 3

11 Victoria and Albert Museum neg. no. 66273

12 *ibid.*, neg. no. 27382, ref. 1374–1904 ·

13 *ibid.*, neg. no. 66907

14 *Notes on Quilting*, drawing taken from plate 2

15 *The Draper's Dictionary*, qu. p. 249

16 *ibid.*, qu. p. 53

17 City of Manchester Art Galleries ref. 1922/2973, neg. no. 3318

18 *Educational Writings of John Locke*, para. 5, p. 117

19 *English Secular Embroidery*, n., p. 60

20 *The Draper's Dictionary*, qu. p. 88

21 *English Secular Embroidery*, n., p. 60

22 *Mediterranean and Near Eastern Embroideries*, Vol. II, p. 42

23 *The Chintz Book*, p. 18

24 *The Draper's Dictionary*, qu. p. 199

25 *The Connoisseur*, March 1942, p. 44

26 *ibid.*, p. 41

27 *ibid.*, p. 41

28 *ibid.*, p. 45

29 *Educational Writings of John Locke*, p. 133

30 *The Chintz Book*, p. 22

Chapter 8

1 *The Tatler*, No. 81 (No. 116 orig. ed.)

2 *English Secular Embroidery*, figs. facing pp. 136, 138

3 City of Bath Corporation, Collection of Costume Museum, Assembly Rooms

4 City of Manchester Art Gallery, Gallery of English Costume, Platt Hall

5 Collection of Civici Musei Veneziani d'Arte e di Storia, Venice. Also illustrated, *The Art of Embroidery*, fig. 425

6 *The Way of the World*, v, i

7 City of Bath Corporation, Minet Collection, Costume Museum, Assembly Rooms

8 Since this photograph was taken, Miss Daniel has presented the cloak to the Bath City Corporation, where it is now in the Costume Museum at the Assembly Rooms

9 *Domestic Needlework*, p. 54

10 *The Household Book of Lady Grisel Baillie*, 1 Jan., 1717

11 *The Art of Embroidery*, p. xxiii

12 *ibid.*, plates 427, 401

13 *Historical Memoirs*, The Duc de Saint-Simon, Vol. I, p. 440
14 *The Tatler*, No. 87 (No. 136, orig. ed.)
15 *ibid.*, No. 131 (No. 245, orig. ed.)
16 *The Spectator*, No. 145, Everyman ed., p. 439
17 *Traditional Quilting*, fig. 6
18 *Needlework Through the Ages*, p. 315
19 *Quilts. Their Story and how to Make Them*, pp. 67–8
20 *Five Centuries of American Costume*, pp. 127, 136
21 *The Russells in Bloomsbury*, p. 245
22 *Country Life Annual*, 1956, p. 168
23 *ibid.*, qu. p. 171
24 *The Spectator*, No. 606, Wed., 30 Oct. 1714
25 Also illustrated, *Picture Book of English Embroidery*, part III, plate 8. Victoria and Albert Museum ref. T. 24–1926
26 *ibid.*, plates 9 (Museum ref. T. 148–1927) and 11 (Museum ref. T. 282–1927). Also *Notes on Quilting*, plates 10 (Museum ref. T. 237–1928, neg. no. 60852), and 11 (Museum ref. T. 236–1928, neg. no. 60851)
27 *Patchwork*, plate 110, *Patchwork Quilts*, p. 33
28 *Needlework Through the Ages*, qu. p. 321
29 *Through England on a Side-saddle*, pp. 364, 277
30 *Traditional Quilting*, qu. p. 157
31 *The Russells in Bloomsbury*, pp. 230, 232, 245, 248, 340
32 *The Household Book of Lady Grisel Baillie*, p. 182
33 *The Travel Letters of Lady Mary Wortley Montagu*, pp. 30, 220
34 *The Beaux' Stratagem*, IV, i, l. 363
35 *English Quilting*, plate 12
36 *Traditional Quilting*, fig. 11
37 *ibid.*, p. 157
38 *Gulliver's Travels*, pp. 79, 93, 113, 115, 121, 161
39 *The Draper's Dictionary*, p. 65
40 *Sophie in London*, pp. 76, 276

Chapter 9

1 *Traditional Quilting*, p. 140
2 *ibid.*, p. 139
3 *ibid.*, p. 140
4 *ibid.*, fig. 7
5 *English Quilting*, p. 4, figs 2, 3
6 Victoria and Albert Museum ref. T. 212–1962
7 *Woman's Day Book of American Needlework*, pp. 116–17
   Textiles in New England, p. 11

8 City of Manchester Art Galleries ref. 1948–250, neg. no. 1736a. Also illustrated, Picture Book No. 3, fig. 14a

9 *The Book of Costume*, fig. 2685, p. 913

10 *Protestant Island*, pp. 133–4

11 *Childhood, Boyhood, Youth*, Ch I, 'Our Tutor. Karl Ivanych.', p. 13

12 *Traditional Quilting*, pp. 29, 30

13 ibid., pp. 45, 46, also Appendix III

14 *English Quilting*, pp. 3, 4

15 *Traditional Quilting*, pp. 33, 39 *et seq.*

16 *Textiles in New England*, pp. 10, 12

17 *A Glossary of the Dialect of Almondbury and Huddersfield*, 'Quilting Feast'. Also qu. *Quilting in the North of England*, p. 77, n. 12

18 *Ulster Folk Life*, Vol. 5, 1959, p. 52

19 *Old Patchwork Quilts*, p. 34

20 *Reminiscences of a Gentlewoman of the Last Century*, c. 1846

21 *The Diary of a Country Parson*, Vol. IV, p. 249

Chapter 10

1 *Traditional Quilting*, p. 47

2 The name of the organisation has been changed and it is now the Council for Small Industries in Rural Areas, abbreviated to COSIRA

3 *Traditional Quilting*, p. 53

4 The Rural Community Council in Monmouthshire, with Mr D. L. Jones, O.B.E., as Secretary and the Keeper in Charge of the Welsh Folk Museum at St Fagan's Castle, Cardiff

5 *Traditional Quilting* (see Bibliography)

6 *Daily Telegraph*, 28 Feb. 1967

7 *Woman's Day Book of American Needlework, Quilting as a Hobby*, both available in Great Britain

8 *The Sunday Times*, 20 April 1968, p. 53

9 *Scott's Last Expedition*, Vol. I, Ch. III, p. 81

10 *The Worst Journey in the World*, p. 93

BIBLIOGRAPHY

BOOKS, POEMS AND PLAYS

An English Garner, Ingatherings from our History and Literature, Edward Arber, Constable, 1897. Containing verbatim 'The History of Wyat's Rebellion with the order and manner of resisting the same.' Made and compiled by John Proctor. Second ed. *Mense Januarrii, anno 1555.* (Each page dated 10 Jan 1555)

Arthurian Legends in Mediaeval Art, R. S. Loomis, London 1938

Art of Embroidery. The, Marie Schuette and Sigrid Muller-Christenson. Translated by Donald King, Thames and Hudson, 1964

Beaux' Stratagem. The, George Farquhar, published 1707

Body and Soul, attributed to Walter Map, MS. Laud 108, Camden Society No. avi, 1841

British Handicrafts, Charles Marriott, Longmans, 1948

Canterbury Tales, Geoffrey Chaucer, *c.* 1387. Extracts taken from the text of W. W. Skeat, Oxford University Press, 1958, reprint of 1906 edition

Castel of Helth. The, Sir Thomas Elyot, LONDINI in edibus Thomas Bertheleti typis impres. Cum privilegio ad imprimendium solum. 1541. 'THE FORTHE BOKE. Of Distillations called commonly Rewmes, and of some remedies against them ryght necessary, Cap.2.' From a facsimile edition made from the original now owned by Dr A. S. W. Rosenbach. Scholars' Facsimiles and Reprints, 106 Seventh Avenue, New York

Childhood, Boyhood, Youth, Leo Tolstoy, 1852

Chintz Book. The, McIver Percival, Heinemann, 1923

Contemporary Embroidery Design, J. Nicholson, Batsford, 1954

Costume in Detail. 1730–1930, N. Bradfield, Harrap, 1968

Craft of Quilting in the North Country. The, Beatrice Scott, Dryad, 1932

Diary of a Country Parson. The, Rev. James Woodforde, ed. John Beresford, Oxford University Press, 1968

Discovering Embroidery. W. Douglas, Mills & Boon, 1955

Dives Pragmaticus. 'The Great Marchaunt Man', A Child's Book, Thomas Newbery, printed by Alexander Lace, 1563

Domestic Needlework, G. Saville Seligman and Talbot Hughes, numbered edition, no. 343, Country Life

Educational Writings of John Locke. The A critical edition by J. Axtell, (Yale) Cambridge University Press, 1968

English Embroidery, A. F. Kendrick, Newnes, 1904. Reissued Batsford, 1913

English Historical Embroidery, B. Snook, Batsford, 1960

English Quilting. Old and New, E. Hake, Batsford, 1937

English Secular Embroidery, M. Jourdain, Kegan Paul, Trench, Trubner, 1910

Faerie Queene. The, Edmund Spenser, 1589. Reprint of 1912 edition of *The Poetical Works of Edmund Spenser*, ed. J. C. Smith and E. de Selincourt, Oxford University Press, 1942

Five Centuries of American Costume, R. Turner Wilcox, Scribner, 1963

Gulliver's Travels, Jonathan Swift, 1728. Reprint taken from *Selected writings in Prose and Verse*, Jonathan Swift, ed. John Hayward, Nonesuch Press, 1964

Habsburgs. The, D. Guis McGuigan, Allen, London, 1966

Henry IV, William Shakespeare, 1597

Here foloweth a Compedyous Regyment or a Dietary of Helth, made in Moutpyilour. Compyld by Andrewe Boorde of Physick Doctor. Imprinted by me Robert Wyte, Dwelling at the Synge of Seynt John the Evangelist, in S. Martyns Paryssche besyde Charynge Cross, MUSEUM BRITANNICUM. Published 1542

Historia Naturalis, Vol. VIII (Book XXIX), Pliny the Elder, A.D. 23–79

Home and County Arts, W. R. Lethaby, Home and Country, London 1930

Honest Whore. The, Part ii, Thomas Dekker, 1630

James I, David Mathew, Eyre & Spottiswoode, 1967

Journeys of Celia Fiennes. The, Through England on a side saddle in the reign of William and Mary; being the diary of Celia Fiennes 1888, Cresset Press 1947

Lay of the Last Minstrel. The, Sir Walter Scott, 1805

Maid of Honour, Philip Massinger, 1632

Marmion. A Tale of Flodden Field, Sir Walter Scott, 1808

Mediterranean and Near Eastern Embroideries, Vol. II, A. J. B. Wace, Halton, 1935

Mary Thomas's Embroidery Book, Hodder & Stoughton, 1935

Needlework Through the Ages, M. Symons and L. Preece, Hodder & Stoughton, 1928

Old Patchwork Quilts and the Women who Made Them, R. Finley, Grosset & Dunlap, 1929

Patchwork, A. Colby, Batsford, 1954

Patchwork Quilts, A. Colby, Batsford, 1965

Protestant Island, Sir Arthur Bryant, Collins, 1967

Quilting, Traditional Methods and Design, M. FitzRandolph and F. M. Fletcher, Dryad Handicrafts, 1955

Quilting as a Hobby, D. Brightbill, Sterling Publishing, U.S.A. 1963

Quilts. Their Story and how to Make Them, M. D. Webster, Tudor, New York 1948 edition

Reminiscences of a Gentlewoman of the Last Century, Letters of Catherine Hutton, edited by her cousin, Mrs. Catherine Hutton Beale, Cornish Bros., New Street, B'Ham., 1891

Romance of the Patchwork Quilt, C. Hall and R. Kretsinger, The Caxton Printers, Caldwell, Idaho, 1947

Russells in Bloomsbury. The, G. Scott-Thomson, Cape, 1940

Scott's Last Expedition. The Journals of Captain Robert Falcon Scott. Arranged by Leonard Huxley in 2 vols. with preface by Sir Clements Markham, Murray, London 1913

Sophie in London. 1786. The Diary of Marie Sophie von La Roche. A translation of the portion relating to England, of *Tagebuch einer Reise durch Holland und England* by Clare Williams, Cape, 1933

Spectator. The, Richard Steele and Joseph Addison, 1711–1712, Everyman

Standard Book of Quilt-Making and Collecting. The, M. Ickis, The Greystone Press, New York 1949

Tatler, The, Richard Steele, 1709–1711, Everyman

Travel Letters of Lady Mary Wortley Montagu. The, Cape, 1940

Travels of Pietro della Valle. The, A Nobel *Roman into East-India and* Arabia Deserta. In which, the several Countries together with the Customs, Manners, Traffique and Rites both Religious and Civil, of those Orientel Princes and Nations, are faithfully Described; In Familar Letters to his Friend Signior *Mario Schipano*. Whereunto is added A Relation of Sir *Thomas Roe's* Voyage into the *East-Indies*. (Edward Terry) Printed by J. Macock, for John Place and are to be sold at his Shop at *Furnivalls-Inn-Gate* in *Holborn*. 1665

True Use of Armorie. The, William Wyrley, The Honourable Life and Languishing Death of Sir John de Gratby Capitall a Buz, one of the knights elected by the first founder of the Garter into that noble order. And sometime one of the principall Governors of Guyen Ancester to the French King that now is. 1592

Tudor Cornwall, A. L. Rowse, Cape, 1941

Voyage to East India. A, With a Description of the large Territories under the subjections of the Great MOGUL. (See travels of Sig: Pietro della Valle.)

Way of the World. The, William Congreve, 1700

Woman's Day Book of American Needlework, R. W. Land, Batsford, London; Simon and Schuster, New York; 1963

Worst Journey in the World. The, Apsley Cherry-Garrard, Chatto & Windus, 1922 (1937 ed.)

CATALOGUES AND ARTICLES

Embroidery, Vol. IV no. 1; Vol. IX nos. 2 and 3, Vol. X no. 1; Vol. XI no. 3; Vol. XII no. 2; Vol. XIII no. 2; Vol. 16 nos. 2, 4; Diamond Jubilee Number, 1966; Vol. XIX nos. 1, 4; Vol. XX no. 3

Connoisseur, March 1942, 'The Craft of the Coffer and Trunk Maker in the 17th Century', R. W. Symonds

Country Life. 6 May 1963, 'The Wearing of the Gorget' G. B. Hughes. Annual 1956. 'Old English Quilting' T. Hughes

Catalogue of the Kretschen von Kienbusch Collection of Arms and Armor, Princeton University Press
Journal, of the Royal Institution of Cornwall, XVII. 'Tristan and Iseult' T. C. Peter, 1906

DICTIONARIES AND ENCYCLOPAEDIAS

Concise Oxford Dictionary, 1954 Reprint, Clarendon Press
Dictionary of Needlework. The, An Encyclopaedia of Artistic, Plain and Fancy Needlework, S. F. A. Caulfeild and Blanche Saward, L. Upcott Gill 1882
Draper's Dictionary. A, A Manual of Textile Fabrics: Their History and Applications, S. William Beck. The Warehousemen and Drapers Journal Office, *c.* 1875
Encyclopaedia Britannica, 'Arms and Armour', p. 39, 1950
Glossary of the Dialect of Almondbury and Huddersfield, Alfred Easther, English Dialect Society, 1883
Latin Dictionary. A, Lewis and Short, Oxford University Press, 1962 ed.
Middle English Dictionary. A, F. H. Stratmann, 1891. New edition H. Bradley, 1963, reprint
Oxford Companion to English Literature. The, Compiled and edited by Sir Paul Harvey, 1932, 1960 ed.
Oxford English Dictionary. The, Ed. J. A. H. Murray, H. Bradley, W. A. Craigie, C. T. Onions
Penguin English Dictionary. The, G. N. Garmonsway, 1965
Thesaurus of English Words and Phrases, P. M. Roget, 1805, 1952 reprint
Third New International Dictionary. The, Webster, 1961 edition

MUSEUM PUBLICATIONS

Bolling Hall Museum, Bradford. *Quilting in the North of England,* Anne Ward, 1966
City of Bath Corporation, *Guide to the Museum of Costume* at the Assembly Rooms
Bowes Museum, Barnard Castle. Catalogue to the Exhibition, *North Country Quilting, 1963*
Manx Museum, Douglas, Isle of Man. 'Notes on Quilting in the Isle of Man' from *Manx Folk Life Survey*
Old Stourbridge Village, Mass. U.S.A., *Textiles in New England*
Royal Ontario Museum, Toronto. Catalogue to the Exhibition of *Japanese Country Textiles, 1965*
Shelburne Museum, Vermont. Catalogue of *Pieced Work and Appliqué Quilts, 1957*

Ulster Folk Museum, Holywood, County Down. 'Quilting in Glenlark, County Tyrone.'

Ulster Folk Life, Vol. 5, 1959

Victoria and Albert Museum, H.M.S.O. Publications,

  Flowers in English Embroidery, Small Picture Books. No. 2, 1950

  History of English Embroidery. The, B. J. Morris

  Notes on Quilting, 1949

  Picture Book of English Embroideries. A, part III 1928. Published under the authority of the Board of Education

NEWSPAPERS

The Daily Telegraph, 28 Feb. 1967

The Sunday Times, 20 April 1968

INDEX

The numerals set in italic type denote the figure numbers of the illustrations and photographs.

Acciaiuili, Laodamia 16
American eagle pattern 61: *82*; frames 36; Museum at Bath 32, 33, 60, 81; patchwork 81; quilts, 18th cent. 126; 19th cent. 140, 148–9: *148*; 20th cent. 164; petticoats, 18th cent. 116–18; quilting *see* wadded quilting
Anorak 165–6
Apprentice quilters 139, 140
Arming doublet, ?German 16th cent. 84, 94: *99*
Armour, quilted, medieval 8–13 *passim*, 21: *5*; 16th cent. 84–6: *99*; 17th cent. 91, 93–4

Backstitch 2, 67, 74, 79, 94, 105; in cord quilting 187–92: *177–82*; flat quilting 183; stuffed quilting 193; wadded quilting 177–9: *169, 170*
Baillie, Lady Grisel 114, 123
Bargello quilt *see* Sicilian quilt
Bed covers, medieval 13–16, 18–19
Bed furnishings, 18th cent. 121
Bird pattern 100: *108*
Bishop, Francis 42
Black Prince, surcoat of 12, 25
Bodices, English, 17th cent. 94; 19th cent. 134–5
Boorde, Dr Andrewe 83
Bowes Museum 42, 151, 153
Brigandine 8
Burtt, Mrs R. A., cushion by *156*

Cabinets, 17th cent. 102–3
Callamanca petticoat, 18th cent. 116
Candlewick cotton, padding 149
Canterbury Tales 11–12, 26
Caps *see* Cord quilted
Carpet, funerary 5–6: *3, 4*
Cendal, lining 25–6
Chain stitch 3, 74, 121, 183: *134, 174*
Chalice cover (?), English, *c.* 1700 77: *95, 109*
Chasse of Saint Ursula 9: *5*
Checklaton 26
Chintz, Indian, in patchwork 27; quilts, 17th cent. 99, 100
Christening coat, 18th cent. 63, 112: *121*; jacket, 18th cent. 79, 112: *120*; 20th cent. 155: *153*
Church window pattern 56, 70, 72: *71*
Cloaks, infants', 18th cent. 63, 112: *121*; 19th cent. 134
Coat, English, 18th cent. 63, 112: *121*; 19th cent. 134; of Joseph 16–18: *11*; Syrian, ?19th cent. 67, 156–7: *154, 155*
Coffers, 17th cent. 91, 102, 126
Cord, candlewick 24; cotton 24, 186, 9–127 *passim*; upholstery 24
Cord and tassel pattern 53, 118, 120: *59*
Cord quilted, baby's jacket, 18th cent. 112: *120*; bed cover, 17th cent. 101: *108*; 18th cent. 96: *129*; 19th cent. *142*; caps, 17th cent. 98: *106*; 18th cent. 106: *111*; lappet caps, 18th cent. 106: *110*; quilt, 16th cent. 75, 89, 100: *97, 100*; 18th cent. 121; robe, 17th cent. 94: *104*; waistcoat, 18th cent. *117–19*
Cord quilting 22–9 *passim*, 37, 68–74 *passim*; 17th cent. 103 *passim*; 18th cent. 104–27 *passim*; 19th cent. 128; 20th cent. 157–9 *passim*; method 75, 186–92; patterns 75–9
Cornucopia pattern 47, 62, 81, 118, 120

Cottage work, wadded quilting as 24
Couched work 73
Council for Small Industries in Rural Areas 33, 37, 198
County Durham, quilting tradition 153, 160; strip quilt, 19th cent. *147*; modern work 151: *150*
Coverlet, English, 17th cent. 101
Cradle, French, 19th cent. 136: *140*
Cross diamond pattern 6, 91–166 *passim*
Cuff, English, 18th cent. 78: *117*
Curioser Spiegel, 33: *20*
Curtains, English, 18th cent. 77–8
Cushion cover, English, 20th cent. 157: *156*
Cut backing 76, 89

Darning stitches 89, 105
Darnley, Lord, quilt of 87
Dictionary of Needlework 45, 131, 136, 137, 149
Diptych, Milanese ivory 16–18: *11*
Dives Pragmaticus 41, 84
Domestic Needlework 112
Double-ring embroidery frame 31, 37: *14*
Dressing-gowns, 18th cent. 115; 19th cent. 135

Eastern influence, in 17th-cent. work 82, 91, 93, 99
Eastern patterns 100
East India Company 99, 100
Economy, in corded work 78–9, 104
Edgell, Mrs, quilt by 152
Edwards, Mrs, jacket by 153
Eiderdown quilt 151
Elyot, Sir Thomas 82–3, 88
Embroiderers' Guild 157, 159
Embroidery, on flat quilting 72–3
Embroidery frame 31: *13*
England, north of, quilting work 160, 163–4: *158–60*
English armour, medieval 8–13, 21: *5*; 16th cent. 84–6; 17th cent. 91, 93–4; bodices, 17th cent. 94; 19th cent. 134–5; caps, 17th and 18th cent. 67, 78–9, 94, 97, 98, 106, 108–9: *106, 111, 113–16, 122*; patchwork quilts, 18th and 19th cent. 126, 128, 130, 143–4, 150; 20th cent. 153; petticoats, 17th cent. 97; 18th cent. 104, 115, 116–20: *123–8*; 19th cent. 130–1; quilts, 16th cent. 87, 88; 17th cent. 96, 99–101: *101*; 18th cent. 96, 121–4: *134*; 19th cent. 128–9, 143–4, 146: *146–7*; 20th cent. 151–2, 154, 160–4: *149–51, 158–60*; gathered patchwork 167–8: *163, 164*
English quilting *see* wadded quilting
English Quilting 32, 154
English Secular Embroidery 78
English strip quilt, 20th cent. *147*

Faerie Queene, The 9, 10, 13, 26, 86
Fan pattern 56, 91–166 *passim*: *68, 69*
Farthingale 89, 94
Feather pattern 50–2, 72, 73, 75, 91–166 *passim*: *47–56, 95, 96, 125*
Figure, Egyptian 4: *1*
Filling patterns 58–9, 70, 80, 91–166 *passim*
Finishing 64, 66; with fringe 74; flat, cord, stuffed work 79, 81; wadded work 179–80
Finley, Mrs Ruth 31, 36

Firefighting clothes 134, 135; *139*
FitzRandolph, Mrs Mavis 32, 153, 154
Flat quilted, chalice cover (?) 77: *95, 109*; coverlet 121: *101*; pillow sham 72, 74, 96, 97, 121: *105*
Flat quilting 37, 68–71 *passim*, 75–81 *passim*; 17th cent. 91–103 *passim*; 18th cent. 104–27 *passim*; 20th cent. 154–7 *passim*; method 181–5; patterns 71–4
Fletcher, Mrs, quilt by 37: *158*
Flockes 21
Florentine stitch 79, 109
Flower patterns 68, 70, 73, 80, 88–166 *passim*: *90–2*
Flower, Francis 42
Flower-basket patterns 77
Frame pegs 34–5: *16–18*
French knots 79, 108, 114: *117, 118*
Fringe as finish, 74, 77, 79, 81
Frontispiece quilt 64, 65, 101, 124
Furniture, 17th cent. 91, 102
Fustian 25, 86, 99, 102

Gallery of English Costume, Manchester 112, 133
Gambeson 10, 11
Gardiner, George, 43, 44, 118, 139, 153: *22, 23, 151*
Gathered patchwork, 19th cent. 167–9: *163, 164*; method 195–7
German arming doublet 84, 94: *99*; military skirt 84; quilt 75, 89, 100: *97, 100*
Gold thread, medieval work 18, 19
Great Tangley quilt 96: *129*
Griffith, Elizabeth *135*

Habergon 10
Hake, Mrs Elizabeth 32, 154
Haketon 10, 11, 20
Hall, Miss, quilt by *149*
Hammock pattern 53, 120: *56–8*
Hangings, 18th cent. 105
Hardwick Hall quilt 87–8
Harp pattern 60: *79*
Heart pattern 55: *63*
Hedley, Joseph 42, 118, 126
Homespun quilts 28
Hoods, 19th cent. 132, 133
Hospital quilts 23

Indian chints 27, 121; quilt, 16th cent. 87–8
Indo-Portuguese designs 90
Inventory, medieval 13; (1459) Sir John Fastolfe 21; (1466) Durham Priory 19; (1551) Powys Castle 87; (1584) Kenilworth 87; (1592) Carew Castle 87; (1603) Sir Thomas Kyston 99; (1614) Earl of Northampton 99; (1710) William Wogan 121; (1742) Robert Jones 126
Italian quilting *see* cord quilting
Ivory carving, Milanese 16, 17, 18: *11*

Jack, the 8–10, 21, 25, 84–6, 90: *5*
Jacket, 17th cent. 72, 94, 97: *94, 103*; 18th cent. 79, 112, 114: *120*; 20th cent. 155: *153*
Jupon 11, 12

Knotting 28: *12*

Lappet caps, 18th cent. 106: *110, 122*
Leaf pattern 48–9, 75–6, 77, 79, 80, 91–166 *passim: 32–41, 108*
Levens Hall, patchwork 121
Lewis, Miss Rosamund *145*
Linen Armourers, charter of 12–13
Long stitch 74
Lough, Mary 66, 163: *159, 160*
Lover's Knot pattern 54, 91–166 *passim*
Lozenge *see* cross diamond pattern
Lute-string 26

McCaughey's Quilting 143
McCrea, Mrs Mary 149: *148*
Machine quilting 131, 134, 149, 150, 159, 160, 165
Manor-house, sewing at 67
Mantle, Egyptian 4: *61*
Marcella quilt *see* Marseilles quilt
Marriage quilts 137; 19th cent. 144, 145: *144, 145*; 20th cent. 163: *159*
Marseilles quilt 149, 150
Materials, 16th cent. 82–90; 17th cent. 91–103; 18th cent. 104–27; 19th cent. 128–49; 20th cent. 150–66; padding 20–5; top and backing 25–9; wadded quilting 170–1; flat quilting 181; cord quilting 186; stuffed quilting 193
Meander pattern 40, 72, 77, 197: *21*
Metropolitan Museum of New York 84
Middleton Collection 72
Military skirt, 16th cent. 84
Military wear, Middle Ages 8–13 *passim*, 22:5
Mining districts 137
Morgan, Mrs Irene *141*
Museum of Costume, Bath 76, 117

Needles 38
Needlework Through the Ages 4, 5, 88, 126
Nightcaps 83, 98, 106
North Country strip quilts 28: *147*
Nottingham Castle Museum 72

Old Patchwork Quilts 31
Origins, of quilts 1–19

Padding, materials 20–5; wadded quilting 170–1
Paisley pattern 50
Panier, the 118
Patchwork, 18th cent. 126; 19th cent. 128, 130, 140, 143–4, 140–9: *148*; 20th cent. 153; gathered 167–9, 195–7: *163, 164*; Indian chints 27; influence on quilt patterns 60: *147, 150*; method 172
Patterns, American eagle 61: *82*; Animal 6: *2, 4, 100*; Bird 100: *108*; Church Window 56, 70, 72: *71*; Cord and Tassel 53, 118, 120: *59*; Cornucopia 47, 62, 91–166 *passim*; Cross diamond 1–166 *passim*; Diamond 1–166 *passim*; Eastern 100; Fan 56, 91–166 *passim: 68, 69*; Feather 50–2, 72–5, 91–166 *passim: 22–3, 47–56*; Filling 58–9, 88–166 *passim: 93*; Flower 68, 70, 73, 88–166 *passim: 90–2*; Flower basket 77, 96; Hammock 42, 53, 120: *56–8*; Harp 55, 60, 63: *19*; Heart 55: *63*; Leaf 16, 48–9, 75–6, 88–166 *passim: 32–41, 108*; Lover's Knot 54, 91–166 *passim*; Lozenge *see* cross diamond; Meander 40, 72, 77, 197: *21*; Paisley 50; Rose 16, 46, 75, 77, 88–166 *passim*: 10, 25–7, 31; Pineapple 60: *80*; Scallop shell 50, 72, 75: *45*; Scroll 5, 6, 79, 91–166 *passim*; Sea-wave 56; Shell 59, 164: *161, 162, Spider's Web 61: *81*; Spiral (snail creep)

5, 6, 56: *64, 65*; Tudor-rose 118: *124*; Tulip 47, 118: *28–30*; Twist 54, 91–166 *passim: 60, 61, 108*; Vine 80, 116; Welsh pear 50; Wineglass 59, 73: *73*
Pattern-makers, professional 41–4
Pattern marking 172–4
Pertian (Persian) 26
Petticoats, 17th cent. 97; 18th cent. 104, 115–20: *123–8*; 19th cent. 130–1, 149
Pieced-work patterns 81
Pillow cases, 18th cent. *121*
Pillow sham, 17th cent. 72, 74, 96, 99, 121 *105*
Pin-cushions 112
Pineapple pattern 60: *80*
Pitt-Rivers Museum 85
Pliny the Elder 21
Poor Law Institutions 22
Portuguese quilt, 17th cent. 76, 101: *108*
Pourpoint 10, 11
Prick and pounce 69, 71, 173, 182
Privy Purse Expenses of Earl of York 25
Proctor, John 85
Professional quilters 139
Pulled stitches 3, 79, 97, 109: *117, 118*

Quilt, definition 2; derivation 4
Quilts, 15th cent. 13–16, 122–3: *6–10*; 16th cent. 75, 87–9, 100: *97, 100*; 17th cent. 76, 99–101: *101, 108*; 18th cent. 121–4, 126: *frontispiece, 130–5*; 19th cent. 128–9, 143–6, 148–9: *142–8*; 20th cent. 151–4, 160, 164: *141, 149–50, 152, 158–60*
Quilts. Their Story 32
Quilt clubs 137, 139
Quilt frame, construction 33–5: *16, 17*; ratchet types 32, 33; self-supporting types 32, 37: *15*; setting up 174–7
Quilt nails 102, 103, 136
Quilting Bee, the 140
Quilting hoop 31; medieval domestic 13; parties 142, 143; songs 143
Quilting Party, The 143

Romance of Arthur of Lytel Brytayne 18
Rose pattern 16, 46, 75, 77, 88–166 *passim*
Royal Wardrobe Accounts 102
Running stitch 67, 76, 79; in stuffed work 193; in wadded work 177–9: *169, 170*

Sanderson, Miss Elizabeth 43, 44, 60, 144: *149, 150*
Sarcenet 25, 26, 82, 87, 99, 102
Satin stitch 74, 114: *134*
Scallop shell pattern 50, 72, 75: *45*
Scott, Sir Walter 9, 10, 85, 86
Scroll pattern 5, 6, 79, 91–166 *passim*
Scytho-Siberian carpet 5–6: *3, 4*
Sea-wave pattern 56
Sendal *see* cendal
Shadow quilting 24–5
Sheckladon 86
Shecklaton 86
Shell pattern 59, 164: *161, 162*
Short stitch 74
Sicilian quilts, 15th cent. 13–16, 80, 82, 122–3: *6–10*
Signatures, on quilts 66, 79, 81; 18th cent. quilts 123, 124: *134*; 19th cent. quilts 149: *142, 148*; 20th cent. quilts 163: *159*
Skirts, 19th cent. 131–2
South Pole, expedition to 166
South Wales, quilting tradition 154, 160
Spenser, Edmund 9, 10, 11, 13, 26, 86
Spider's Web pattern 62: *81*

Spiral pattern 5, 6, 56: *64, 65*
Split stitch 74: *134*
Stab stitching 196, 197
Stays, 19th cent. 133: *138*
Stem stitch 74: *134*
Stitches, back 177–8, 183, 187–92, 193: *177–82*; chain 3, 74, 121, 183: *134, 174*; darning 89, 105; florentine 79, 109; french knots 79, 108, 114: *117, 118*; long 74; pulled 1, 79, 97, 109: *117, 118*; running 177–9, 193: *169, 170*; satin 74, 114: *134*; short 74; split 74: *134*; stem 74: *134*
Stomachers, 18th cent. 112
Strip quilts 28, 62–4, 130, 144, 172: *147*
Stuffed quilting 13–16, 67–79 *passim: 6–10, 142, 143*; bedcovers 13–16, 122–3: *6–10, 142, 143*; method 193–4; patterns 79, 81
Suit, 17th cent. 94
Swanskin 28
Syrian coats, 19th cent. (?) 156–7: *154, 155*

Tangley Manor quilt 77: *129*
Templates, basic equipment 37–8; drawings 198; flat and corded work 69, 71; gathered patchwork 195; wadded work 172, 173
Textiles, Early Middle Ages 8
Thompson, Mrs Mary *142*
Threads, buttonhole twist 181, 186; cotton 1–197 *passim*; gold 18, 19, 123; linen 1–197 *passim*; metal 73, 123; silk 1–197 *passim*; silver twiste 87
Traditional Quilting 28, 60, 154, 169
Transfers 69, 71, 159
Tristram, legend of 15, 16: *6*; quilts *see* Sicilian quilts
True Use of Armorie, The 86
Trunks, 17th cent. 91
Tudor-rose pattern 118: *124*
Tulip pattern 47, 91–166 *passim: 28–30*
Twist pattern 54, 91–166 *passim: 60, 61, 108*

Underlay, quilted 19
Underskirt *see* petticoat
Upholstery, 17th cent. 91, 103; 18th cent. 126; 19th cent. 136; *140*

Victoria and Albert Museum 15, 18, 63, 72, 75, 76, 77, 94, 121
Vine pattern 80, 116

Wadded quilting, 20–5 *passim*; 67–81 *passim*; 16th cent. 82–90 *passim*; 17th cent. 91–103 *passim*; 18th cent. 104–27; 19th cent. 128–49 *passim*; 20th cent. 150–66; armour 93–4; coat 16–18: *11*; dressing-gown 135; early examples 4–5, 16–18: *1, 11*; equipment 32–7; jacket 154: *153*; mantle 4–5: *1*; method 170–80; patterns 40–66: *21–89*; petticoats 116, 118, 120, 130–1: *124–8*; quilts 87, 88, 123, 126, 143–6: *frontispiece, 134, 135, 144, 145, 151, 152, 158–60*; skirts 131–2; upholstery 102–3, 126–7, 136; wadded work, 16th cent. 84–7
Waistcoats, 17th cent. 67, 94: *102*; 18th cent. 79, 112, 113: *117, 118, 119*
Wales, South, quilting in 44, 153, 154, 160
Welsh flannel 28
Welsh patchwork quilts 143–4
Welsh pear pattern 50; petticoats 130–1; quilts 124, 144, 145, 153, 154: *130–3, 135, 141, 144, 145, 152*
Widow's quilt, the 60
Wineglass pattern 59: *73*
Woods, for frames 36